STEALING THE FUTURE

(AND HOW YOU CAN STOP IT)

By Neil Crofts and Mark Thompson

Stealing from the future and how you can stop it

First Published in 2018

Holos Change Ltd

www.holoschange.com

ISBN 978-1-9993292-0-4

Authors Neil Crofts and Mark Thompson
Editor Sally Dellow
Proof reader Rima Cotran
Design Studio Tangerine
Illustrations Sam Chesterman

STEALING FROM THE FUTURE
(AND HOW YOU CAN STOP IT)

By Neil Crofts and Mark Thompson

Dedication

Neil's Dedication:

My first book was dedicated to my wife Benedicte, shortly after we married. My second was dedicated to our daughter Minnie. My third was dedicated to our son Casper. This book is dedicated to our as yet unknown grandchildren and your grandchildren and all of their children. It is for them that this book was written in the hope that it can contribute in some small way to helping our generation and our children leave a beautiful and habitable planet for our grandchildren and our great-grandchildren.

When I was younger it was frustrating to find that no achievement was truly my own. Today I can relish all of the thousands of people who have contributed to this proud articulation of my and our learning. This book is also dedicated to everyone who has ever taught me anything, most especially my wife, our children and my business partner and co-author Mark, but also everyone I have worked and learned alongside, every client who has ever allowed me the privilege of working with them and their people, every workshop participant who has made a challenge, asked a question or appreciated a piece of learning, everyone who has ever given feedback on my writing and everyone I have ever coached. This is their book, for every one of those interactions was a learning opportunity and I hope that I grasped enough of them.

Mark's Dedication:

Whilst change may be easy, creating a collaborative view of leadership is not. My first dedication is to my co-author, Neil Crofts. Neil, finding our way through this writing journey together has been for me a role model example of interdependence. Whilst (very) occasionally frustrating, often challenging, and usually complex, it has always been a genuine collaboration, with no view superior nor turn of phrase sacrosanct; and never a conflict. Thank you for the courage and commitment to see our intentions through to completion. I am proud of our work together and the way in which we have gone about this project in particular.

There are many other people without whom a project like this cannot be fulfilled, ranging from the incredible support and encouragement of loved ones, to the professional critique, feedback and appreciation from peers that help to hone messages and sharpen thinking.

In the loved ones category, thank you so much to my wife, Susie Thompson, whose belief in me has enabled me to see around corners more successfully, and my teenage son, Freddy Thompson, whose pragmatism and simplicity of observation has given clarity to me on many occasions.

Professionally, thank you to Irina Filippova and Daryll Scott, great spirits both, whose keen eyes and unfailing insights assisted us in many improvements.

Special thanks to Sally Dellow, our Editor, for her laser-like skills and unflinching feedback, as well as working through Typhoon Mangkhut to meet deadlines!

Acknowledgements

Special thanks to Simon Croft and Sam Chesterman of Studio Tangerine for the jacket design and interior illustrations.

We further acknowledge and list below the many authors whose accumulated insight on change, leadership, and behaviour has contributed to the body of knowledge around systemic and adaptive change, and has been trialled in some way in our work over the last ten years.

Barry Oshry, Dr Spencer Johnson, Mike Abrashoff, Jim Collins, Stephen Bungay, Yuval Noah Harari, William Bridges, Stephen MR Covey, Lazlo Buck, Fritjof Capra, EF Schumacher, Ed Catmull, Elizabeth Kubler-Ross, Al Gore, Tony Seba, Simon Sinek, Hans Rosling, James Lovelock, Anthony Robbins, Matthew Syed, David Rock, Daniel Pink, the Dalia Lama, Jeff Bezos, John Kotter, Mac Macartney, David Whyte.

About the authors

The journey to this moment has been varied for both Neil and Mark - it has included military service, racing cars, visiting Everest, cycling over the Pyrenees, acting and directing plays, writing business books and novels, running a classic car business, senior positions in multiple corporations, and being at the heart of some of the largest and most challenging corporate transformations of the 2000s.

After each spending a decade as independent consultants in the leadership and change industry, Neil and Mark joined forces to form Holos in 2014, with a vision of Universal Authentic Leadership. Holos is a business that operates without offices or formal employees, but has a global reach through its networks of partner-level facilitators and coaches. We wanted to connect this combined experience that totals thousands of years into a consulting capability that can actually help our clients to change and become adaptable.

If it is about one thing, Holos holds context at its core. Leadership and culture need to be understood from inside this 'crucible of reality'. Reality in 2018 is a different one than that of even ten years ago and the need to steal less from the future has become pressing.

This is something both Neil and Mark put into their daily lives as well as professional. Neil speaks often to companies about the current global Megatrends and how to lead better in this context. In 2015 Mark trained with Al Gore to become a Climate Reality Leader, spending time working with leaders in organisations to acknowledge and mitigate the effects of climate change.

Neil is an author of three business books and lives with his family in Surrey. Mark is an aspiring novelist and painter and lives with his family in Devon.

Contents

LEADERSHIP IN CRISIS

Leadership is about the future, not the present. As a species, we are generally, and for the most part blindly, stealing from the future. This is a crisis of leadership.

Popular culture seems to be a reflection of our fears. Is the world about to end? The climate is changing and the environment is facing collapse. Politics is in tumult. Technology is runaway, with social media degrading how we relate to one another. War, terrorism, resource depletion, fears over our food and water supply, plastics everywhere, the energy transition, religious extremism, misogyny, pornography, unbridled immigration, fake facts, and widespread depression; all of these stressors and more, have set the hot, red light of crisis blinking in our global culture. Many of us feel we are at breaking point. We fear the potential outcome of these multiple challenges, and that leads us to speculate wildly about some impending extinction event.

Many of these deep challenges are urgent, but this is not a book that supports the 'doomsday' view. What seems to be true is that the threats we face today are so global, so complex and so nebulous, it feels impossible to respond purposefully, or the way our ancestors did to other challenges such as the Great Depression or Nazism. Humanity fears what is unknown and we behave in our own interests. Because of humankind's unprecedented power, we are now reaping the results of our myopic behaviour. Never before have we felt and been so fundamentally and personally responsible. This state of affairs has arrived so swiftly and with so little fanfare that it is causing simple and predictable reactions such as shock, bafflement, denial, anger, blame, resistance and retreat.

In 2014, the authors co-founded Holos as a leadership, culture and change consultancy for the digital age. Holos means 'whole'. We have worked across the world, developing leadership, culture and change as a professional discipline for the last fifteen years. Separately and together, we have participated in and helped to shape some of the most demanding corporate change efforts of the early part of the 21st century, including the rehabilitation of BP after the Gulf of Mexico accident in 2010, Barclays Bank after the LIBOR and PPI scandals from 2013, and others we will explore below. Our research pool comprises tens of thousands of leaders, thousands of teams, hundreds of peer practitioners, and dozens of businesses, from Brisbane to Birmingham, and Stockholm to Soweto.

While we cannot hope to have answers to the world's problems, we do have some clarity on the power and interconnectedness of leadership, culture, and change, and some great examples of how they can work together brilliantly. We also have some understanding of just how poorly leadership is understood in business and much of the public sector. Leadership, culture and change have come to be treated as three separate subjects or disciplines when, in fact, they inter-relate as one. By exploring the nature of what is happening across our planet in these early years of the 21st century, we hope to inspire an optimistic and unified view of a type of leadership that also pays attention to social or cultural outcomes. History shows there is vast potential in human collaboration based on interdependent principles and the pursuit of shared vision.

There are thousands of books on leadership, each valid in their own way. How does this book add to that body of work?

We will attempt to explain the wave of extreme disruption currently breaking over humanity. The disruption is, of course, created by humans, yet it is not planned and our species has never experienced it like this before. That means unique challenges, opportunities and responses. Political events such as Brexit and the presidency of Donald Trump add to an already disrupted economic and social landscape. They bring into focus the risk that a void in authentic leadership means change which may be led or influenced in ways we did not intend or desire. However, while many global indices are improving, climate change and environmental depletion are urgent, game-changing imperatives that have elevated the need for a different kind of leadership. In case we had forgotten, we are re-learning that leadership which minimises conflict and division is critical to human well-being.

Below, we make a critical distinction; divorcing the subject of leadership from the personal traits and whims of individual leaders. Our focus is on the necessity for inclusive and interdependent vision. We will also make the case that the alternative to "stealing from the future" is "sustained success", and not, as some fear, loss of competitiveness.

We will cover the general and specific skills required to be great at understanding, mastering and leading agile, vision-led change, in this era of constant disruption. With our observations gleaned from our extensive, intensive and practical work, we want to re-shape the hackneyed idea that change efforts are difficult, long, and doomed to fail. We want to embrace and reinforce the truth that change is universal and easy, occurring constantly everywhere. Using this concept as the key, we hope to further unlock and accelerate widespread leadership of the plural, inclusive and transparent values that are on the rise all across the world.

We reference and give examples from business and corporate life, and some of the modelling in Part II of the book refers to organisational change, however, this is not a strictly business book, nor one aimed exclusively at CEOs and senior leaders. We want it to be in the hands of everyone who aspires to lead positive change more authentically, purposefully, and successfully in their own lives, families, communities, organisations and societies. Our intent in writing is twofold: to develop and extend the body of thought on leadership as a skill accessible to everyone and, second, to inspire people to lead, whether for the first time or through expanding the scope and influence of their existing leadership.

In Part I we will look at the 'why' of leadership: the context, philosophy and argument for the promotion of authentic leadership that creates sustainable cultures. In Part II we will offer examples of the 'how' for you to dip into: our accumulated insights into the personal habits and disciplines that individuals and organisations can adopt.

Lastly, we hope to share a new leadership language that we will explain, both in the Glossary above and in the relevant sections below. We will explore why, simultaneously, there exists leadership that divides loudly next to leadership that unites quietly. If the problems we face are created by short-sighted, extractive management, the solutions will require a huge increase in long-term, invested leadership. There is a huge community of authentic and purposeful people out there who are already making a profound difference to each other, to their communities, and to the flora and fauna of our planet, and we must unite if we are to make material differences to the global outcomes.

In our leadership language, Bosses and Rulers have been our past. Our future must be led by Visionaries and Authentics, so that we avert the doom so many predict.

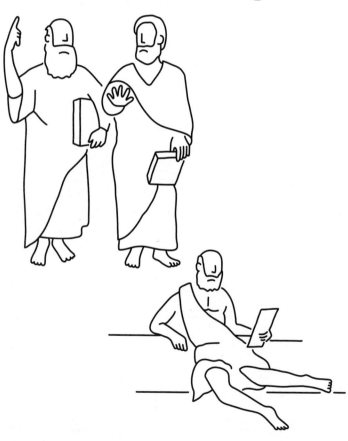

PART 1

PERSPECTIVES

The secret of change is to focus all of your energy,
not on fighting the old, but on building the new.

Socrates

"Change is the law of life, and those who look only to the past or present are certain to miss the future."

John F. Kennedy

CHAPTER 1

THREAT IS THE CHANGE YOU ARE NOT LEADING

"Who wants to be a leader?" Hands up! Anyone? ...Anyone?
In our workshops and research we often ask this question. In rooms of relatively senior people, for example Heads of Divisions or even those running Functions (ie, people who already hold leadership accountability, but are within the system, not heading it), about one in twenty will raise their hand. There then follows a short silence, everyone looks at the one person, and there is either nervous laughter or some humorous name-calling.

But then we ask a different question: "Who wants to make a change to what they see around them?"

All raise their hands. In this game (which we've seen produce roughly the same results across cultures), we see a microcosm of the problem at the heart of leadership. It's a problem of perception.

"I want to be a leader" marks us out publicly as different, so we feel alone, burdened, and responsible. To declare ourselves "a leader" may feel pushy; we appear to desire power, be ambitious; we are revealed in those intentions to our social group, which can be a mistake. It's seen as hubris and ego.

"I want to make a change" is much easier, somehow. If I can influence, collaborate, and plan, it's pretty likely that I can successfully alter something. To publicly intend to make change is acceptable. It's equally OK to do so under the radar, without having to put our timid head above the parapet or stand out. Making change is perceived as healthy, authentic and well-meaning.

Yet making change happen and leadership are one and the same activity. Change requires leadership and leadership is about change. There is no other function for leadership than change. If you are not leading, you are not mitigating threat, and in today's world, this means you are simply managing your own decline. Leadership is also essential for bringing about the world we long for, and for bringing others with us on that journey.

Many aspire to make change, yet few aspire to leadership. Why?

Part of the answer may lie in separating 'leadership' from 'being a leader'. This may feel like a semantic distinction, but it is entirely necessary if we are to liberate our perceptions from the belief that 'leading = ruthlessly tell people what to do'.

On the one hand, there is our desire for he-roes and she-roes to come and lead us safely out of the latest crisis. On the other, there is what we (as mere humans) feel we are capable of doing, and how we define or value that.

Leader is a term many use to refer to individuals who hold positional authority. We are conditioned to view leaders as those at the top, or those who hold decision-making power over us. For many, the term has become pejorative.

As authors and practitioners, we believe **Leadership** is the practice and art of bringing something new into existence, by inspiring and engaging others to participate. It is an active behaviour that can be shown by anyone. It is not a permanent state, but one we manifest dynamically. Sometimes we lead. Other times we follow. Other times we manage. Sometimes, we do all of these things in rapid succession.

'Leadership' is based in skill, and is universal and democratic. 'Leader' is an appointment and is usually personality led, or tied to a title. The two concepts are fatally confused in our shared understanding, partly due to a number of assumptions that go unchallenged. Watch any leadership-related interview in the media, and you will see interviewers automatically refer to leaders as providing leadership through force of personality, being in control, having the answers, being politically strong, demanding loyalty, and making irreversible decisions. As viewers, we associate such 'strong-man' behaviour with leadership (and label anyone who does not 'get a grip' as weak). But this is only one mode of leadership, and not an especially productive one.

The complexity of true leadership is that it is a personal choice backed up by skill, integrity and commitment. It is not an appointment. Because someone is appointed Minister for Housing, it does not mean that particular individual can necessarily write a brilliant Housing Policy, nor lead people to deliver the policy effectively. There is a powerful argument that leadership should not necessarily require the highest level of technical expertise. Yet skill is something that the general community should always demand of those who seek to hold power. It is always reasonable to expect those with appointed authority have (or can learn) the leadership skills to motivate and mobilise diverse teams to execute their remit. We will discuss this further in Chapter 5.

Leadership is not taught in schools or Universities (beyond passing references to historical figures or two weeks of an MBA). In practice, it is generally learned either by osmosis or by example, without rigour around quality.

People aspire to the status of leader, instead of the opportunity to use leadership to bring about positive outcomes.

The tension between **Leaders** and **Leadership** poses a problem. **Leaders** have a bad name because the mechanics of leadership are so interwoven with our perception of character, position and ego. As a result, many potentially outstanding individuals avoid **Leadership** because they don't want to be a 'Boss' (see glossary).

Many talented people choose not to take on the responsibility of leadership because their only role models have been either the overbearing bosses they do not respect, or public figures who lack integrity and authenticity. Who, with any sense, would want to be like that? So firstly, we need re-education about the essential nature of leadership.

When we do make change, there is also an uncomfortable truth to address. Passively calling for 'better leaders', rather than making change ourselves, is to abdicate responsibility to others. In those circumstances, we get, and have, the leaders we deserve.

When we blame others, we give away our own power to create change.

Who has not shaken a fist at the TV and angrily demanded better leadership to improve the state of the world? Who has not wanted to be saved by a powerful and visionary leader who has all the answers?

Happily, because the world is changing so fast, we may no longer need to wait for 'saviours'. As appointed leaders have faltered and failed, there has been a parallel and corresponding rise in plural authenticity, otherwise known as 'getting off your arse and doing it yourself'! Many individuals are taking the decision not to wait for a 'leader' to solve their problems, but to chart their own course for change. In just the last twenty years, global levels of activism, entrepreneurialism, consumer-driven change, protest and lobbying movements have led to many living more simply and organically, to new social structures, political revolution and technological innovation. These are dramatically re-shaping our everyday world to the degree that government and policy-makers can no longer keep up.

These activities would previously have been dismissed as fringe, or irrelevant to the mainstream. Aided and enabled by the internet however, individuals are finding like-minded communities, and their democratic power is growing. This is not happening because titled leaders are willingly letting go or giving up, but because true leadership will always find ways to supersede status-driven structures, and create positive change where it is not being sponsored. It takes power and influence to make effective systemic change, but the internet is shifting that power to a point that upsets the mainstream structures supporting appointed leaders.

Although there are occasionally very successful visionary leaders with mass appeal (Mandela and Gandhi for example), most such leaders end up being authoritarian. Yet despite this we should never underestimate the continued attraction that individual (elected or non-elected) "personality cult" leaders hold for the masses who are still looking for a parent figure to tell them what to do and to solve their problems (often the ones the leader has told us we have).

We've all asked, "How can I, little me, feel as though I am making a difference?" Given the unprecedented nature and sheer complexity of the global threats we face, it is hard not to sigh and submit. We feel that swapping to long-life lightbulbs didn't really work; and we wonder whether cutting down on plastic in our weekly shop will even make a dent in the problem.

But the first step towards successfully addressing a set of challenges is to be aware of them. The next is to understand them. Then we need to apply ourselves, in whatever way seems the most valuable, to making positive change. When our actions involve change, we are using leadership.

Awareness - Understanding - Application - Achievement. Repeat at your own level. A person leading 5 others has a more limited reach and perspective than one who is leading 80 people, or even 300m. But the way to make progress remains the same. Restless searching and relentless application is everything.

Throughout this book we will look at four emerging global trends as the context for **Leadership**, that ancient art and practice that has been so misunderstood. We will then seek to support you in your own practice of leading, beginning with yourself. We will also explore what we have learned about how intentional change can work. Lastly, we will explore a system for effective and agile adaptability in this new world of constant change.

Eliminate despair. Forget hope. Exercise purpose.

Our quest is for universal, authentic leadership in service to the world, our home. Leadership is what we need to navigate these unprecedented times together, not with fear and division, but with a resolute inclusivity that goes beyond merely 'hoping for the best'.

Decarbonisation   Digitisation

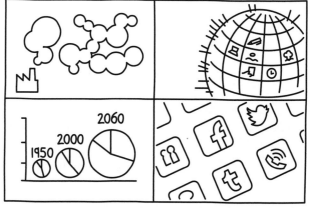

Ageing   Social Transformation

"We are drowning in information but starved
for knowledge."

John Naisbitt

CHAPTER 2

THE MEGATRENDS SHAPING THIS CENTURY

Since World War II we have embarked on three simultaneous grand experiments as a global society. The experiments were not consciously co-ordinated, but resulted from advancing technology and social dynamics, combined with unbridled possibilities. Reactions to those experiments, as well as proactive and innovative ideas have changed the social fabric, creating a 'fourth dimension'.

The causes are the "Megatrends" and they are: Decarbonisation, Digitisation, and Ageing.

A little like the Renaissance in 16th and 17th century Italy, and the Industrial Revolution in 18th and 19th century Europe, the Megatrends of the 21st century are changes humanity has never experienced before. During the Renaissance, humans had no way of knowing that the explosion of art and science would give rise to the Enlightenment and the advance of secular identity across the world, forever changing our freedoms and how governments conducted their work. The Industrial Revolution changed how we depended on people to support an economy, creating new ways to bank, manufacture goods, and transport ourselves. In turn, these changes shifted society from agrarian communities to cities. We still live out the ramifications of both of these immense changes. In some ways, the current Megatrends are extensions of both those previous advances in thinking, technology and society.

We don't know what the outcomes of the current Megatrends will be. We do know they are already producing unprecedented levels of social change, ambiguity and chaos. What we can be sure of is that they are reshaping society, how we organise ourselves and our individual careers. They are generating plurality and opportunity: there will be winners and losers at personal, organisational, national, and international levels. Some call the Megatrend changes the 'Fourth Industrial Revolution' but, they are in fact bigger than industry and the ramifications of these Megatrends go way beyond the seismic shifts if the First Industrial Revolution.

Our purpose in this book is not to provide an exhaustive analysis of the Megatrends. (At the end of this book we have provided a list of sources and further reading). We are not privy to some arcane mystery: all of the material identifying the Megatrends is freely available today in the public domain. It is just not being discussed as much as it needs to be, and the pace of change is, for many people, so frightening that it induces defensiveness and retreat.

Leadership cannot be exercised without a shared understanding of context. That global context is no longer simply the sector in which we work, the geographical area in which we live, or a national agenda, (although for some the nation is everything). In fact, we are all inside and affected by a global context. Like it or not, the planet is global, and no nationalistic move to make anywhere 'Great Again' can stop that, and no argument by revisionists will alter its nature. Our runaway global connectivity is now irreversible.

Individually, each Megatrend is overwhelming. Taken together, they inspire deep feelings of insecurity, bewilderment and loss. As authors, we believe these feelings are necessary:

1. Because they engender appropriate awe and a sense of individual insignificance, and

2. We need to move beyond any resulting downward spiral of fear to develop the right approach and solutions for our future context.

Ageing

The first Megatrend is human. In many ways, this trend is the originator of change. It is from our shifting profile as a species that ideas, technology, innovation and energy derive.

What Is Ageing?

"The... stages a population goes through as it moves from a pre-industrial population with high fertility and mortality, to a modern industrial country with low fertility and mortality. The model is based on the experiences of Western European countries.

In stage one (pre-transition), both birth and death rates are high so the population grows only slowly. In stage two, social and economic changes, most notably improvements in the quality and quantity of the food supply, lead to a fall in death rates. This in turn causes rapid population growth. By stage three, birth rates also start to fall and as a result population growth slows. Stage four represents the stable situation following the demographic transition, where both birth and death rates are low and the population size fairly constant. The model assumes that net migration is zero."

The UK population: Past, Present and Future
by Julie Jefferies

Most of the global north has been through the demographic transition, and is now beyond stage 4, into decline. India is in stage 3, and Africa is in stage 2.

Why Does It Matter?
To illustrate the pressing changes presented by Ageing, it is useful to look first at an example. In the UK, one of the best examples of the impacts of Ageing is seen in the National Health Service. Despite real term increases in funding during the Blair and Brown Governments, 1997 to 2010, the NHS is now

permanently stretched. By 2018 the NHS had a massive and ever-widening funding gap to the tune of billions of pounds. Executives, used to old models of efficiency and cost management, and ruled by successive and interfering regulators looking for the same goals, are at their wits' end wondering how to close the gap and provide a more sustainable service. Attempts to make the service more efficient through measures such as the Carter Report and the Sustainability Transformation Planning process have served only to stretch the stretched even further. Many talk of a permanent crisis in the NHS, even with a national population that is relatively stable.

Only some of the pressure on the National Health Service can be put down to money or poor management. From our work with the NHS, we have observed extremely motivated and professional people doing an amazing job under stresses that would cause many others to buckle. However, the NHS has been chasing its tail for too long. It is run by managers and problem fixers, largely not by skilled leaders or visionary change agents.

The fundamental problem for the NHS is Ageing. It is Ageing that will eventually trigger root and branch reform of the NHS. Too many chronically ill people are living longer and requiring more treatment. Because of advances in technology, treatments are improving (so elderly patients live longer) but also becoming more expensive. Food quality over the last fifty years has improved, but food additives such as sugar and salt have increased individual weights and complicated treatments. Ageing in a healthy population creates demographic risks; but ageing in an unhealthy population increases those risks exponentially. Without visionary leadership to first improve the health of the population, along with industry reform and legislation to curb the use of additives, sugar and salt, the UK's NHS will continue to struggle in a culture of ongoing crisis, robbing Peter to pay Paul. Even if action is taken now, these issues will still take decades to work through.

This example illustrates that problems exacerbate when governmental policy runs on an extractive, short-term basis, rather than an investing one, in which social systems are viewed through a long-term perspective. Scandinavia faces the same Ageing challenge, but its systems drive different decisions and increased resilience, relative to the short-term policies of boom and bust seen in the UK.

Ageing Examples

Ageing in the Western world is a cause of a unique and unprecedented set of global challenges that feed into national demographics, available talent, immigration, GDP, and economic performance. The facts are stark. Let's begin with a look at median ages:

Median Ages

Europe

Europe has a high median age. Median means there are as many people above that figure as there are below it. According to the CIA World Fact book, in 2017 the median age in Germany was 47.1; Italy 45.5; Greece 44.5. Europe as a whole was 42.9. Much of the global north and the global south is in its late 30s or 40s. In the UK, nearly a third of the population is likely to be over 65 by 2050.

The birthrate required for a stable population is about 2.1 children per woman. In 2015, Spain had a birth rate of 1.27, and Europe's birth rate as a whole was 1.55. Spain's population has been shrinking since 2012, Portugal's since 2010. If the trend continues, Portugal's indigenous population will fall from 10.3 to 6.5 million by 2060. In Galicia in north-west Spain there are over 1,500 abandoned villages driven by a combination of urbanisation and depopulation.

Germany has had far more deaths than births for decades, 153,000 more in 2015 alone. With a birth rate of 1.4, the government expects the population to fall from 81 to 67 million by 2060. The UN predicts that by 2030, only 54% of Germans will be earning. To compensate, Germany needs an average of 533,000 immigrants per year.

Japan

Again, the CIA World Fact Book states that in 2017, the median age in Japan was 47.3. In Japan the ratio of workers to pensioners will go from six to one in 1990, to two to one by 2025. Japan's population peaked around 2010 with 128 million people and had fallen by about 1.6 million by the end of 2017. Japan is on track to lose about one third of their population, or 40 million people by 2060, when 39% of Japanese will be over 65. Local Japanese authorities are concerned about the safety issues presented by a growing number of empty buildings. They need to decide which roads and bus routes to keep or cut. Some villages are buying mannequins to place in the street so it does not look so empty, and over 500 schools are closing each year. Immigrants still account for less than 1.7% of the population, including tens of thousands of Koreans who were born in Japan but are not Japanese citizens. Perhaps it is not a coincidence that Japan leads the world in animatronic robotics.

USA

By contrast, the USA attracted more than 16 million immigrants between 2000 and 2016, with foreign-born people now making up about 13% of the population. This success with immigration protects the US from the demographic decline threatening most other developed countries. The fifth stage of the demographic transition is that rich countries see depopulation with attendant economic decline. The US and UK have so far been unusual amongst developed regions in being able to attract sufficient numbers of immigrants to mitigate this. Recent UK and US policies which have at their heart a move away from an inclusive immigration policy will ultimately also shrink those economies.

Northern countries that fail to attract sufficient numbers of immigrants are depopulating. The polarisation of politics and the absence of clear policy direction are, we believe, indicative of a global mid-life crisis!

Asia-Pacific

Countries in the global 'middle' are younger, and growing. India's median age was 27.9 in 2017, with an elderly dependency ratio of 8.6 percent. Over 50% of people in India are under 25 and more than 65% are under 35. By 2020, the average age will be 29 years, compared to 37 for China and 48 for Japan.

Africa

Much of sub-Saharan Africa has a median age of less than 18. Zambia, Malawi, Mali, Uganda and Niger all have a median age of less than 17; 41% of the African population is under the age of 15. In 2016, Africa had a population of about 1.2 billion at a density of about 65 people per square mile, as compared with about 700 in the UK and 85 in the USA. The population of Africa is predicted to double to about 2.4 billion by 2050.

A "dependency ratio" is the ratio of working people to dependent people, typically children and retirees. Africa's current dependency ratio is high at about 80 percent, with only 56 percent of the population at working-age. This is a significant contributor to poverty. However, most of those dependent Africans are very young. As the birth rate slows and Africa moves from stage two to stage three of the demographic transition, those young dependents will enter the work force and the dependency ratio will fall to 60 percent by 2055.

With by far the youngest median age globally, Africa is set, beyond 2050, to be the powerhouse of innovation and growth for the future world economy.

The Meaning of Ageing

These rather bald statistics mean one thing above all: the developed economies of today will be more and more focused on supporting the elderly. This will take up time, resources and money that is already scarce. The developing economies will have youth and wealth at their disposal and economic power will shift, along with changes to the dynamics of global talent, innovation, and disruption.

Falling birth rates and ageing populations combine to increase the dependency ratio at the wrong end of the age spectrum. Eurostat research says that Europe will be most seriously affected, with a dependency ratio of 76% by 2055.

> "The average age of the engineers that built the most powerful rocket ever built in human history, which landed a man on the moon, had an average age of 28. Now the average age of a NASA engineer is 47. I don't want to sound ageist, but it's been a good long while since anyone's been on the moon."

Robert Allen

Coincidentally, in 2016 the median age of employees at Space X was 29; they seem more likely than NASA to get the next human to the Moon or Mars.

Just like countries, businesses age, and ageing has consequences. As of 2016 the median age of Facebook was 29, Linkedin 29, Google 30 and Apple 31

Meanwhile the median age of IBM is 36, Oracle 37 and HP 38. There is a reason why corporations staffed by immigrants are hotbeds of diversity; it is because immigrants tend to be younger. (Data: US Payscale survey).

Innovation, economic growth (and, potentially, conflict) follow youth. Countries and companies tend to enjoy their greatest creativity when the average employee age is in their mid-to-late 20s. Once the average age is in the 40s, countries and organisations run the risk of excessive conservatism, along with stagnation and decline.

All of this adds up to a picture already being played out on the world stage. Europe and Japan are falling victim to political in-fighting and struggling to develop social or commercial strategies to cope with their ageing populations. The US is keeping pace, but stirring up nationalism and anti-immigration to win an election, won't beat the long-term demographics. Supporting immigration is not the answer either; Brexit and the US both show that resident populations cannot cope conceptually with the new global context and prefer a fortress mentality over opening up their nation to young and vibrant immigrant talent.

At an organisational level, the war for talent will focus more and more on the young. So younger countries and companies will lead innovation and disruption.

So What?

As populations age, the quality of leadership at all levels becomes more critical. Solving issues through the simplistic deployment of numbers of people, or greater effort, is no longer possible. Leaderless ageing populations are at risk of polarisation as older people become more conservative and younger people push the liberal boundaries (as evidenced in the UK in 2016). Paradoxically, ageing populations create problems in housing, welfare and healthcare that can only be solved by young people, and yet older people are often resistant to the changes that younger people want.

It is the role of leadership to align and inspire people through change. It is leadership that can explain the context and the challenge, and engage people to co-create the solution. The case for political leadership in response to ageing populations is clear. But ageing also requires stronger leadership in business. The "grey" market will expand, and products and services will need to be tailored to it. All sectors will need to look carefully at how an ageing population is likely to affect their plans and good leadership will inspire organisations to adapt.

How long will a healthier, fitter, older population need to work? How will it affect pensions or health insurance? Will we need more care homes? How will they be funded? Who will staff them if there are fewer young people or immigrants? How can technology help? These are just a few of the many challenges that could become great business opportunities, or disasters waiting to happen. Probably both.

How the Megatrend of Ageing impacts our lives and society will be defined by the quality of leadership. A visionary leader in business or government could inspire and align a group of people to come up with brilliant new ways to use technologies and investment to create self-funding solutions. Or, the problems could be dealt with as they arise, and the opportunities ignored until the stress of the situation becomes so acute that any sort of fix is cobbled together and accepted so we can scrape by for a bit longer. Which will it be?

Digitisation

What Is Digitisation?
Widely hailed as the 'Fourth Industrial Revolution', rapid and full-scale digitisation is upon us.

In 1965, Gordon Moore, one of the founders of Intel, predicted with remarkable accuracy that the number of transistors on an integrated circuit would double every two years, and halve in price, making computer processors faster, cheaper and smaller. The Apollo guidance computer of 1966 had a memory of 4 KB and ran at a speed of 2 MHz. A 2017 iPhone X has 128 million times more memory than Apollo (<256GB), and a processor that runs 1,250 times faster (2.5 GHz).

In 2003. the number of connected devices in the world was 500 million, or less than one device per 10 people. In 2020 there will be over 50 billion, or 6.5 devices per person. (Source: Internet Growth Follows Moore's Law Too, Lisa Zyga, PhysOrg.com, January 14, 2009)

During the Dotcom boom in the late '90s, Neil worked for a digital agency called Razorfish that hoped to change the world (and did change parts of the entertainment industry!). Razorfish had a strap line: "Everything that can be digital, will be" (which is not to say that it should be, but that it will be anyway). Digitisation has come a long way since then, and is now rapidly changing the world.

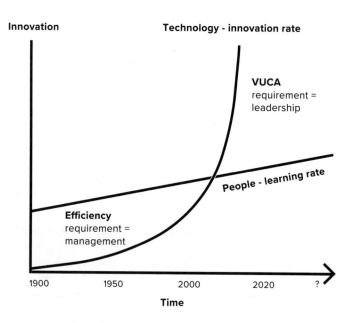

The VUCA environment shown in the graph above is Volatile, Uncertain, Complex and Ambiguous. What the graph illustrates is why many of us feel so powerless, and why businesses that focus on management to incrementally improve how they "crank the handle" are only managing decline. Technological innovation has accelerated to such a degree that it has outstripped our rate of learning, and our ability to respond to each change. The only option available to us in this environment is permanent adaptability.

Why Does It Matter?
At one level, digitisation refers to the shift from analogue, mechanical systems to digital, computer-based systems -"doing digital". However, at another level what digitisation really enables is disintermediation, or deliberately collapsing value chains - "being digital".

Disintermediation is the removal of intermediary stages in a process. A good example of disintermediation is the transformation that took place in the music industry. The product transformation was from a physical product (the compact disc), to a downloaded or streamed product, the music itself. The value chain collapse began with the decline and disappearance of high street music retailers, then the move to direct artist sales (removing the record labels), to the current shift from sales to subscriptions, and music as a service rather than a product (through providers such as Spotify and iTunes).

In about 1999, shortly after the emergence of Napster, a revolutionary peer-to-peer music service, Neil met with UK retail chain, Our Price Records. When Neil remarked that their business model was over, the Head of Marketing countered, saying that could not be the case, because they had just signed off their five-year plan. Ironically, Our Price Records went out of business five years later. This story illustrates the absence of one of the main attributes of effective leadership: ***horizon-scanning to foresee rapidly changing markets and develop an adaptable vision to cope.***

Our Price Records were not the only ones to struggle in that first wave of the digitisation of the entertainment industry. Blockbuster and Kodak were also high-profile victims. Since then, digitisation has enabled other disintermediations: Uber with taxi firms, Airbnb with hotels, Netflix with TV networks, Google and Facebook with traditional media, Amazon and eBay with retailers, Skype, WhatsApp and FaceTime with telecom companies, and so on. These disruptions have changed our lives in many ways, not least by getting services to the consumer cheaper, or even free, which breaks previous economic models entirely. Yet these changes are modest compared to the coming wave of digital disruption.

More Digitisation Examples

Financial Services

There is now a specific word for digital disruption in financial services: Fintech. Already around 97% of the money in circulation in most countries is digital, with only 3% made up of notes and coins (Source: Positive Money), and hard currency is becoming an endangered species in places like Sweden.

Unlike other sectors, the big banks are unlikely to face a single competitor. Instead, hundreds of specialist new entrants have emerged to bite off the easy profits in financial services, leaving banks to service the most expensive, most regulated and least profitable channels.

Armed with the latest software, operating in the cloud and reaching customers largely through apps, these agile new competitors enjoy massively lower operating costs. Many early players like Zopa, Kickstarter and Lending Circle are disintermediating banks through marketplaces that connect funders directly with those seeking funds, whether in the form of loans, investment or pre-sales.

Others like M-Pesa, Paypal, Bitpay, Bitcoin and Ethereum will nibble away at the payments business by offering alternative and cheaper ways to transact directly through servers with no bank involved. Yet others like Tandem, Atom Revolut and Monzo will simply offer regular banking with better service delivered more cheaply through apps and online. Clear Bank uses technology to challenge the conflicts of interest inherent in clearing services being offered by major UK banks to their competitors.

The crucial challenge for the legacy banks to address, if they want to compete, is twofold: the core banking platform, and fractional reserve banking.

Through the high margin 'good times', legacy banks built up enormously complex core banking technology platforms to run all of their services. These platforms, constructed of layers of new technology sitting on layers of old and very old technology, are mostly mainframes that take thousands of people to run. Many of those people are now approaching retirement and are not easily replaced.

Into this market have come new, cloud-based core banking platform competitors including Temenos, Finacle (an off-shoot of Infosys) and ThoughtMachine, a well-funded start-up set up by some former Google employees.

> "Vault OS creates banks that run in the Cloud. It provides secure, fast, reliable end to end banking systems, capable of managing users, accounts, savings, loans, mortgages and more sophisticated financial products. Our customers are banks who want a modern banking engine. Everything runs as 'Software as a Service', so a bank can scale from one customer to tens of millions without having to incur any hard costs. Vault OS is completely flexible, smart contracts are used to create products, so any type of loan or deposit account is configurable."

ThoughtMachine - An Operating System for Banks

Cloud-based core banking systems massively lower the barriers to entry for new banking services. The first legacy bank that takes the bold decision to move to cloud-based banking will trigger an earthquake in the banking world. At the time of writing most of the legacy banks see themselves as integrated, end-to-end service providers. Shifting to a third-party cloud-based system would make them just a service company outsourcing the whole technology infrastructure to someone else. To avoid that, the legacy banks will have to up their game and compete with the top internet companies for talent and technology. Either way, fewer people will be required to run banks.

The second challenge is with fractional reserve banking. Fractional reserve banking is what has allowed banks to be so phenomenally profitable: it is also what makes them systemically risky for the whole economy. The concept and practice of fractional reserve banking is a major reason banks are so heavily regulated.

Fractional reserve banking has its origins in the Renaissance. When merchants began to find gold inconvenient, heavy and insecure as a medium of exchange, they began to store their gold in the vaults of goldsmiths, initially overnight, in return for a receipt. Over time merchants started to trade the receipts that the goldsmiths provided for the deposits, rather than lugging gold around. The goldsmiths twigged that since the merchants didn't all come to collect their gold on the same day, it was safe for them to issue receipts to a higher value (up to ten times higher) than the gold they held, and fractional reserve banking was born. (Source: Wikipedia) To this day those with a banking licence can effectively create money out of thin air, as long as they hold a sufficient reserve. A loans officer with a computer plugged into a regulated bank can invent money by pressing 'enter'; if you or I did this it would be illegal!

Fractional reserve banking can only be offered by those with a banking licence, a significant barrier to entry for competitors. However, since the financial turmoil of 2007/8, governments have sought to encourage competition in the banking sector and, in the UK, 40 new banking licences have been issued to the likes of Monzo and Atom. Perhaps more significantly there are other players who eschew the banking licence and its heavy regulation. Paypal, Holvig, Zopa and others offer bank-like services without a banking licence, adding to the competitive threat to banks.

The trajectory is for increasing competition and innovation from niche players, leading to a far more diversified sector. Big banks are highly likely to shrink or split as, with a few exceptions, they lack the digital expertise to keep up with, or acquire and integrate the Fintech startups.

New smart, app-based products, powered by artificial intelligence and blockchain will facilitate loans, investments, transactions and all of the other financial services we might need. It is also possible that one of the big players (Apple/Google/Amazon/Facebook, etc.) will decide it is time to get into financial services and will buy up a swathe of start-ups to accelerate the process. (See Chapter 14 for more examples of AI-based financial services offerings).

This all means more change and less security, not just for the banks but also for employees.

While Financial Services is the sector currently having its "Amazon moment", almost every other part of society will experience a tsunami of digital change.

Automation and AI

Think of your favourite fictional robot: Marvin, Hal, C3PO, Wall-E, T-850, Her, or Ultron. Are they real? Could they be possible? Our concept of what a robot is or could be is evolving exponentially as our development of technology progresses. An entirely new species.

> "The accumulated doubling of Moore's Law, and the ample doubling still to come, gives us a world where supercomputer power becomes available to toys in just a few years, where ever-cheaper sensors enable inexpensive solutions to previously intractable problems, and where science fiction keeps becoming reality."

> Erik Brynjolfsson and Andrew McAfee

The first phase of technological change is subtle; the technology develops and improves, and costs come down. Once a tipping point is reached, the growth graph goes nearly vertical. At this stage, the new technologies enter our daily lives. For example, 'email' was invented by Ray Tomlinson in 1971 off the back of earlier inventions that created the infrastructure of the internet and computer-to-computer communications. Email did not enter mainstream usage until the mid-90's, and even then, with cumbersome processes such as 'replication'. By comparison, the global penetration of smartphone technology was 2% in 2005. By 2016 it was 81%, cutting the technological adoption rate from 25 years to 10. (Source: Statista)

Robots

Many technologies other than smartphones and email have been through this curve and are already vertical: plasma TVs, computers, the internet, online streaming, etc. These changes are here and driving our behaviour now.

Robot technology is still in the early phase, but the tipping point is approaching. The Henn-na Hotel in Tokyo is run by animatronic robots. Robot mowers and vacuum cleaners have been on the market for some time, and cars have long been built by robots. All of the big tech companies are into robot voice assistants like Siri, Cortana, Alexa and so on. The development of artificial intelligence, big data and machine learning takes robotics much, much further.

Healthcare and medicine are areas where robotics and artificial intelligence are starting to become relevant. Computers can hold unlimited data points and access them rapidly with zero confirmation bias. Once there is a natural language interface, people can list symptoms and instantly get diagnoses that are far more accurate. IBM's supercomputer, Watson (the one that won the TV quiz show Jeopardy) and Enlitic are already offering this. A UK start-up named Babylon takes this further by making AI health diagnostics available through an app that also connects patients with live doctors via video call, and maintains a detailed personal health record on your phone.

Diagnostics is just the first foray for machines in healthcare. Robots are also starting to be used to analyse scans and x-rays with better results than humans, and robot-assisted surgery is already here. The future will move towards virtual GPs and hospitals where robots do much of the manual work such as portering, cleaning, and catering as well as the processing tasks such as registration (already happening), diagnosis, resource allocation and prioritisation. Humans will still play important roles in the more caring and relational aspects, working alongside their unsleeping, smart, robot assistants.

For some time, Tesla have had an "autopilot" feature available in their cars, and many other car manufacturers are releasing or working on enhanced cruise control and self-driving modes. Beyond car manufacturers, Uber is experimenting with a fleet of autonomous taxis in Pittsburg. Google have been working on their own autonomous pods and ULTra Global PRT have been running the automated pods at Heathrow Terminal 5 for a few years. The autonomous treatment extends to trucks, vans and buses as well.

Robot vehicles using lasers, cameras, satellites and the data from millions of previous journeys by other vehicles will be intrinsically better at driving than we humans are. On major roads, autonomous vehicles are already more precise in their driving. They don't change lanes suddenly, they never get tired, they don't get angry, and they don't drink.

Fully autonomous cars will change the dynamics of car ownership, particularly for city dwellers who will be able to summon a ride at short notice and will never need to worry about parking again. Most private cars spend 95% of their time parked and idle (Source: Reinventing Parking). The switch to autonomous cars will not only ensure far higher utilisation of cars, it will also free up the space currently dedicated to car storage. (According to the Journal of the American Planning Association, in 2010 Los Angeles had about 200 square miles or 15% of its area dedicated to parking). Once autonomous vehicles are also networked and communicating with each other, they will dynamically manage the use of road space and seamlessly filter in at junctions, without even slowing down. It is likely that human drivers will be banned from cities and main roads for safety and flow reasons.

Publicly available cars provided by Uber or local authorities may end up being rather utilitarian and not always clean. So it is also likely that people will continue to want to own cars and some may want to have the option to drive the car themselves on roads where they are allowed to. Tesla is already experimenting with valet and summon modes so the car drops you off at your destination and goes off to find an available parking space, returning to collect you again at your request.

Vans, trucks, boats, trains and planes are all likely to get the robot treatment. Trucks will ply the highways in efficient nose to tail convoys to reduce energy consumption (Nikola One truck will do this). The trucks will be loaded with cargo from robot ships (Rolls Royce are planning one for a 2020 launch), using robot cranes. The trucks will make their own way to their destination, where the cargo will be unloaded by robot forklifts straight on to robot vans such as the UK made Charge. These autonomous vans will deliver our orders and mini-robots or drones will take deliveries right to the door; Mercedes Benz have already built a prototype.

By the time the UK's 400km/h HS2 conventional high-speed railway is completed in 2033, it may be badly out of date. Hyperloop could be the future of ground-based, high-speed transport. By 2020, Hyperloop One propose to operate their first system covering the 124kms from Dubai to Abu Dhabi in 12 minutes at a speed of 1,220 km/h. Passengers will travel in capsules in the Hyperloop vacuum tube, gliding with very low air resistance. Hyperloop systems are all electric and many incorporate solar generation into their designs. Hyperloop was conceived by Elon Musk as another way to accelerate the energy transition, by replacing many popular overland air routes. Proponents of Hyperloop claim it is cheaper to build, operates faster, and is less disruptive to the communities it passes through than conventional high-speed railways.

Although the idea of the skies over our homes being polluted with hundreds of small passenger craft may not be entirely appealing, there may come a time when we can summon a flying passenger-carrying robot (rather than an autonomous car) to take us wherever we want to go, and then release it to its next task. Lightweight, electric, self-flying, vertical take-off passenger aircraft like the Ehang 184 raise the possibility of individuals who are not pilots avoiding ground transport altogether and flying directly point-to-point. In 2018 police in Dubai user-tested electric hoverbikes as pursuit vehicles. These drone-like aerial motorbikes are not limited to roads.

All of the above will also apply to the military, who for some time have been using robots in all sorts of roles from robot trucks and planes, to bomb disposal and mine clearance. Agriculture will also automate repetitive tasks like ploughing and harvesting, through systems such as the John Deere Auto Steer.

Robots are also getting involved in other areas of life. Legal Robot uses AI to review contracts and draft legal letters. AI is also already used for legal research and case preparation. Narrative Science turns numbers like sports scores, stock performance and earnings into reporting. LeadGenius combs the web for business leads, learns as it goes, and emails prospects. The Grid creates websites that bring results.

X.ai is a diary assistant that can find and book meeting times. Google Duplex is a prototype of the next stage of Google's existing Assistant service. This voice robot can hold an entirely realistic human conversation, albeit limited initially to booking appointments and checking opening hours. Imagine a similar voice interface for call centres. All calls would be answered immediately as there would be no constraint on the number of call handlers. The robot would know everything necessary and could therefore answer any relevant question. The robot could operate to the same brand standards all the time and in any language. Now think of the future of all the people currently working in call centres.

Most international stock, finance, and currency trades are now conducted automatically by algorithm. Trillions of transactions are already conducted each year without one single intervention by a human hand or thought. The data running these systems is now so complex that there have already been a number of algorithm-based 'glitches', in which seemingly rogue trades occur against predictions or protocols, and new algorithms rise to the surface in the manner of a self-learning system. This may seem like bad science fiction, but there are now many cases of such algorithms manifesting, not least in early 2016 when markets saw a sudden and unexpected drop which was recovered, again automatically, within minutes. Experts are at a loss to explain these incidents, but they are here to stay.

Automation is not just about robots and artificial intelligence. There is also the "internet of things", which effectively means putting internet connectivity into everything, like fridges that order replacements when the milk, eggs or cheese run out. Shot Genius makes golf clubs and balls that share their speed and location with your phone so that you can see how hard and how accurately your golf swing struck. They keep score and the balls never get lost. MyPort, made by Schindler, automatically summons lifts or elevators as you approach, using your phone. There are pet collars such as the Whistle that track or call pets wherever they happen to be. New safety equipment will automatically call for help when deployed, and so on.

3D printing can automate the manufacturing of anything from pizzas, to custom-made surgical implants, to bridges, buildings and cars.

Perhaps both things and transport will be made obsolete by high-definition virtual reality, 360 degree cameras and telepresence devices. Why would we need to transport ourselves or even objects when we can experience them virtually? Why travel to an office or a meeting when everyone can be brought together in a completely realistic virtual space? How about spending time with friends and family who live in different parts of the world, in an immersive virtual environment? Or inspecting a hard to reach or dangerous structure with a combination of telepresence, 360 degree camera and a headset?

Of course, we will also want real human interaction where it is convenient, but to be able to have meetings virtually in London, San Francisco, Shanghai and Mumbai all in the same day would be cheaper, more convenient and less environmentally damaging. And, of course, it is already happening. Similarly, we want to spend physical time with friends and family, but when they are on a different continent, perhaps having a virtual lunch together is better than not seeing each other at all. The military have long used telepresence devices for bomb disposal, but as the technology becomes both better and more accessible we might be able to use it for clearing our gutters or trimming our trees as well.

And for those tricky intercontinental day trips when we really do have to be there in person, SpaceX are planning to use their rocket landing technology to enable travel to anywhere in the world in under an hour (via space), for the price of an economy flight. SpaceX are also planning a mesh of low earth orbit satellites that would provide cheap high-speed internet anywhere in the world. The combination of Hyperloop, truly immersive virtual reality, augmented reality, and cheap reusable rockets could disrupt the entire aviation and communications industries.

Jobs, speed and pace of life, our values, relationships, connection to the planet and each other, social structures, communities, and our sense of identity will all be impacted by the digitisation-driven revolution.

So What?
Once again, the key to survival and success in the digital transition will be leadership. Legacy businesses will have to intentionally collapse their existing value chains or watch while competitors do it. The accountancy business is ripe for disintermediation, as well as insurance and re-insurance. For accountants to survive they will have to find new ways to create value for their clients. Banks already hold many of the relationships and much of the data they use. Or, the threat could come from software companies, who have the tools and in many cases the data and the relationships; we may find banks radically re-drawing their roles and changing the financial industry.

It may well be that some aspects of leadership itself are given over to robots; decision making being the obvious one. We already delegate many decisions to robots; from what to wear, to weather prediction, to 'how to get there' route planning, health diagnosis, and so on. Inspiration, culture and collaboration will remain human activities for a while yet.

Organisations, both commercial and non-commercial, need to shift from "doing digital" to "being digital", or risk being left behind simply to manage their own decline. In every case this will require courageous and skilled leadership to see both the threats and opportunities, and to inspire and facilitate the cultural change necessary to make it happen. Virtually every sector will need to rethink their offering and their role, as the robots and algorithms take over everything that can be digital, just as machines took over manual labour during the Industrial Revolution.

If we link this picture to that of ageing, it even brings into question the need for so many humans. Certainly, the ratio of available jobs to the number of humans (whether shrinking or growing) will be massively disproportionate. This brings into sharp focus the purpose and meaning of a human life. In ideal circumstances, technology will release most, if not eventually all, of us from the burden of working 'to earn a crust'. Instead we will be free to spend our time in pursuit of leisure and contentment, and/or finding purpose through altruism and service. More dystopian versions of the high-tech future also exist. In the Wall-E version, humans served by robots become so idle that they lose all sense of purpose and capability. Or we may face vast swathes of angry, disenfranchised people who have lost their jobs to digital estate agents, self-service supermarket checkouts, autonomous cars and cleaning robots, and so end up living lives of addiction and crime.

As individuals, the difference between living a utopian or a dystopian life may well be access to money, and we already see an ever-widening wealth and equity gap in almost all developed societies. As a society, the outcome we create through our choices will be driven in large part by the energy of our personal, social and corporate leadership.

Scared yet?

Decarbonisation

What Is It?
The Decarbonisation Megatrend is different from ageing and digitisation. Ageing is a consequence of natural social development. Digitisation is an expression of our innovation, and our genius. Decarbonisation is a radical behaviour change forced upon us by a major shift in technology and economics.

Those of us reading this book may like to imagine that the relative affluence we enjoy compared to other periods in history, is because of human brilliance. This is only partly true. The greater part of the affluence we enjoy has come from burning ancient sunlight in the form of fossil fuels. This is not so much brilliance as selfishness: putting into place a global system of burning our collective inheritance for the short-term gain of a few, and to the long-term cost of many.

We have been addicted to the convenient and potent power of fossil fuels for at least 150 years. Indeed, possibly the first anti-fossil fuel pollution legislation was enacted in 1306 by Edward I of England, in response to the thick smog created over London and around his castle in Nottingham by burning sea coal, which people could collect from beaches. Perhaps a harbinger of later efforts at pollution control, the legislation was ineffective. People needed fuel for cooking and heating. As the populations of cities grew, wood became scarce and expensive; sea coal was easily found and we are drawn to easy solutions to our individual problems, even if they come at a cost to the collective and the future.

During the industrial revolution, coal from underground mines replaced water power as the fuel of choice because it meant factories could be sited closer to markets or transport links, rather than needing proximity to streams and rivers to power water wheels. In 1772, Richard Arkwright opened the first factory of the industrial revolution in Cromford in Derbyshire, not because it was close to markets, or even had a ready supply of labour, but because it had a reliable supply of water to power the mill. The mill closed when coal-powered steam engines enabled factories to move closer to markets and labour.

In 1870, JD Rockefeller founded Standard Oil and sold the benefits of mineral oil-based kerosene for lighting. It was cheaper and more reliable than whale oil (so, in the process he probably helped avoid whale extinction). A waste product of kerosene production was a volatile aromatic known as petroleum, which for a time was dumped into rivers. Karl Benz came to the rescue in 1885 by choosing this virtually free waste product to power the first car. (Otto Diesel originally fuelled his eponymous engine with peanut oil).

In the following century, governments saw the geopolitical power created by fossil fuels and started both to shape the market, and own shares in it. In the UK, after William Knox-Darcy discovered oil in what was then known as Persia, (and establishing what was eventually to become BP), the First Sea Lord, Winston Churchill, changed the Royal Navy fleets from burning coal to oil in order to give them better range and more efficiency. All over the world, fossil fuel production boomed. Coal provided electricity, and oil provided everything else: plastics, animal feeds, fabrics, fertilisers, paint, lipstick, chewing gum, and (of course) fuel for planes, trains, cars and ships.

Cheap, portable and full of energy, the use, control, and wide dissemination of fossil fuels has enabled enormous wealth, started devastating wars, facilitated globalisation and, eventually, created the final result of indiscriminate carbon emission: climate change.

So, history shows us that, far more than idealism, it has actually been economics that changes our habits. Even faced with the existential 'perfect storm' of threats related to climate change, we find great difficulty in changing our behaviour (more on this in Chapter 3). Luckily, if we're struggling to change our behaviour for its own sake, technology and economics generally morph and change it for us. Most of us change when our income is affected, and not before. This is hardly something of which we can be proud.

Why Does Decarbonisation Matter?
Just as everything that can be digital will be, everything that can be electric will be. Renewable energy from solar and wind, together with batteries, are on track to make electricity so cheap that we will use it for everything. In 2016 solar electricity officially became cheaper to install and produce than gas, oil, coal or nuclear in many parts of the world.

Both domestic and utility-scale electricity generation and storage are plummeting in price. Storage is also improving in watts per kilo, per cubic meter and per dollar, increasing the range and performance of batteries for electric cars and for domestic and utility scale storage. We are fast (and by 'fast', we mean within the next 5-7 years), approaching a tipping point where combustion engines will be uneconomic for virtually all applications. Tony Seba, author, thought leader and entrepreneur, is predicting the end of petrol and diesel-driven vehicles by 2030. Many national governments, including China and India, have already banned the sale of ICE vehicles (Internal Combustion Engines), from either 2030 or 2040.

Some Examples

Solar cells are becoming transparent, or integrated like the Tesla roof-tile cells launched in September 2016, and will reach a point where all surfaces can be electricity-generating surfaces. Roads have been constructed in France with in-built power generation capability. France is also requiring that roofs on new commercial buildings must either generate electricity or be covered in plants. In the Netherlands an electricity-generating bike path was built in 2014, and by 2017 all trains were powered by renewable energy. Transparent solar cells like the ones pioneered by Ubiquitous predict a time when not only the tops and sides, but also the windows, of buildings will generate electricity.

In the US, Kickstarter campaigns such as Solar Roadways are accelerating change by generating millions of dollars of consumer funding through a combination of digital access and new generation 'cool' technologies. Solar Roadways replace metalled roads with a system of hexagonal glass solar plates that generate energy. They can also light up to indicate traffic flow, speeds, the edges of lanes, etc, and heat up to melt snowfall. Solar Roadways estimate that if all the tarmac areas in the US were paved with solar cells, it would generate enough electricity to power three times the total US energy need! They are already paving car parks and sidewalks, and at the time of writing have been commissioned to replace a section of Route 66 under reconstruction. Their solution is based on a complete road 'system' not unlike the way the Romans built roads, provisioning on one side for drainage and on the other a channel for access, cabling and fibre-optics. This makes the roads compatible with new forms of smart road construction and traffic management, as well as assisting in the wider distribution of broadband internet. Later editions of their specially developed solar cells will have the capacity to charge electric vehicles through induction, making generation and charging simultaneous, extending battery life and range. Though the price will need to come down and durability will need to increase for widespread deployment to happen.

Generating unlimited quantities of electricity during the day alone is not entirely helpful: we also need to be able to generate electricity in the dark, and then store it. Wind turbines are getting cheaper and more efficient, both on and offshore. The renewable generation story will not be about one or two systems but about an array of forms operating at different scales, from single home, to community, to utility; and will include solar cells, concentrated solar, wind, hydro, tidal, biomass, geothermal, and more.

Storage solutions won't be limited to chemical batteries, but will include hydrogen, molten salt (heated by concentrated solar), mechanical systems and compressed air. Examples include General Electric's wind turbines near Munster in Germany that are being built to pump water from a lake to elevated storage inside the wind turbine when wind and electricity are plentiful, and then generate electricity from the downward water flow when it is not. A rail system being built in 2017 by ARES in Pahrump, Nevada drags a heavy train up a slope when electricity is cheap, and releases it to generate power from gravity when scarce. Gravitricity in the UK secured £650,000 of government funding to turn disused mineshafts into giant mechanical batteries, using a 2,000 tonne weight to store up to 20 MW of electricity by winching the weight up and lowering it according to demand. Much older hydro systems have been in place for decades, (like Dinorwig in Wales, created in 1974), which pump water uphill and release it to generate power. Dinorwig has a total stored capacity of about 9.1 GWh.

Most renewables generate when they can, rather than when they need to, and so the requirement for storage is central to their effectiveness. Gas-powered generation, on the other hand, can be switched on and off according to demand.

This power revolution could have happened 130 years ago and was on the verge of being created by Nicola Tesla, the electrical genius, who wanted to make universal electricity available for free. It is said that his ideas were shut down by vested interests who supported his rival, Edison, who wanted to charge for electricity.

The first electric car was made in 1835, 35 years before the first petrol, and 65 years before the first diesel, vehicles. By 1900, 40% of all cars on the road were electric, 38% were steam and only 22% were petrol. It was by no means certain that cars in the future would run on fossil fuels. At the time, chauffeurs were required for petrol cars because combustion engines required hand cranking to start them, which was hard work and not regarded as seemly for ladies, or indeed gentlemen. Electric cars were popular because they did not require cranking and most journeys were short. In 1900, in New York alone, there were 15,000 luxurious Baker electric cars with a 100-mile range.

Ford and Edison, working together, sunk millions into making an affordable electric car, but by 1914 it was clear that batteries were just too expensive and their range too limited for the longer journeys being undertaken on the rapidly improving roads. Petrol won out over electric and steam cars after the electric starter was invented, when roads were surfaced, and people started to drive further. In the end, the killer blow was price. Henry Ford marketed his mass-produced Model T for $260, compared to a conventionally built electric car at $1,750. From there, the infrastructure required to refuel was built, and the electric car was consigned, temporarily, to history.

If Tesla and Edison had won their respective races towards free electricity and cheaper batteries, would fossil fuels ever have had their 150 years of dominance? A hundred years after Henry Ford's fateful choice, the economics are now changing fast. Gas, coal and oil are all commodities that are both subject to market forces and are finite. There comes a point when they become too expensive to extract and transport. Solar cells, batteries and most other renewable options are subject to a different economic path because they are technologies, not commodities. The path they follow is subject to Moore's Law, has a longer experience curve and greater economies of scale: as we get better at making them, and as we make more of them, they continue to get cheaper. Once the tipping point is passed, commodities cannot compete with technologies on price.

It is already possible to buy a solar cell and battery combination for your home and for houses to be off-grid, managing their own power and heating or cooling independently. In the highly populated areas of Europe, North America and Northern Asia this technology could reduce electricity bills to zero in the summer, pay for itself in less than 10 years and provide free electricity for many more. Solar PV and batteries reduce in price by around 20% per year meaning, in real terms, that by 2020 payback time will have halved, and will halve again by 2025. In more solar-rich areas of North Africa, the Middle East, India and Central America, the payback time is far less.

For utility-scale generation, as of November 2016, the lowest generation bid price for solar and onshore wind was about $0.03 per kw/h for projects in Morocco. By September 2017 this had fallen to $0.017 per kw/h for two projects in the Middle East. The average price of electricity from coal and nuclear in 2015 was around $0.09 per kw/h and gas was about $0.075. Solar and wind generation will inevitably continue to get cheaper, whereas the economic case for coal, nuclear or gas generation continues to worsen.

In this change scenario, the economics of fossil fuel and nuclear generation fall apart. We've already seen this happening in Germany where there is large scale uptake of solar cells and wind generation. During May 2016 there were times when the price of electricity went negative because there was not enough storage, and the sun and wind cannot be turned off. Germany now regularly generates more than 75% of all its daily electricity needs through renewables. Once there is enough storage in the system, the problems of intermittency go away. Electric vehicles with their built-in storage may well also be part of the solution - allowing so-called "Vehicle-to-Grid" systems where owners charge their cars when electricity is abundant and sell some of it back when it is scarcer. Nissan enables owners of their Leaf cars to do just that. A pilot project in Utrecht in the Netherlands is linking 200 electric cars in a neighbourhood to balance out renewable electricity supply.

By contrast, imagine the billions of dollars and decades of time it takes for even the most capable oil & gas exploration company to extract its resource. Imagine the cost of funding a licence to explore, the exploration itself, discovery, well assessment and design, development of the field, laying pipelines, building and placing rigs, technical manufacture and safety, and then connecting that system to one of the 658 refineries around the world plus the subsequent cost of refining and distributing product. Compare this to the simplicity and efficiency of building a solar array and connecting it to the national grid. Or, in the developing world, connecting to a local or micro-grid for the town or village. In a cheap solar/battery world, the oil & gas behemoth is just plain out of business.

The top renewable players in 2018 are countries like Sweden, Costa Rica, Nicaragua, the UK, Germany, Uruguay, Denmark, China, Morocco, the USA and Kenya. Being ahead in the renewables game increases national competitiveness and reduces national climate impact.

As electricity and storage become cheaper they will incentivise new ways to use electricity, particularly for transport. Further incentives will come from the urgent need to improve urban air quality. At least 1,800 cities around the world are committed to air quality targets that cannot be met while combustion engines are allowed in the city.

London, for example, is planning that by 2020:

- All 300 single deck buses operating in central London will be zero emission (either electric or hydrogen)

- All 3,000 double decker buses will be hybrid

- There will be 9,000 zero emissions taxis (from 2018 all new taxis must be zero emission capable (ZEC))

- There will be an Ultra-Low Emissions Zone in central London

- In addition they will work on:

- Complete electrification of the rail network

- Moving goods from road to rail and water

- Further cycling growth, with over £1bn of investment in dedicated cycling infrastructure by 2025

- Increased electric vehicle charging points

In September 2018 a number of streets in East London were closed to combustion engined vehicles during peak hours because of pollution concerns.

Paris is even more ambitious, adding the AutoLib public electric car-sharing program, banning diesel engines and implementing significant closures of roads to traffic.

According to the BP Statistical Review 2017, oil demand in Europe peaked in 2005 and has been declining ever since, mostly due to improving energy efficiency. Shell broke ranks with the rest of the oil industry in November 2016 by projecting that oil demand globally might peak as soon as 2021. Whenever the peak comes, it is clear that demand for oil and gas will dry up before the wells do.

The slump in oil prices since 2014 was largely driven by a recognition of this reality, and the desperation of oil-rich states to minimise their volume of stranded assets in the form of unsellable oil and unusable infrastructure. At the same time, some engineering talent has left the big oil & gas companies to work on wind and solar projects.

Dong Energy (Danish Oil and Natural Gas) saw the writing on the wall some time ago and has become a big player in renewable energy. In October 2016, Dong Energy announced that it would sell the remaining 20% of the business that remained in oil and gas. In 2017, Dong Energy changed its name to Ørsted to reflect their transformation. Total too, are taking renewable energy seriously. Other players like BP and Shell are starting to make gentle moves in the renewables direction (BP led the field in 1997 under Lord John Browne, but after the Gulf of Mexico accident in 2010 their renewables programme lost momentum). In 2018 BP bought the Chargemaster network of electric car charging points in the UK. Exxon, Aramco, and Rosneft had still not made any substantial moves by the end of 2017, although the Vision 2030 programme in Saudi Arabia (Aramco) does involve selling potentially stranded oil & gas assets and a move towards solar.

Low oil prices from 2014 to 2017 reduced exploration activity and increased debt for oil companies and nations. In August 2016, Shell, BP, Exxon and Chevron had a combined debt of US$184 billion. In October 2016, Saudi Arabia issued a bond which raised $17.5 billion to prop up its national finances, which were suffering from the low oil price.

The reduced exploration activity will inevitably result in reduced production, which will result in increased prices. However, this price spike will only further accelerate the drive to renewables.

Weaning Ourselves Off Dependency

Giving up oil is not without discomfort. Nations that have depended on oil for their existence will suffer. Some 31 million people live in Saudi Arabia, in an environment that can perhaps support a tenth of that without a revolution in dry farming. All food is imported and most water is desalinated after an experiment with irrigation depleted much of the historic aquifers.

We only have to look at the chaotic state of Venezuela in 2016-18 to see what a falling oil price can do to societies dependent on oil income.

So far, much of the reduction in demand has been caused by global efficiency standards applied to cars. By 2016, these are thought to have reduced demand by 2.1 million barrels of oil per day, according to the International Energy Agency. The real impact of the electrification of transport has not happened yet, but as new models come to market with greater range and lower prices, the transition will be dramatic. As Tony Seba likes to say, "It only took 10 years for the horse to be replaced by the car". Once tipping points are reached, things happen quickly. As a telling example, in April 2000, at the height of its game, Nokia was worth €203bn. It was bought by Microsoft in 2014 for $7.2bn, due solely to the invention of the smartphone. In 2015, Microsoft wrote off $7.6bn, admitting to "grossly overpaying" for Nokia.

In 2010, there were only a handful of relatively expensive electric cars available, like the Tesla roadster or the G-Wizz, only suitable for particular niches. Significantly, the first modern mainstream electric car, the Nissan Leaf, was launched in December 2010. By 2016 there was a far wider selection of cars available with models like the Renault Zoe, the Tesla models S and X and the BMW i3. By 2020 they will be joined by electric models from Audi, Toyota, Hyundai, Volvo, Jaguar, Mercedes, VW, Kia and more.

In August 2016 Tesla announced that in 2018 their Model 3, the world's first fully electric mass market car, would be launched. Over 400,000 people placed deposits of upwards of $1,000 to secure one. The car industry had never seen anything like it and was shocked. Mercedes Benz had an emergency Board meeting. In the event, Tesla were beaten to the punch by Chevrolet, which launched the Bolt at the end of 2016, a mass market long-range electric car. By the summer of 2018 the Tesla Model 3 was the best-selling compact luxury car in the US. Together with the VW diesel emissions rigging scandal, which confirmed that diesel engines simply cannot be made to meet coming emissions standards, many in the automotive industry have started to pivot away from liquid fuels and towards electric.

By 2023, not only will countries such as the Netherlands and Norway be phasing out the sale of combustion engine cars, but a far wider variety of electric cars will be available to suit a far wider range of uses. China is the world's biggest market for electric vehicles. In 2015, domestic manufacturers sold 331,092 vehicles, according to the China Association of Automobile Manufacturers. This put them well on the way to their target of 3 million units a year by 2025, aided by subsidies that can amount to 60%. In 2016 there were 4,000 electrified car models in development, with the government moving to licence manufacturers because of fears about poor quality products. In December 2017, 102,000 fully electric cars were registered in China, a 130% year-on-year increase, taking annual sales to over 600,000 (up 71%), or 3.3% of all car sales. The electric single decker buses in London are made by BYD, a Chinese manufacturer.

Driven by a combination of simple economics and urban air quality targets, vans, trucks and buses will all be electrified. As battery prices come down, electric vehicles will be cheaper to run and cheaper to buy than ICE ones. Electric vehicles have massively fewer moving parts to manufacture, assemble or wear out. They are up to three times as efficient in their conversion of energy into movement, and electricity is now cheaper than petrol or diesel. In 2017, the Chinese city of Shenzhen converted their entire 16,000 bus fleet to fully electric. By the end of 2016, London reached around 170 fully electric buses (more than any other European city at the time) and will reach 2,500 hybrids in 2018.

Electric vans are so simple to manufacture that when Deutsche Post could not persuade VW, their usual supplier, to make a suitable electric van for them, they started to make their own! They put 1,000 of them on the road in the first year and will build another 5,000 of them for their own use; they will also decide whether to sell them to others.

In 2017, Tesla launched Semi, an electric haulage truck. With extraordinary performance, different models have ranges of 300 and 500 miles, allied to 'Megachargers' that can add 400 miles of range in 30 minutes. They will be expensive to buy, but cheap to run at 40 to 60 cents per mile. Other manufacturers like Nikola, Cummings, Bosch and Mercedes are all exploring the electric truck market.

NASA and Airbus are both working on electric planes. In 2016, Airbus flew their test plane, the E-Fan, across the English Channel. NASA believes that electric planes can be faster, much more energy efficient and 40% quieter than gas turbine engines. As anyone living anywhere near an airport knows, noise is a key consideration for airlines, and nearly silent electric planes would transform the lives of anyone near a flightpath, thereby reducing landing and take-off restrictions at controversial urban airports like London's Heathrow.

At the opposite end of technologies, small consumer appliances such as electric and robot mowers like the Electric Tractor Corps OX2 and Husqvarna's range will all contribute to reducing carbon emissions and demand for oil.

Why Does It Matter?
The case for decarbonisation is not just economic. Decarbonisation is a planetary imperative. It is driving and accelerating changes to the fabric of all our systems. Despite the climate deniers, 97% of climate scientists and many activists have succeeded in proving the phenomena and trends behind the changes we are experiencing. In fact, changes to our climate due to carbon in the atmosphere are accelerating faster than even the most extreme models predicted. The climate is changing. Within this complex and diverse subject group the following seems to be true:

- The earth has already warmed to 0.9 of 1 degree from pre-industrial levels, with evidence released in 2018 by the IPCC that the rate of warming is not proceeding in a linear fashion but increasing.

- This warming has taken place over the last 150 years at a rate unprecedented in all of recorded history (recorded history going back 800,000 years, measured from air locked in old ice, and the geological record). This accelerated change coincides exactly with the industrialisation of the earth, widespread use of fossil fuels and factory-farm meat production

- Public health is at risk in countries such as Indonesia, China and India, all of which vie for 'planet's most polluted' on a yearly basis

- The United Nations Climate Conference (COP 21) held in Paris in November 2015 was a watershed moment in global political history. No other issue (not even the Second World War) has produced agreement from 195 countries. Yet in 2017 the USA gave notice it would withdraw from this agreement

- As a species, humans pump 110m tonnes of carbon into the atmosphere and oceans every day; up by 20m tonnes each day since 2009. Just from a public health perspective this can't be good, even if you disregard the greater destruction of the Earth

- We have lost 50% of all coral reefs due to ocean acidification and warming; this is already having a dramatic impact on marine life and food chains

- We are felling and burning forests in the Amazon, the Congo, and in rainforests across Asia Pacific (the lungs of the planet), to create palm oil plantations and cattle ranches

- Large areas of previously fertile land are becoming desert, including the American midwest and the Middle East. In 2016 the Middle East saw its worst drought in 900 years

- Using industrially desalinated seawater for irrigation, industry, and drinking is salinating both the Arabian and Red Seas at unprecedented rates, asphyxiating marine life and destroying those ecosystems

- The fossil fuel industry accounts for a large proportion of all carbon emissions and is perennially seen as the carbon 'bad boy'. However, agribusiness and the meat industry are almost equal in emissions when the clearing and burning of forests, supplying water, animal feeding, and food distribution systems are all taken into account

- One of the hardest truths about sustainability is that a low impact economy has to be founded on minimal meat consumption:

- Relative to pork or chicken, red meat needs 28x more land to produce, 11x more water and results in 5x more climate-warming emissions. It requires 160x more land and produces 11x more greenhouse gases than potatoes, wheat, or rice. In a world in which 1-in-7 people are hungry, the preference in developed nations for feasting daily on red meat will have to become a thing of the past. 16% of all emissions are methane (from melting permafrost and livestock), which is 23x more carboniferous than CO_2

These facts mean that carbon emissions have to, and will, become regulated. Although there is no sign yet of a carbon tax, COP 21 laid the groundwork for this eventuality.

So What?

All businesses in transportation and energy will be subject to what is already being called the 'Energy Transition'. Electricity generation and distribution; the movement of people and goods via land, sea and air; oil, gas and coal companies and the suppliers to all of these sectors; lighting, heating, etc will all be transformed.

Even non-energy/transport businesses are already taking advantage of the transition. Google, Apple and Amazon are aiming for, or achieving, energy independence through a mixture of renewables and storage because it is the right thing to do and is good for their brand.

For oil, gas and coal businesses the transformation will be the most dramatic. These companies have to reframe their entire business model based on what they are actually good at, beyond the product. Core strengths of these businesses are often engineering in hostile environments and accessing or handling tricky materials deep underground.

Like Dong Energy/Ørsted these companies could deploy these talents building offshore wind farms or finding ways to access the potential of geothermal energy in more locations. They could also get involved in electric car charging, as Shell and BP have already done in the UK, solar power provision, batteries, onshore wind and so on.

The challenge is not so much in identifying the opportunity as pivoting the business towards it. This is the challenge of leadership: to shift the business from simply cranking a profitable but unsustainable handle, to leading the entity through a likely dip in profitability to a new paradigm. In doing so, leadership needs to create a culture which can both crank a different, reliable handle, but also undertake continuous innovation. Failure to do so soon enough will almost certainly result in irrelevance over the long term.

Doing this is probably both easier and riskier if you are the CEO. CEOs have more influence than most; a trusted CEO might get the Board and the Executive team to go along with the shift but would be scrutinised heavily if the change failed to deliver quickly.

We are currently involved in supporting just such a transformation for a company that has had the same business model for over 100 years. The first challenge is to correctly identify and calibrate the crisis. Is this just a dip in the traditional market or a long-term trend? And if you feel you are on to something, how will you persuade others?

All of this was preceded by decades of experimentation. A few innovative (disruptive) thinkers inside the company were able to secure resources to explore new ideas. Eventually they got to a point where they had a marketable product. This coincided with what looked like an accelerating decline in sales of the conventional product. At this point, the CEO was persuaded to pivot the business.

The next challenge is realigning the business systems and processes and, most significantly, the culture, to a new way of operating. In the conventional model, cranking the handle for a well-established and highly profitable product required minimal creativity and plenty of obedience. It could successfully be managed by 'managers' in a hierarchical structure where everyone knew their place and did what they were told. The new business model requires people to be creative, to think, to come up with ideas, and to experiment. These practices were antithetical to the old model. Achieving the shift will require two cultures to exist in parallel for a time. The challenge is how to avoid creating resentment and antagonism between them.

This particular company has made the choice, so far, to retain their people, their name, and the overall geography of the business. Another option would be to start a separate and parallel business from scratch in order to avoid the difficulty of getting mature people to change their ways.

The other choice when facing disruption is simply to fail. As Amory Lovins says: "Survival is not mandatory". There are plenty of examples of companies that failed to take the right decisions when the writing was on the wall. Blockbuster and Kodak had some warning, while Blackberry and Nokia had less, yet none of them succeeded in transforming when their market was disrupted.

Throughout this book we will try to understand why.

Social Transformation

None of these Megatrends have had sufficient public debate or discussion. The consequence of this is that the immense ethical and social questions implicit in the changes don't get adequate answers, politics clings to the status quo, and the careless way in which change happens creates far too many losers.

In a relatively stable environment, most organisations prioritise management over leadership. In a stable environment, leadership is annoying and disruptive because of its appetite for change. Management, on the other hand, refines processes and gets the job done reliably and repeatedly, which why it is beloved of large legacy organisations like banks, and oil & gas companies. Doing anything different is heresy and not wanted. As the business environment becomes more turbulent, established businesses with a preponderance of managers struggle to keep up with the changes, and begin to seek out leadership.

Conventional organisations are extremely vulnerable in current circumstances. With size and weight comes an inherent inertia. Shareholders get used to receiving fat cheques, and any new CEO who recognises the trends will be criticised and often ousted for attempting to make change. Consequently, CEOs are often not the best proponents of change. CEOs want their tenure to be successful, and so they play along. We are currently living through a generation of CEO-managers, not leaders, people who are essentially and imperturbably not about change. However, this simply kicks the 'need for change' can further down the road.

The same is occurring in government. For example, in the UK, a very experienced manager was appointed to run the country's exit from the EU. 'Appointed' because the popular vote in favour of Brexit left a catastrophic vacuum in leadership, and the appointment of an uncontested Prime Minister in some of the most dramatic political events since World War II. Mrs May has since won her own General Election by the slimmest of margins and with the need to be propped up by a 'confidence and supply' arrangement with the Irish DUP. So the UK's exit from the EU, the most profound transformation the country has seen for decades, is being led by an efficiency manager who herself voted to remain in Europe.

Given the degree of turbulence being faced in the UK, all organisations and agencies will need to upgrade their leadership capability and their bench strength. The question is how to make that happen.

Alongside other causes of liberal and social inertia, the Megatrends are also contributing to a backlash. Those who feel marginalised by the pressures of globalisation are kicking back against them: unfathomable changes to business, climate, immigration, and the economy are driving a psychological retreat all over the world. It may not be long before technology companies pursuing AI and robotics are seen as 'the enemy', just as the Luddite movement protested the automation of textile manufacturing in the UK in the early 19th Century. There have already been clashes between legacy taxi firms and Uber, for example.

As a society, we need to talk about this. Banks and supermarkets are struggling to cope with digitisation; the whole fossil fuel-based energy and transport supply chain is either traumatised or in denial about decarbonisation. Health services in the global north are being overwhelmed by ageing communities. The backlash has begun in the UK, Europe and the

USA: more and more older people, struggling to understand their role in a digital landscape, challenged by the very idea of climate change, failing to get treatment for their conditions, and losing their pensions as the oil companies they relied on crumble, are looking to past certainties for security. This kind of nostalgia is dangerous.

Governments are blindsided by the speed of events and confused by forces they do not understand. They are too used to managing transactionally by virtue of status; political leaders are profoundly ill-equipped to deal with nimble, tidal inevitability.

Is There Purpose?

And yet... And yet, an optimistic rise in openness, transparency, and social mobilisation has also been in evidence for some years. Social standards have all been improving. Movements such as #MeToo are suddenly and dramatically rebalancing gender bias. The sheer number of people working to alleviate hunger, provide clean water, reduce poverty, supply shelter, fight addiction, and advocate against war is staggering. One of the main indicators of change is the noise created in the system: think of recent moves to address racism, such as #blacklivesmatter, or movements to improve female safety with legislation against 'upskirting', or the agonised, dignified and powerful calls for social justice in the wake of the Grenfell Fire in the UK.

These are high profile examples, but many other initiatives and efforts go unreported. The global thirst for democracy through peaceful means has increased exponentially. Even the incidence of war has diminished to 1% of that experienced in 1945. Communities are driving change for themselves rather than relying on slow-moving or self-interested leadership at national and international level. Because of this, we assert that visionary leadership has, of necessity, now moved outside the mainstream.

Hope is the medium for change while we wait for a new or better leader. Purpose occurs when we start to do it for ourselves.

"There is no coming to consciousness
without pain."

Carl Jung

CHAPTER 3

MAMMALIAN PERSPECTIVES

Neither Mark nor Neil are qualified psychologists. However, along our journeys we have learned a good deal about psychology, and the subject is integral to our work. Leadership is a behaviour after all. Understanding some fundamentals in the way that our brains are wired, the ways that we operate collectively and the ways that we mature, is crucial to understanding our topics of leadership, culture and change.

The pressing challenges and opportunities we all experience mean one thing for sure: more, and constant, change. The less consciously we, as a species, address those changes, the more wild and unpredictable their effects will be.

Those of us hoping to return to some stable, rose tinted past will be disappointed. Technology will continue to disrupt, meaning old business models will fail, new ways of working and developing our careers will evolve, in turn causing changes to family life, the social fabric, and our daily individual experiences. Building fortress countries is an attempt to hold back the tide. Building fortress businesses will simply be managing their decline. Building a fortress career may be possible, but would be at odds with everything else occurring around you, and change will be thrust upon you at some point, except for a tiny number of hyper specialists. Paraphrasing the words of Aragorn in J.R.R. Tolkien's *The Lord of the Rings*, "Change is upon you, whether you would wish it or no."

We have a choice, but it is not a choice about whether or not we change. It is a choice about how we engage with change. The opportunity open before each of us is to learn to lead ourselves more effectively, building a whole new mindset and skillset to help us and our communities in the years ahead.

The skillset and mindset we need is one of **change agility**, a core component of leadership. Alongside that, we must consciously build the capacity to hold a long-term vision, whether that be personal or a contribution towards something larger. And our vision must no longer allow us to steal from the future.

Evolution has armed us with a host of amazing attributes, including a very large brain, capable of dealing with multiple activities at once, such as simultaneously running your liver, regulating your temperature, feeling wistful about your lovely romance, and learning to use a great new app. There is also an added benefit: you are a learning animal, able simultaneously to cross-compare sets of experiences from the past with what is happening to you right now, and matching both of these to an imagined set of behaviours we might need in the future. Therefore, you are already superbly set up for change agility.

We Are Animals

There are some critical dimensions in human behaviour that are never mentioned in discussions of leadership. Leadership is typically treated as a set of traits we should ideally aspire to, and rarely as a lived experience. We experience leadership all the time, frequently without recognising it. As humans, we are:

1. Produced by evolution and the world, and therefore a part of the environment on which we rely.

2. Mammals, conforming to evolutionary principles of how animal (social) groups interact.

3. Post the Enlightenment, and accelerated by good research and technology, becoming more and more consciously aware of how systems behave, and hence able to make new kinds of decisions that may be at odds with our mammalian habits and heritage; this creates tensions.

As mammals, evolution has built us to co-operate within social systems in which we all have a role. Alphas, Betas, workers, scouts, mothers, warriors, foragers, and so on. There is even the role of outcast. Co-operation mixed with exclusion is an evolutionary mechanism to increase the likelihood that our children grow up, and the group survives. Whether this appeals to our ideals of human supremacy or not, it is present and observable in our behaviour.

These dynamics also affect our response to leadership. Animal groups need 'strong' leaders at their head, because without them they fall apart. Humanity has built an incredibly complex global system in which our identity as 'animal group' is becoming less and less important. We still have farmers and warriors, but we don't know them personally; they operate in a co-ordinated way under the national Alphas and Betas: my clothing is made in Indonesia, my beef comes from Patagonia, my wine from France, my shoes from Italy and my interior design from Sweden. Yet as individuals in a political system we still have the power, just as we did when we were kicking around the savanna in small family groups, to boot out the Alphas when they appear not to serve our interests any more. We especially do not like Alphas to achieve their position by manipulation, and we do not like to be lied to.

Later we will examine the different kinds of leadership roles we expect to see, and our responses to each. At the same time, the nature of what we respect in leaders is changing. In addition, the leadership styles that have got us to this point (strong, controlling, vested interests), will not serve us in the future. We increasingly need inclusive, distributed, shared interests.

Many of us understand instinctively that a new kind of leadership, one which cannot have all the answers, is required. Now, we need to step up and lead in that way.

The environment of constant change goes against our programming. Evolution has prepared us for a slow pace of life with occasional intense bursts of excitement and activity. We are still what we have always been. Because of this, we are neither physiologically nor psychologically set up with the right kind of alarm bells either for a constant state of hyper-vigilance (brought by constant change), or for long-term future threat.

In evolutionary terms, humans are best at responding to (rather than anticipating) short-term threats. We are all capable of dealing with medium-term threats such as mitigating a job loss within a year, or working through a process of divorce, but these threats only come into focus when they are specific, known, and affect us personally. Neuroscience tells us that new forms of long-term, existential threats such as climate change, nuclear confrontation, millions of economic and climate immigrants, business decline, mass job loss through automation, the end of oil and gas, and water and food scarcity are not the kind of dangers humans can easily address, or even, perhaps, care about.

When these kinds of super-threats start to affect us personally, we may look (often in vain) to government to change policy or big business to keep our jobs. We like to assume that large entities are capable of bringing about large-scale change. But though they may care about us, there will be little they can do about our individual circumstances, as they have to deal with the 'good' of the whole.

The larger the social system, the more important are the stories that hold it together. In his books, *Sapiens - A Brief History of Humankind* and *Homo Deus*, Yuval Noah Harari describes in detail the mechanisms of mythology and belief that we employ in order to make sense of the world and the systems in which we live. A mythology could range from a religion, to a political doctrine, to a business model, to an internal personal narrative such as ego or self-worth. The mythologies give us a belief system - comfort and light in the darkness - and are so powerful that we will, in fact, continue to believe in these cherished narratives even after facts have proven them different. We will make an enemy of someone who challenges our stories, even though the challenge may be correct: "My book about my invisible friend is better than your book about the same invisible friend, and I will kill you for being opposite." We may prefer to continue as we are without making change, though it is not the change itself we resist, but *believing a new thing*.

According to Harari, in co-located groups of up to about 150, it is possible to organically manage a single mythology without too much trouble. Stories and gossip are shared and there is enough social contact for it to self-sustain (think of a large family or a small start-up). However, above that size, groups tend to fracture into sub-groups and spin-offs, and these spin-offs create their own sub-cultures and stories as they go. Now think of a large multinational across many countries, each with their own different mentality and approach to the same business, or any large religion and how it fractures into smaller, but related, micro-belief systems. None of them can claim the absolute truth, but all will fight to protect their version of it.

Consequently, in very large groups such as countries or political structures, powerful mythologies need to be created in order to glue millions of people together into the same social construct. Nazism, Liberalism, Socialism, Nationalism and Capitalism are all examples of this. Some of them can work in tandem with one another, such as Nazism and Capitalism, others just don't go together, such as Capitalism and Communism. Those dogmatic tensions underpinned the global conflicts of the 20th Century. Used manipulatively, it becomes possible to send a generation to its death simply because 'Your Country Needs You', or in a more benign version, for billions of people to buy the new iPhone X because it's better at *everything* than the last virtually identical version.

Mythologies make large cultures work. All are built on shared stories and attract the people who believe, and buy into, the way in which the culture is presented.

So, up to this point, it seems everything is either programmed (genetics that shape our behaviour) or a superstition (subjectively experienced with myths and stories to explain it). Using scientific principles of critical observation enables us to become more objective. Scientific investigation is the application of curiosity, and unlike religion or a value system, does not claim to know the absolute truth, but treats outcomes as undetermined. Rigorous science gradually uncovers the cause of what is, using observation, experimentation, and trial and error (which, incidentally, are the true mechanisms of evolution, and hence change). New discoveries are built on old ones and tend to move along with what works. Scientific theories exist but are constantly tested and re-examined in the search for facts. (It is only when our biases turn them into mythologies that they fail to serve their intended purpose).

It is important to state that how we choose to apply science and technology is wholly different to the scientific process itself. Decisions on how to apply scientific discovery come from the subjective realm, becoming victim to our own biases, superstitions, and beliefs. Science is not good, it just is. What we do with science can only manifest from the consciousness and intent we are capable of holding at the time.

In summary, it is entirely possible for us to argue with mates down the pub that the Green Party should be in power, then go off to work at our job for an oil company at 6am the next morning, in our diesel 4x4, eat drive-through McDonalds for breakfast without recycling the packaging, and remain fully convinced we are concerned about climate change and social justice! We don't make the big personal changes because we are more firmly entrenched in our convenient Capitalist mythology than we are in our Socially Responsible Citizen one.

How would it be if we could rid ourselves of beliefs entirely? Would that enable a less conflicted world?

Clearly, there are people who can address existential, long-term threat. What makes them different? How are they able to marry their purpose to their commitment, their emotional life, and their actions? How is it possible for someone like Al Gore personally to connect to and coordinate activity aimed at fixing the hazy distant future, while the rest of us debate and argue about whether or not climate change even exists?

This level of commitment is in its simplest expression just a behaviour, and is about three things:

1. **Reach**: one's ability and capacity to affect levels of a system, for example yourself, a family, a team, an organisation, a region, a country, a bloc, the world, etc.

2. **Motivation:** what truly underlies your intentions in wanting to effect a change; usually aligned to either status or purpose.

3. **Perspective:** related to personal maturity, perspective concerns your relationship to the mutual interconnectedness of things, and the way in which you solve problems or take advantage of opportunities.

Perspective relates to leadership. We suggest that the first task of anyone who aspires to have positive influence through leadership is, first, to grow themselves.

No system can exceed the consciousness of its leaders.

Brain Science

There are roughly three centres in our amazing, evolved brains; each centre processing information differently.

The youngest and outermost part of the brain - the cauliflower-looking part - is the neocortex. This part of the brain is responsible for rational and logical thought; it problem-solves, creates, uses tools and communicates. It is also responsible for sense-making and imagination; without imagination we cannot conceive any other possible future. It is the source of debate, possibilities, options, choice and planning.

Underneath the neocortex sits our limbic system; a collection of parts which are older and deeper. Also known as the mammalian part of our brain, this centre is responsible for cooperation, parental care, love and attachment, status and social pecking orders, role specialisation, sympathy, empathy, war and peace. The limbic system attaches importance or meaning to the thinking done in the neocortex. Decisions made here are stronger because they have emotion attached to them and have a somatic or bodily impact. Sometimes the decisions we take seem to others to be completely irrational and not based in facts. That is because they may have different motivators driving them, such as the achievement of power, social positioning, retaliation, or winning.

The limbic brain has no capacity for language but conditions the body for action by creating floods of peptides, cortisol and adrenaline designed to prompt a physiological response. If, for example, we need to engage our body to evade a charging rhino, then developing imaginative options to persuade the charging rhino not to hit us might just get us killed. We need to engage our body to procreate, yet in my experience developing and sharing sophisticated arguments as to why I'd be a better DNA donor than the fellow next to me just doesn't work. We need to be *involved*.

The third, oldest and deepest part of our brains is the medulla, which many call the reptilian brain, and is just a bulb at the top of our brain stem. This has three functions only: to stimulate fight, flight, or freeze. Remember the last time you were in this state (and maybe you have only been here two or three times in your life)? The experience was powerful and stays with you; you tell stories about it. This is evolution ensuring that the next time we are in a perilous or threatening situation, we remember and hide, motionless, get the hell out of there, or form our hand into a fist. What predicates changes to our mental state, or progression downwards through the levels of the brain, is conflict, or the degree of perceived assault on our self-worth.

As we encounter difficulty, disagreement and conflict, what occurs is a natural selection process to obtain the right response to the environment we are in. The deeper the potential conflict, the less logical and more physiological we become. In the neocortex we can consider ourselves, the problem, and the others involved. The limbic brain can only deal with our relationship to the problem and ourselves. In the medulla, we can only be concerned with self-preservation. Once down there it takes extreme conscious effort and personal mastery to intentionally return to neocortex-driven behaviour.

This separation means it is possible to rationally know and understand a thing without it having one scintilla of meaning; we do not feel involved. This connects to the term 'existential threat'; long-term threats are not a rhino charging down on us right now but exist only in the imagination. A cognitive flight of fancy such as, "If we don't change, our business will be over within ten years", may not stimulate the right response for us to care sufficiently about it (remember Neil's example from Our Price Records). To care about it, we need to reach into the limbic areas, and form an emotional connection.

Research around change says that in prompting action, emotional commitment is four times more powerful than rational commitment, because our body becomes engaged.

There is another effect more related to our upbringing and our experience than our evolution. The work of psychologist Clare W. Graves on what came to be known as Spiral Dynamics describes how the brain physically develops as we mature and learn. Brain plasticity causes observable and consistent physical differences in the neural connections between the brains of people at different levels of maturity. One of the key differences between those at a dependent state of maturity (red or blue in Spiral Dynamics terms) and those at an Independent or Interdependent level of maturity (orange, green and yellow in Spiral Dynamics) is that at a dependent level of maturity, we are likely to see beliefs or myths as having equal status with facts. When and if we reach an Independent or Interdependent level of maturity, we would see facts as being of a higher order than beliefs or myths.

This is important for change and leadership because while it is relatively quick to change our habits or to shift from our medulla or limbic brain to our neocortex, it usually takes much more time (or a more powerful stimulus) to rewire our brain and change our maturity level.
(See Vertical Development below).

So, the difference between Al Gore and some of the rest of us, may simply be that he has succeeded in connecting his limbic brain to his higher functions and maturing his neocortex to an Integral level. This produces in him an aligned response that is able to understand through facts, feel through emotions, and relate to the distant 'existential' threat of climate change on behalf of all life and in service of a long-term future.

Al Gore is using the full extent of his Reach, Motivation, and Perspective. As a former Vice President of America, he understands, has access to, and can affect very large, supra-national bodies. His Motivation cannot be for himself - he has been vilified and criticised in his effort to draw attention to the long-term perils facing the world; so he cannot be status-driven but must be motivated by purpose. Mark has never met Al Gore in person but has spent a day in a conference room being trained by him and understands from this experience, that Gore's purpose is closely linked to his children and grandchildren (and ours too) and therefore his limbic system, giving him four times more commitment than just his rational understanding.

Lastly, Gore's Perspective is an Integral one, seeing the whole of the world as an interconnected web of life. Thus, a grave threat requiring urgent action is presented by significant changes to climate and rampant overuse of the Capitalist mythology. He sees the systemic impacts not just to humanity, but to our very sustenance, or the ecology of the world. By all three definitions, Reach, Motivation and Perspective, Gore is knowingly and intentionally exercising conscious leadership; his behaviour is designed to disrupt the status quo and bring about change.

None of this is to say that we all can or should be Al Gore. We must recognise and work from where we are in our own lives and personal journeys. However, it's a simple truth that if we aspire to live authentically, we are aspiring to leadership, which means the double-whammy of both standing out a bit (by bucking the trends of our established social groups) and growing our Perspective (expanding our sphere of awareness and influence). Authentic leadership commits to continually raising our awareness in all three dimensions of leadership behaviour. There is a resulting application to changing the self, reducing ego or personal significance, and being of service at bigger and bigger levels. In doing this, authentic leaders accept that however many fans and followers might support you, there will also be detractors and saboteurs, especially if your purpose challenges their myth.

In years gone by, many people who felt this way gave their personal journey a spiritual significance and removed themselves from the mainstream to contemplate nature and the web of life as an ascetic, joining a nunnery, or studying art or philosophy. Today, we can no longer 'drop out' in that way.

We have a family, a career, a social group and pastimes, while we develop our spiritual awareness. Facebook carries more uplifting humanist messages around the world in one second than the whole of all historical spiritual literature combined. So it's easier to journey among friends.

In years gone by, a high Perspective leadership response would also have been a matter of personal conscience. When the world had fewer than 3 billion people, we could pretty much do what we liked as individuals, and the only thing that mattered was whether or not we had harmed anyone else, and felt fulfilled (without the two necessarily being connected). Now, we are facing a range of pressing societal issues that anyone with even a moderate level of Perspective can no longer ignore. The context has changed, and it is this particular change that means anyone who aspires to authenticity also aspires to purpose-driven leadership.

All of this means you.

Leadership Perspectives: The Definitions

Contrary to popular belief, most people are not afraid of failure but of success, of becoming everything they ever wanted to be. That bright light is intimidating because it demands that we upgrade ourselves and stick to living at that level of consciousness. We must put into place the standards and discipline required to maintain that Perspective and continue to act on those standards and disciplines. And that can feel hard, at least at the beginning.

We need to begin to look at leadership through the Perspective lens. Happily, this is neither a theoretical concept nor a mythology. This is measurable and definable, developing through clear stages. Perspective grows quickly during our childhood and more slowly during adult life. For some, this progression can stop or slow earlier than for others. This can be caused by specific events, or more usually by the way we are raised and educated. In many cultures, there is a need to reach a certain standard of education; after that, we are expected simply to contribute through work. For those who follow the path of growing their Perspective, Reach, and Motivation, learning is for ever.

We are all familiar with the effects of 'horizontal' development, where we add skills that enable us to be more effective. Learning to drive, building fluency in a new language, apprenticeship, developing business skills; all of these are horizontal development. Developing our Perspective is a challenge of 'vertical' development because it is the pursuit of personal growth. What exactly grows when we talk about this? It is our awareness, or consciousness. The higher our level of consciousness, the greater the potential impact and sustainability of what we do, and the wider and more durable our influence.

Vertical Development - A Matter of Perspective

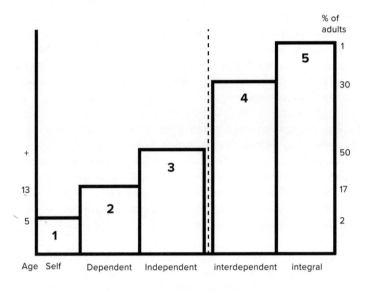

| 1 | The world exsists to serve me. |

| 2 | The world should be the way I view it. Rules or other people give me validation. |

| 3 | Life is a competition with individuals, winner and losers.

Me and people like me against the world. |

| 4 | Life is a collaboration.

Vulnerability and trust go hand in hand.

The possibility of deeply trusting team relationships exists. |

| 5 | All life is interdependent.

Responsibility is global and indefinite.

Understanding of the complex interrelatedness of everything, and seeking universal solutions to enable sustained success. |

Based on work by the Centre for
Creative Leadership

Level 1: Self

As infants, our preoccupation is ourselves, our needs are immediate, and we don't care about those around us. Learning that there are other people in the world who we must consider is a traumatic experience manifested in the "terrible twos", although it can last much longer than a year. At this stage of development, we think nothing of lying on the floor and screaming at the top of our voice in public places, simply because some minor limitation has been placed on our freedom.

It is important that we retain a moderate level of "self" consciousness through our adult life for our own protection. Too little or too much "self" consciousness and we are either open to abuse and exploitation, or we may become selfish and inconsiderate. However, those who hang on to this "self"-centred stage of development can also be dangerous to others, and may later show signs of psychopathy or narcissism, having failed to learn to empathise with or respect the needs of others.

Having self-oriented people in powerful leadership positions is potentially extremely damaging to everyone and everything else around them. They create dog-eat-dog systems in which no assumptions or values can be reliable and constant beyond their own whims.

If you find yourself having very strong reactions when things 'aren't fair' to you, or when you don't get what you want, or if you tend to blame others or the general situation rather than looking to your own behaviour, you may still have an excess elements of your 'Self' Perspective in play.

Level 2: Dependent

For the 98% who make it past the first stage (generally age 5 or 6), we move on to a state of 'dependence' characterised by obedience. You may recognise this in the strict rule observance of children around the age of 8 to 13. By that age, we have learned about the needs of others and have accepted or formulated rules that control our behaviour. Our sense of fairness also resides here, as in this state we feel that the rules should apply to everyone equally, whether that is workable in life or not. As we mature, it is important that we become less obedient. While appropriate level of conformity is essential to the social compact, excessive obedience can be a serious problem in organisations and societies when people are unable to take the initiative or challenge authority figures. In the days before the data-led culture change in aviation, there were a frightening number of aircraft crashes attributed to excessively obedient cockpit crews who felt unable to challenge the Captain.

Failure to move through dependence to what lies beyond is a key enabler of particular kinds of leadership. Dependent adults will often seek out strong authority figures (as a kind of surrogate parent) and will trade loyalty for the sense that someone else is taking responsibility for them. This plays out at all levels, from domestic abuse right up to authoritarian political or corporate leaders.

Dependent Perspectives may find themselves wishing that someone would come in and take away their problems, or they may be slavish to rules, regulations, policies and procedures. Dependent leaders look to their seniors for decision-making and can create stifling, wait-till-we're-told systems.

Level 3: Independent

By the time we are into our teens, most of us will be showing signs of independence, or at least a transference of our dependence from our parents to our peers. At this stage, many of us would prefer to make mistakes, sometimes quite big mistakes, than listen to advice. You may find some comfort here if you are a parent and find yourself pondering why little Freya will only listen when her friend tells her the exact same thing you did just last week. In addition, many developed societies have education systems that generally see co-operation and collaboration as 'cheating', so you will have to prove yourself as independent through the individualised nature of passing exams. In the West, it is source of pride when people become independent and 'stand on their own two feet' so as not to be a burden on anyone. Independence is both admired and aspirational. In India and the Middle East, this trait is frowned upon as the family is the more important body, and individuals exist to serve that greater good. In China, the social group is most important, and taking pride in being an essential 'cog in the machine' is a prerequisite for success.

Many people in powerful leadership positions hold on to an independent mindset well into adulthood. However, getting teams, departments or organisations to collaborate with each other is a big part of life. Essentially this involves moving on from your 'Independent' Perspective. Many of us need to unlearn this independence in order to be effective team collaborators and exercise leadership that is not limited by our need for control.

The 'independent' mindset is at the root of feelings about 'us and them', or 'in-group versus out-group'. In teen years this commonly leads to bullying and exclusion. In organisations, this mindset contributes to competitive silo structures, where parts of the organisation fail to collaborate because of excessive loyalty to their own mythology. In countries, this leads to caste systems or the victimisation of minorities. In global blocs it leads to a nation or group peremptorily removing itself from longstanding international communities or agreements in the belief that it is better to go it alone.

Adults who have not matured beyond this 'Independent' level are vulnerable to manipulation. Cynical manipulation of vulnerable mindsets is extremely powerful. If a leader can project a "same is safe, different is dangerous" belief, s/he can gather one section of the population in opposition to another, masking many other troubles.

If you find yourself frequently blaming others, feeling victimised or believing your expertise or specialist area is never good enough, you may be feeling a high degree of separation and independence. If you are highly competitive and always need to win, you are fiercely independent. The problem is that for one person or group always to win, someone else must lose, which perpetuates an imbalance. This is an unnatural scarcity mindset. Nature is not scarce, but abundant, and seeks balance. In unhealthy minds, independence can also lead to dissociation and sociopathic behaviours.

Independent leadership tends to attract either hero or 'saviour' style personalities, who are motivated by status and ego rather than purpose. It also draws in fiercely competitive Bosses who mainly enjoy control and dominance.

Level 4: Interdependence

The fact of the matter is that we are all connected. There may very well be a spiritual side to that statement, but there is also a very practical one. As we stated above, we are a product of the earth, not separate from it. Our actions affect our species. If we poison our water, we poison ourselves. If we burn the lungs of the planet, we asphyxiate. Our world is complex and ambiguous; truth is also a perspective. Learning to deal with plural perspectives as a leadership characteristic is one of the issues of our time.

The majority of adults do not make it to a fully interdependent mindset. The fully interdependent mindset bases choices and their life on our interconnectedness with other humans and with our environment. Many of us will achieve a partial level of interdependence where we are aware of the need to be open to and respectful of difference, and we become aware of our reliance on our family, friends, or work colleagues. We struggle to convert that knowledge to wisdom because interdependence also requires that we take off the armour of independence and make ourselves a little bit more vulnerable. It means that sometimes we might lose out and not get 'everything we deserve'. Sometimes, it might mean we don't get anything at all.

Interdependence is a risk: it is trust, but not in the same way as dependence. Dependence asks that we place ourselves at the mercy of something or someone else. Interdependence suggests there is a mutuality to all exchanges of energy or power, and that while we have something to lose, we have much to gain. Interdependence asks that you put yourself in the hands of another, and vice versa. In our society, many of these lessons come only when, for example, we abandon a destructive first marriage and get it right the second time, finding a partner with whom to grow and change. Or we learn interdependence after having a child and seeing their 'self' stage from the outside. Or perhaps we are fortunate enough to work in a high functioning team or organisation where a mature culture of interdependence carries us along too.

Interdependence is slower, less fraught, and less anxious, because there is also a huge degree of comfort in knowing that at least a few other people have your back. We can stop pushing and work together. Many people we work with tell us that they are far too busy to take on any additional work such as regular one-to-one meetings with their direct reports or other employees. Tasks and delivery are more important than the social or business systems in which they spend their lives. Many business systems have at their core a fear of betrayal, or a political basis to relationships. None of those businesses can perform as well as the businesses that work with trust.

Interdependent leadership takes more time, celebrates diversity (invisible as well as visible), and builds for the long term. Interdependent systems can be frustrating because they need to take account of multiple perspectives and stakeholders. However, if they can be made to work, they are often purpose-driven and extremely robust. Interdependent leaders have the rather annoying habit of calling us out on our bullshit, being adult and balanced, and in many cases can generate real love in others. They can also create jealousy in those who are not as advanced.

Interdependent leadership is often viewed as weak or ineffectual from independent or dependent perspectives. Both of these can undermine and attack interdependence as being worthless, time-consuming, or 'too nice'. Truly interdependent leadership, however, has teeth, because as well as knowing the ideals it espouses, it also knows its values-driven red lines and no-go areas. Living authentically to a clear value set is neither weak nor ineffectual. Truly interdependent leadership is inspirational because it asks us to raise our own standards.

If you regularly feel that your vulnerability is held safely in someone else's hands, and you value this so highly that you also take care of theirs, you are likely to be quite firmly in the realm of interdependence.

Level 5: Integral

Interdependence is a high level Perspective which only a small minority attain, let alone transcend. Integral is the level at which we are able to fully integrate all of the previous levels in a balanced way. We have a healthy sense of ourselves that is objective and humble. We are willing to be vulnerable enough to depend on others and yet assertive enough to be prepared to stand out. We are able to collaborate effectively, even with people we disagree with or find annoying. The work we do has a high degree of sustainability because we naturally honour the past and the future, as well as the present.

82

We can be respected and loved by all of the other levels because of the ways in which our communication, humility, integrity and dignity touch those around us. Integral leadership sees the whole and operates from it but is not itself lofty or disconnected. Integral leadership raises others up, finding purpose and meaning in the work itself. The work is to be integral, and integration is the work. To be integral is to hold a vision, and the limitations of the system, in mind simultaneously. To be integral is to build for the long term and in sympathy with the behaviours and needs of the people involved and of the natural systems and resources on which the work of building is based. Integral is investing, long term and systemic. It requires an alchemical understanding of how things are, as well as the influencing skills of a prophet, to succeed in re-shaping things not just in line with how they are, but how they can become better.

Within this ideal we remain flawed and human. We are weak as well as strong and can succumb to temptation and triggers that provoke lower level behaviours. Examples of truly integral leaders are rare, but recent global examples include Pope Francis, Elon Musk, Malala Yousafzai, Steve Jobs (towards the end of his life), Al Gore, Desmond Tutu, Oprah Winfrey, Margaret Atwood, George Soros, Jose 'Pepe' Mujica, Ariana Huffington, Michele Obama, Sirimavo Bandaranaike, APJ Abdul Kalam, and Youyou Tu.

Integral leadership does not build solely for the purpose of the enterprise of which it is part. Such leadership sees further, building beyond that, for a social cause or for humanity. Integral leadership is noteworthy because it often creates or adopts an idea or mission before the wave has crested. Integral leaders do not follow band-wagons but set the trend. Tesla and Dong Energy are two integral businesses. Integral businesses have massive potential for success because they offer so much life-enhancing value to so many and can profit by taking even a small percentage of that value for themselves.

Integral leadership respects and serves all life, the past and the future. Integral leaders develop products and strategies that seek to make things better for the broadest spectrum of life, while minimising or eliminating harm to the rest. They understand the lessons of the past and don't feel the need to repeat them. They also understand and honour those on whose shoulders they stand.

Triggers

Whatever level of perspective we are operating at we all remain vulnerable to being triggered back to previous levels. Even when we are firmly Interdependent we can be triggered back to Independent competing with those in an out group, to Dependent helplessness where we need others to take decisions for us, or even to Self-oriented, lying on the floor in the supermarket screaming our lungs out (metaphorically speaking).

Triggers will vary from person to person but tiredness, overload, insecurity and stress are common ones. Triggers can apply not just to individuals, they can also be cultural and apply to groups.

Working with a large energy company our initial working assumption, based on extensive briefing, was that many of the individuals were operating from an Independent level of perspective. We designed an intervention that would accelerate vertical development from Independent to Interdependent. However as we came to know the people we realised that individually they were fully Interdependent outside work. It was when they came into work that they were almost universally triggered to Independent and even Dependent levels.

Since that insight we have seen that many organisations trigger people to Independent and Dependent levels. Sometimes this is due to a crisis, but more often it is the nature of the hierarchy they operate in and the stresses placed on them.

Visionary Integral Leadership

In terms of change, disruption and leadership in business, Elon Musk stands tall at the moment (recent press notwithstanding), although he follows in a rarified line of visionary integral business leaders including Isambard Kingdom Brunel, who led disruption in land and sea transport, Oprah Winfrey, who transformed broadcasting narratives and social mores simultaneously, Thomas Edison, who led disruption in communications and energy, Tim Berners-Lee, who gave us the internet and Steve Jobs, who defined what we think of as personal computing and led disruption in animation, mobile phones, music and photography.

Even among such august company, Musk is special. A high-level view of the disruptions he is leading includes:

- **Tesla** - cars, trucks, batteries, solar PV, virtual power stations, gigafactories

     Disrupts - automotive and energy sectors
     Revolutionises - power grids, manufacturing

- **Space X** - cheap space flights, satellite internet, reaching Mars

     Disrupts - space and communications industries
     Revolutionises - long haul flights and which planets we live on

- **The Boring Company** - cheap tunnelling, fast point-to-point urban transport, bricks

     Disrupts - tunnelling and urban transport
     Revolutionises - where to live and work

- **Hyperloop** - fast intercity transport

     Disrupts - Rail and airline sectors
     Revolutionises - speed and efficiency of travel

- **Neuralink** - Neurotechnology or brain implants

     Disrupts - the human being (think Matrix-style enhancement of humans
     Revolutionises - human interaction with just about anything

As a visionary integral leader, Musk is driven by a need to make things better for all life. In doing this, like many in the list above, he is a divisive figure. His visionary thinking inspires passion and loyalty, as well as fear and derision. Musk's habit of setting super-aggressive deadlines for ground-breaking technologies (none of which his companies ever seem to meet), drives some investors and commentators to distraction and heaps pressure on employees.

However, it is undeniable that he does deliver remarkable achievements - just not every one he promises, and certainly not on time. But time is often a random measure.

Musk's work ethic, attention to detail and overall standards can make him an unpleasantly harsh leader to work for, or a quasi-messianic figure to the faithful. There is no doubt that he is incredibly demanding and not always skillful in his communication.

The same extreme character traits are also true of other visionary integral leaders. After his wife died, Gandhi took to testing his celibacy by sleeping with naked women much younger than himself. Emmeline Pankhurst supported the bombing of the Chancellor of the Exchequer Lloyd George's house. Marie Curie died from aplastic anemia after long-term exposure to radiation after working without precautions, carrying radioactive isotopes in test tubes in her pocket and storing them in her desk drawer. She never really acknowledged the risks of radiation. Steve Jobs lived in a fourteen bedroomed mansion for a decade with virtually no furniture.

Perhaps it is in the nature of such people to be extreme. Many seem to arrive into the world seemingly fully formed, with the energy and capacity to see further, do more, and lead us to places we had hitherto only dreamed. Certainly, it is often only when such figures pass on, that we really understand the importance of their legacy. Perhaps they are not meant to be universally loved but to serve the purpose of advancing us all a little further, if only in our sense of what is possible.

The evidence of a life well-lived is not in what we think or the values we espouse, but in what we do. The impact we have is through the actions we take, how we make others feel, and what they do as a result of our inspiration. You cannot be such a leader in your bedroom: you have to be tested by the world.

Perhaps this quality of experiential stress-testing is the real legacy of visionary integral leadership.

Doing Vertical Development

The vertical development challenge is that we cannot operate from a level we have not yet achieved. You can see back down the road you have traveled and understand the levels and triggers that have brought you up (and down) that path to where you are now, but you cannot know the crags in the mists above you until you have actually been there and explored them. Of course, you can imagine; you may even know what it looks like from afar and have planned your route, but that is not the same as doing it. Like mountaineering, vertical development takes effort, and the air gets thinner. Your route will always deviate from your plan. Sometimes there is a cost, and at times that cost can feel like a death, or a re-birth.

To intentionally move up from our current level takes determination, humility and time, although time alone does not guarantee progress. Progress requires that we change our habits of behaviour, and also of thought. Like all learning, effort and application are needed to open up new neural pathways in our brain and keep them open by repeating them until they are ingrained. Elite athletes train a new action they want to learn 200 times to give them the muscle memory that allows them to embody the learning. Research says it takes three months to change a habit, and 10,000 hours of practice to master a skill.

While it may take time to experience and embed, other research indicates that change can occur in one instant, in a heartbeat. This is the moment of decision. We can spend years pretending we are fit and healthy and losing weight, but if we have not truly made the decision to commit to our fitness we may never lose a gram. When we decide 'it is time', and fully commit, it suddenly feels easy. Kilos drop away.

So we must get to the place where we can make the honest decision to change, and then we must practice and develop ourselves in alignment with the decision, and get to know the terrain.

Neil says of his own experience,

> "I learned independence at a young age and became strongly independent. I felt I had to compete with everyone; it was exhausting and unfulfilling. Eventually in my 30s I found an environment where I no longer needed to compete and where trust was offered. One of the first signs of this was that I became physically ill as I adjusted to this new environment. This started me on my journey to interdependence. Since then my approach has been to seek out and identify the next thing I need to learn. To then rationalise it down to a simple word or phrase and then to work on being that concept until it is embodied. Among the challenges I have set myself are: 'Be with love' and 'From knowledge to wisdom'. In each case I first set out to understand the words - what is love? What is wisdom?
>
> Love, I discovered, is the bit beyond the rational. We may have lots of rational reasons for liking a person, activity or thing, but if our relationship cannot be explained by the rational bits alone, whatever is beyond that is love.
>
> If wisdom is the enactment of knowledge, we can know that we must be humble, but it is only when we are consistently humble in our behaviour that we can consider ourselves wise in terms of humility.
>
> Once I have an intellectual understanding or explanation of the topic, I need to move it from my head to my body. I use two techniques to achieve this, the first is that I make the lesson present for me, so that it is in my way. For example, messages or images on the lock screen of my phone, on the fridge or desk.

The second is that I work to bring my awareness of my failures closer and closer to the moment of choice. Initially I might only become aware of my failure after the event, sometimes long after, sometimes because I have noticed and sometimes because I have been told. Gradually I can bring that awareness back to moments after the event, then during the event and finally before the event to the point where I have choice, and I can choose to do something different.

Being in a loving and interdependent relationship means that I never feel alone, this enabled a period of growth and creativity for both of us. Vulnerability and trust are givens and this creates the confidence to do things that neither of us would attempt alone."

Some lessons take months or even years to embody, others can be learned in days. Even when we have learned them thoroughly, events can still trigger us back into old habits. At these moments we have to catch ourselves again and remind ourselves of our intention.

There are many lessons on the journey between the levels and particularly between Interdependent and Integral. Some of the lessons are in this book. You will know what your next lesson is because, as it creeps into your consciousness, you will start to notice discomfort around it. It will be a word or a concept or an expression that you keep noticing and will be in feedback from others. The discomfort is the truth of it. However, you will only notice it if you are open to it. If you are afraid or complacent or simply unconscious, the messages will slip past you until they turn into a crisis that you cannot ignore. How you choose to deal with those crises will determine whether you transcend or succumb to them.

Meditation, self-reflection, quiet moments and deep conversations where you allow yourself to be vulnerable and listen to feedback are all useful ways to notice what the next lesson is.

Mark's experience was less considered, originating in a 'crash':

> "For a long time, I struggled with lack of self-worth and a profound imposter syndrome. Although able to do and even be many things, from the outside appearing to be a normally functioning member of society, inside was only judgement and turmoil. I had been an Army Officer, an actor and a business executive, accustomed to leadership, yet I was held back by the belief that none of those things truly defined me, and by a series of early life experiences that limited my ability to value myself.
>
> This was a state of dependence and independence in profound conflict; a condition I managed to bask in/ignore for a long time. I needed value and recognition from others on the one hand, but rejected such advances on the other. Unattended, my inner life spiralled downward into a series of poor relationships and bad (unconscious) decisions. My breakthrough into interdependence was a forced entry, emerging from crisis. In that moment I faced a binary decision, which was either to stop existing and end the pain, or choose to live - but, if I chose that path, to live well.
>
> This single intention did more for my sense of self than any other. What did living well mean? How had I not been living well before? What was the potential to live better?
>
> It was the first in a series of conscious, resolute moments that formed the basis of a much more supportive and nurturing way to be. I learned how to trust myself and to stop seeking value and approval only from others, balancing that with my own sense of value and self. I deliberately sought out ways to demonstrate being authentic, whether that was simply finding the time to do the things I loved, like trekking or oil painting, or more deliberately and consciously seeking out the right social and

life partners. I worked on creating a life purpose and changed careers.

Most tellingly, as Neil explains above, I understood that the brain is plastic, and can change. I bypassed the over-used neural pathways that triggered the thought 'I am not worth anything' with the simple mantra: 'I trust myself.' I grounded that by spending time in natural environments and places where I felt good. What worked was to stop 'thinking' and start 'feeling'. My work also contributed towards bringing them more into balance. I stopped doing damaging things and started doing healing things. Critically, I also talked about where I had been, and when I sought help, I finally understood connection.

All of this ended my dissociation and created a relatively instant leap-frog of states into interdependence. Observing my previous state in many people around me, I took the decision to put my energies into sharing what I had discovered as an occupation, becoming a leadership coach and facilitator of change. Unsurprisingly, this in turn created deeper and more rewarding states of interdependence, which also returned that energy to me."

A Roman proverb says that we 'teach what we need to learn'. So, rather than simply learning interdependence, try also teaching it. You will accelerate your journey exponentially.

The Conscious Mammal

We need to re-examine our global, established, and often unchallenged definitions of leadership and success if we are to embrace higher levels of Perspective.

If you aspire to lead, do not be distracted by the gloom of the headlines or the preoccupations of others. Leadership now exists outside the mainstream: go, be a 'lone nut', stand out and get noticed, attract followers, create a movement, gain a higher Perspective, raise your own and others' consciousness.

Just start. If threat is the change you are not leading, and you see no one leading the positive change you want to make, start doing it. Make a call. Write an email. Connect, talk to a friend. Build a website. Speak publicly and YouTube it. Design your product or service. Engage others.

Get off your arse and start doing it.

(This section on Vertical Leadership Development leans heavily on Spiral Dynamics and the work of Dr Clare Graves and Dr Don Beck, as well as Ken Wilbur. It also references the work of Nick Petrie and the Centre for Creative Leadership, as well as our experiences of our own development, and our work with other leaders across sectors and geographies.)

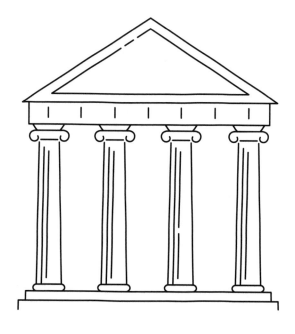

"Do you not know, my son, with what little wisdom
the world is ruled?."

Axel Oxenstierna, Swedish Statesman, 1648

CHAPTER 4

SUSTAINED SUCCESS

At any level you care to examine, from the individual choices we make in life, to the large-scale, geo-political complexities of diplomats and presidents, we cannot separate who we are from what we do. The societies we create are the direct product of our thinking and how we translate that thinking into reality. "Thoughts become things".

Despite all the many great things going on, we cannot deny that overall, our world is based on short-term, short-sighted goals. As a species, we plunder extractively in order to pay for the present, and in so doing, we steal from the future. This condition is the product of our existing communal thinking, but it is not fixed. If thoughts become things, the future will be whatever we imagine it can be... and then, what we do.

If we were to collectively follow only those who act from an integral perspective, would we have a different world? If we shared higher levels of Perspective between us and modelled the education of our children on vertical development, would we create long-term leadership for the future? If we were just to re-shape our definitions of 'success' by 10%, would we create a tipping point of sustainability that would re-define our threat-blindness and our apparently avaricious nature? How can we role model competitive plunder on the one hand, and expect to create holistic sustainability in our children on the other?

In the previous chapter we began to explore how general culture is created by specific behaviour. Here we will examine what it might take to re-imagine a future of sustained success through consciously crafting, and curating, a culture that achieves that vision.

By 'sustained success' we do not mean ecological, although of course that is a part of it; we mean the ability to adapt and shape systems and organisations that do not have to overreach and avoid "boom and bust". A 'sustained success' way of thinking, would use resources in such a way that they are never depleted or polluted and so that results just keep getting better by every metric.

The Megatrends are forcing a radical re-appraisal of our condition and place in the world. Whatever your dominant world view, Creationist or Evolution (or anything else for that matter), as a species, we have become used to thinking of ourselves as superior and dominant; the zenith of life in either model. In those two myths we are either made by a God in His image, or an aware expression of a conscious Earth. Both of them have humanity at the top; marked, special.

We are clearly not. The way in which we are ravaging our own nest indicates we have taken our inability to act on existential threat to its very outermost limit. Our disconnection from ourselves and from nature is a profound and damaging schism in our psyche.

What if the natural state of life is interconnected intelligence, built from the individual experiences of everything? Cosmologically, many scientists are beginning to speculate that life may not be scarce but super-abundant, all of it serving the same function: to connect to all other life. Rather than being a virus as the film The Matrix suggested, what if we are simply an interim technology on life's way towards an intelligence that works in balance with all other things; with no species or organism superior to another? Or some other heresy, such as the succession of AI? In 200 years we might well have become the apes in the zoo, hardly conscious of the gazing multidimensional, super-conscious public come to see the funny human antics. Look, the animal that thought it wasn't!

If we want to avoid the mythological re-balancing of our species from becoming a reality, we need a new paradigm of leadership: one that accepts change as desirable and natural, a long-term view necessary, and which views extractive models as redundant.

One could argue, in fact, that given the challenges of matching lifestyle to population all across the world, this is no longer a Socialist dream but, with full irony, the Capitalist survival imperative.

How then, do we re-define organisational life, achieve adaptability, and sustain our success all at once? How do we keep our technological prowess and reframe our human need to keep everything for ourselves? How do we both satisfy the demands of the markets (which, like it or not, drive most human activity through the flow of capital) and at the same time build long-lasting, healthy communities? How do we maintain our industrial power and the undoubted life-advantages this brings, whilst at the same time arresting climate change, habitat loss and the alarming rate of extinctions?

When we have conversations with powerful people (usually white men) on these topics, a deep yearning seems to enter the room. Many confess to buried feelings of uselessness or the pointlessness in attempting to re-design our way of living. Inside, they are poets, painters and philosophers. Outside, they are hard-headed businesspeople who say of the world they yearn for that 'it's not possible', or 'what we are talking about is a dream world'. And they turn back to their profit statements with wistful sighs.

These are all missed opportunities. Have we become cowards? Are we so ashamed of our guilt and separation that we can do nothing but accept it? Surely, if the money and the power got behind such ideas then different ways of being, that are in relationship with the planet and ourselves, would manifest. The world we all yearn for is perpetually just a decision away; right there, right in front of us, at all times. Why has it not happened?

In order to address this, we need to go from the epic to the microscopic plane: we need to talk about how we can, each of us, actually change our behaviour.

The Mechanics of Change - Linear to Agile

Let's define what we mean by the word 'change'. Conventional wisdom uses this word interchangeably for many things, and sometimes the use of the word itself creates misunderstanding. The main misunderstanding we experience, is in the singular nature of the word itself, change, indicating as it does an individual instance of metamorphosis with a start, middle, and end. By this old definition, post our 'change' there may be a period of relative calm, after which some new imperative will manifest, and we will embark on the cycle again. This was true in the past, perhaps twenty years ago, but that linear, single instance model of change no longer has any relevance at all.

'Change', now, must mean constant change, or we risk doing and being the wrong things in order to try to achieve it. The aim of the change, now, must be to **create adaptability**.

Types of Major Change

Constant change has multiple causes. It is when these causes combine to mean different kinds of change occurring to different parts of ourselves, our organisations, and our lives, that it becomes overwhelming.

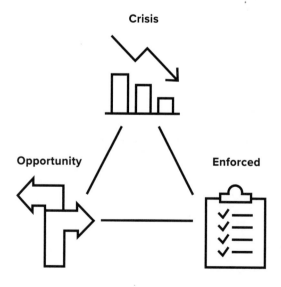

Crisis change occurs when we have to react to a situation or event that is the exact reverse to what we might wish, and have not asked for. Being made redundant, a serious health scare, a family bereavement, and divorce are all variants of personal crisis change. At organisational level it becomes remediation. Examples such as the LIBOR and PPI scandals, the Texas City or Deepwater Horizon accidents, Nokia's sales decline, or or Blockbuster's collapse caused by technology driven disintermediation are business examples of crisis-based change. Sometimes, the change effort we put into place does not work and we are out of business for good.

Opportunity change is when someone sees that there is another, better way to do something and initiates change early, in order to take advantage of circumstance. Opportunity change is where no one is being pressured to make a change and it is done for reasons that can at first seem 'nice to have' rather than essential. In our personal lives this is buying a new house, getting engaged or married, changing to the dream job or switching career tracks, going on a gap year, and so on. This is change we have chosen, are looking forward to, and as a result feel engaged by. In organisations, Reliance Industries' creation of the Jio digital business, Philip Morris International deciding to create a 'smoke free future', and Apple's creation of workable, digital platforms for a whole range of new services and ways of viewing the world, are examples here.

What can characterise an apparently 'nice to have' change is in fact not true on further inspection - someone is taking a leadership position ahead of the curve because they perceive long-term threats approaching fast. So in many cases what seems to be opportunity-based change is really an easier version of deeper, more hurtful change that would have come later on. Interestingly, Nokia's supremacy in the late '90's was also brought about by an opportunity change, taking a business that was previously about forestry, cabling and Wellington boots and creating the mobile networks and handsets that took 40% of the mobile comms market at the time.

Enforced change is when there are conditions created in our context that ask us to change whether we want to or not. They may not create crisis but do cause inconvenience. In our personal lives this can be changes to bye-laws or increases in interest rates or the price of beer and cigarettes. It might be some new boundary or request set by our partner or parents that we do not like. In the business world, enforced changes can be legal or regulatory, market changes, or even talent-based workforce changes. Enforced change can be the hardest to lead because in most cases, no one, not even those pushing it, really want it, but just have to live with it. By its nature, it does not feel like a change for the better because of its enforcement.

In reality, most major change initiatives are some combination of at least two, and usually all three change propellants. In crisis change, leadership has already failed. In opportunity change, leadership is performing its job properly. In enforced change, leadership must step up to find the opportunity and avoid the potential crisis.

Change is not a supertanker. It is a flotilla.

Traditional metaphors for change describe a large management supertanker with a slow turning circle and massive inertia. This in turn creates a mental model of the change, predicting the change approach which naturally slows down, making the change effort more difficult. Our mindset adjusts to move with the slow, grinding responses of the tanker.

Although in many ways the demands of constant change mean increased pace and pressure, change efforts do not need to be dealt with in this way. If we focus on a 'flotilla' metaphor, we can understand the true nature of change in organisations better, as well as the demands of leadership in adversity. In the supertanker metaphor, there is a single destination; some port or refinery we need to get to, where we can relax before the next journey. In the flotilla metaphor, we are in a round-the-world yacht race which never ends; round and round we go, without end, with constant adjustments and adaptation.

Each member of the flotilla brings different and valuable skills, and we must be opportunists. Opportunity change is far more likely to create adaptability. Trimming the sails, reacting to localised weather, changing crews, meeting at waypoints - this is the new metaphor to better understand the constant change context.

No one would think of embarking on a perpetual round-the-world yacht race without ensuring we have both the people and the equipment to be able to do so safely. We need training, experience, structure, rigour, and discipline. We need many qualified blue-water skippers to lead each sub-unit and we need the sat-nav and comms to be able to coordinate effort, such as keeping together in bad weather or avoiding the shallows. In the supertanker, we need a single Captain and a well-practised crew, with many automated processes. In the flotilla, we need a significantly higher frequency of leadership, and resilient, skilled and practical crews who can anticipate trouble and act for themselves. The flotilla must also be bound into a single purpose, but that purpose is again not exclusive. External parties and partners are also relied on for success, such as meteorologists, mechanics, electrical engineers, space centres and satellites, rescue crews, supply ships and depots, doctors, and replacement crews - in short, a whole ecosystem of internal and external stakeholders who all contribute to the general success. Even the competing yachts rely on one another to an extent. A supertanker is solitary and Independent. A flotilla has to be plural and Interdependent.

Motivation Is Everything

This brings us to the key topic of motivation, and hence leadership. The supertanker can easily operate without motivation, other than that required to plod from port to port, unplanned course changes take significant effort and so they are avoided. Without motivation and coordination, the flotilla becomes a collection of boat enthusiasts crashing into each other or spread randomly across the sea.

Motivation is key to any change. In making change, there are broadly only two types of motivation. The first is moving away from something, or a state we do not want to be in. In business this state is often called the 'burning platform' and is by far the most frequently used impetus for change. This is an 'away from' motivation, seen usually in Crisis and Enforced changes. The other is its opposite, a 'towards' motivation, a state we want to be in or become. This is called a Vision and is used during Opportunity change.

Which, for you, is the more powerful? Moving away from the situation you don't like, or moving towards the condition that you do?

One of the most fascinating statistics around the psychology of change is the result from a medical study into the behaviour of heart patients, recounted in an article by David Rock called the Neuroscience of Leadership. Two separate groups of seriously ill sufferers were counselled differently. The first group were given an 'away from' motivation:

"If you don't change, you will die".

The second group were counselled positively:

"If you change, you will be able to... (walk up a mountain, play with your kids, meet the love of your life)".

The patients defined their 'towards' goal themselves, but in all cases created life-affirming and positive pictures.

When we talk about these statistics with business groups, they are usually astounded to hear that in the first group - the threat of death - only 10% of patients changed. In the second group 77% changed, whilst 13% did nothing at all, despite the threat of death or the lure of a different future.

This study should not be taken as the indicator of all motivation, but it does raise a genuine question around how we take on the psychology of change, especially in our current environment. It means that most of the publicly accepted ways we have of communicating, through the media, magazines, books, internet, etc, are only impacting 10% of us to change because most of these messages are narrow, single-cause voices based in fear and negativity, representing restricted views of the world.

We have become too good at presenting the nightmare, but poor at framing the positive cause we can all get behind; and which is, in fact, the far more impactful method. If we were to look around us, where are the central narratives about a different, clean, ubiquitous energy future? Where are the stories of fulfilling the arc of history through the collaboration of governments, and the many astonishing projects under way to tackle these issues?

Where is the common vision of a well-fed, balanced world where no one is starving or thirsty? Where are the powerful voices in support of a resource-based economy, rather than a money-based one?

Perhaps we as a species have become too skeptical, too bound up in the political promise, too marketing-savvy, to risk our precious belief by buying into false mythologies in this way. Perhaps we have become let down too often by cynical uses of our beliefs by those who would seek to profit from or gain by them. But there are winning, powerful, game-changing examples. The best of humanity is truly out there, doing its thing.

In early 2018 SpaceX successfully launched its precursor Mars rocket, the Falcon Heavy, cutting the cost of launches from around £435m for an organisation like NASA, to around £90m, using reusable boosters. The launch also left the profound, enduring image of a Tesla Roadster, piloted by a mannequin in a spacesuit, listening soundlessly and endlessly to Space Oddity by David Bowie, with the words "Don't Panic" on the screen, orbiting the Earth on its journey outward into the Van Allen Belt.

Examples of real vision are plentiful and always supported. Think of the vision of NASA in the '60s to land a man on the Moon, or the entrepreneurs addressing ocean cleanup or creating starch 'plastic' bags you can eat. What makes them stand out and create change is that they define in clear terms something different to what is, and those who believe in the same things - change, creativity, technology, humanity - are all attracted to contribute. Notice, it is all on a wing and a prayer and nothing is certain. And yet the power of purpose, commitment, and a concerted effort to experiment, has indeed changed our world many times over.

So in facing up to change, we need to include the burning platform, but we should not let the 'away from' motivation define our change efforts, because it only attracts 10% of people. All this does is get us out of the burning house and onto the lawn, where we become fascinated with the burning house. We need to become good at describing and refining a positive vision. We will look at what a vision should constitute below, however for the moment, successfully sustaining change is about sharing and iteratively developing two key concepts:

- The vision, story or narrative - the "from-to" journey, and its benefits, which can also change.

- Sharing a way of working that encourages collaboration - the collective implementation of the way we want to do the change, and which should be adaptive in nature.

Both of these concepts apply at individual and group levels.

'Managing' a Bucking Bronco

Do not make the mistake of believing consulting doctrine, that we can 'manage change'. Managing change is like saying we can get a bucking bronco to perform dressage. True change holds the vision in mind for the long term, whilst simultaneously experimenting with the present to work out how to effectively bring it closer to reality. Trial and error, like evolution.

The change narrative - the bucking bronco - will be affected by the long and short-term forces affecting the change. For example, long term, we may hold deep essential values and have created a fine and noble vision for the sustainable health of our organisation, its people, and its impacts. Short term, those who hold the organisation accountable may be screaming for quarterly performance or for rapid progress against targets or regulations. As we have explored above, these two forces are perpetually in motion and usually in conflict, and their paymasters hold even the boldest back.

These factors set up stress in the system, which requires skill and courage to mitigate in practice. Whatever your ambition, whether it is recalibrating the EU without the UK, trying to adopt a new digital technology in your business, or upgrading your own career, it is necessary to step back and appraise what you are trying to achieve, and understand what you need to do in order to achieve it. Then you need to calibrate both where you are in terms of innate ability to accept major change, and the readiness of your leadership to deliver it.

If you were about to start a round-the-world yacht race that never ends, would you not prepare a little bit? And what would you personally need to upgrade about yourself to be successful?

Reliability or Adaptability?

Forget either/or thinking. Adopt an approach that is both/and.

There is already an innate understanding amongst senior leaders that adaptability is the goal. The fact of constant change, if not studied and learned, is understood now as the day-to-day medium of the modern workplace, meaning society needs an agile-minded workforce which can operate autonomously. However, too many senior figures still believe they can achieve adaptability by exercising more and more control. The destination, in many minds, is an empowered workforce coming up with ideas and innovations, but also doing what they are told. The structure is still a hierarchy of up to 10 or even 20 layers, but the expectation is that junior staffs are not afraid. This kind of thinking comes from the existing paradigm of entitlement and the expectation of hereditary rule. It is fatally flawed, made impossible by a limited leadership capacity or bandwidth to implement change, combined with organisational states that are exposed due to over-reliance on heavy management.

At Holos we call this permanent tension condition 'Fix'. Too often, too many leaders and managers are being paid to complete tasks to fix the organisation, in order just to deliver its goals. Whilst understandable, this condition will never elevate the activity of the leadership beyond the simple and transactional, or just fighting fires and running around, burning.

In our personal change efforts, sometimes we desperately want change but cannot draw ourselves away from the self-sabotaging behaviour that keeps us where we are. This is widely known as the 'pyromanic fireman' theory of change.

Having established the essential need for effective and collaborative leadership, the new global context requires that, regardless of the 'white water' of our day-to-day, senior figures also need to de-stress their organisations and create a cultural stability and predictability. It is the same if your desire for change is just for you. There is a direct correlation between leadership bandwidth (time and energy) and ability to deliver change (skill) at personal, team, and organisational levels. Very few large or legacy organisations are fit for this fight.

Getting to an adaptable condition is therefore mostly about increasing leadership capacity (time and skill), and then developing the right culture that re-shapes the organisation from within. In other words, developing culture is the strategy, because it is only though changes in behaviour that you achieve the systemic outcomes you require. These are leadership imperatives that anyone with leadership accountability should be brought into and involved in. Creating adaptability is a need that should also be embodied in the organisational approach to HR, learning and development, as well as organisational design, process design, and policies and procedures. They all connect.

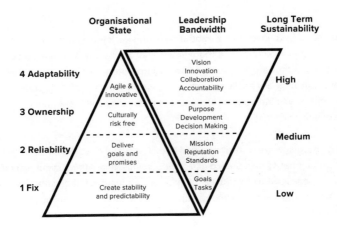

Organisational State	Leadership Bandwidth	Long Term Sustainability
4 Adaptability	Agile & innovative	Vision Innovation Collaboration Accountability	**High**
3 Ownership	Culturally risk free	Purpose Development Decision Making	
2 Reliability	Deliver goals and promises	Mission Reputation Standards	**Medium**
1 Fix	Create stability and predictability	Goals Tasks	**Low**

Sustained Success

The model above defines change readiness aligned to organisational state, and relates that to leadership capacity. In management-heavy businesses, the entire goal and raison d'être of the organisation is to achieve state 2, Reliability. This requires gaining clarity over processes and skills to the extent that performance becomes predictable and reliable. Internal reliability must be as effective as external, or goals and promises are not met.

Most large legacy businesses, such as financial services, large engineering, construction, and oil & gas, realise they need to change, but are not even close to state 3, Ownership. Any organisation still focused on cranking the handle at stage 2 as an objective, is already managing decline. They are realising that their businesses need to become more agile and nimble, and yet are still in the supertanker mindset and capability. The reason is cultural, not operational. The conformity one needs to perform reliably no matter what, is entirely different to the ownership one needs in order to be creative. Management heavy, reliable models hire experts and technocrats who wring the very most out of margins and mechanics. Adaptable, distributed models hire creatives and innovators who love autonomy and space, making the impossible possible. The logics and behaviour required to move from one mindset to the other is about as far apart as it is possible to be on a continuum and are usually different people and skillsets entirely.

Neither is Sustained Success about leapfrogging. It is a maddening reality that you have to progress through the stages one by one. We have tried. The cognitive jumps are too great and, replacing experts with innovators, only results in immediate tissue rejection. Things must be moved deliberately up the chain, with the organisation gathering capability and bandwidth as it goes, over time.

A global player we worked with had hired four world class digital disruptors in senior roles to help them digitise their organisation. After a major reshuffle, their sponsor, who was providing "air cover" for them, left. Soon after, we were asked to coach all four of them, with a brief that basically meant asking them to stop being disruptive. All four suffered "tissue rejection" and left shortly after.

The progression operates at personal level, team level, and organisational level simultaneously. The best way to look at it is to regard the team (the yachts) as a basic unit of performance, team leaders (the skippers) as the change agents, and to change by targeting the ways that teams work, and what they work on (their collective training and direction of travel).

1. In order to move out of **Fix**, the organisation becomes **Reliable** at a granular level, meetings happen on time, agendas are followed, actions are taken. You cannot be reliable on the outside without being reliable on the inside.

2. Once **Reliable**, there is the bandwidth to begin to extend **Ownership** and empowerment, sharing responsibility as widely as possible, the start of the transformational sphere.

3. Once culturally risk-free with widespread responsibility and self-organisation around challenges and opportunities, only then is there the capacity to look long term and create space to innovate.

4. Once in the **Adaptability** space, the full leadership capacity required for sustainability becomes available.

5. There is a fifth stage, **Universality**, which only two or three businesses in a generation achieve. Other types of organisations, such as NGOs and supra-national bodies, have a higher frequency of Universality.

At the same time, there is a new term available here: cultural safety. This refers not to Health and Safety but to the risks inherent in cultures that are not curated effectively. They manifest in their worst forms as risks to business, such as criminality, accidents, lives lost, environmental accident, and severe disruptions such as strikes. In milder forms they show up in quieter ways such as churn, silo working, or resistance to change. Because of this, there is a strong argument for placing cultural oversight within the Risk or Audit department of any business, rather than within HR (having ensured that Risk has the skill to foster the right culture, rather than compliance, of course).

A focus on cultural safety includes the extension and establishment of a psychologically, as well as physically, safe environment in which employees can flourish and be offered the opportunity to bring their very best potential to work. Recent case studies, such as the Bly Report into the BP Gulf of Mexico incident in 2010, and internal investigations in the banking sector LIBOR and PPI scandals from 2013, have proven that a focus on cultural safety exponentially increases process and systems safety. Transactional reliability alone does not deliver such goals.

Leadership Bandwidth

Moving across one column, we must also consider what leadership is available to make our business sustainable. We may be tempted to read the states in parallel, i.e. to correlate the state of Fix with its leadership actions, to set goals and tasks. In fact, that is the risky strategy. In order to elevate the organisational condition from one level to the next, leadership must be operating from the level just above the current organisational state. So to get us out of Fix, leadership must focus on Mission, Reputation, and Standards. If all leadership does is achieve goals and tasks, we stay in Fix. To move from Reliability to Ownership, leadership needs to focus on Purpose, Development (of people), and (distributed) Decision Making.

This poses a very real problem - don't we need to be heading toward Adaptability in order to achieve it? Don't we need to define what that is and include leaders in setting the Vision and the business model in order to get there? Of course. But we also need to go one step further - to educate all levels of leadership in the change modelling, plan, and stages to get there, and to skill up leaders in focusing on the right actions at the right time to progress the organisation according to the limits it can stand at the time. If we focus on the team as the unit of performance, this enables one team, which may be further on than another, to move from Reliability to Ownership, whilst others are focusing on getting out of Fix. In this way, leaders simultaneously learn about becoming adaptable, and practice those skills as they go. Imagine the crew of the supertanker suddenly being asked to crew a flotilla of small yachts. It would be unsafe and disastrous. Agility requires training and practice.

Identify the company goals in this hierarchy of Sustained Success. Teach yourself and individual leaders and teams to re-interpret local priorities based against the organisational Cause, Conditions, and strategies, giving context and shape to all decision making. Do this, and your flotilla begins to take shape and head in a broadly similar direction.

To be clear, this is not a choice between slow and fast change, this is a choice between the mindsets of hard, linear, push change, and easy, cyclical, pull change.

On the following pages there are some definitions for these four primary conditions:

Fix

What does Fix feel like?

- The organisation, or parts of the organisation, are not fit for purpose.
- Execution gaps exist which may be being addressed through new process or system implementation.
- Failures are being observed at higher rates than normal, such as customer feedback or operational exceptions. Goals are not being achieved.
- People and teams are unsure about their role and function, people are being used ad-hoc to solve problems or re-roled at short notice
- Daily tasks consist of fighting fires, resulting in stress and absence.
- There is a feeling of psychological insecurity.

Leadership Bandwidth

Are my leaders in Fix?

- Leaders are spending 90-100% of their time dealing with transactional tasks or ensuring goals are met.
- A high meetings culture in which problems are endlessly debated.
- The vision of the organisation is just a poster on the wall, if that.
- What we do and speed of delivery has supremacy over how we work.
- Changes have increased pressure and decreased morale and capacity.
- A 'just do it' culture.
- No bandwidth to effectively lead change

Sustainability

- Very low
- Leaders and teams cannot raise their heads to see the context
- All time and attention is focused on survival or fixing issues
- There is no future here

Reliability

What does Reliability feel like?

Organisational State

- The organisation is fit for purpose
- People and teams know their role and function, and regularly deliver their goals
- Processes and systems perform as designed and envisaged, delivering quality information
- Decision making is based around mission and standards; standards are increasing
- Employees, customers and stakeholders are increasing trust due to delivery of promises and objectives

Are my leaders in Reliability?

Leadership Bandwidth

- Leadership is focused on delivering mission and goals
- There is capacity for efficiency improvements and variations to standard processes
- Standards are implemented through discussion on how we work over what we do
- Behaviours and habits that support values are developing
- Leaders begin to raise the bar on personal and team development

Sustainability

- Low
- Many businesses believe Reliability is the end state. In reality it is only the start of becoming Adaptable
- Reliable businesses are management-heavy and vulnerable to disruption and competition

Ownership

Organisational State

What does Ownership feel like?

- People and teams have mastery over their role and function, and have capacity to innovate locally
- Problems, challenges and issues are being addressed automatically as part of a self-organising system
- People speak up and feel able to challenge upward
- There is a feeling of psychological safety and an effective feedback culture
- The organisation is becoming culturally risk-free, in which the values and behaviours have come off the wall and are being embodied across all tiers
- The brand begins to become a destination for employees and customers

Leadership Bandwidth

Are my leaders in Ownership?

- Discussion focuses on delivery of organisational purpose
- Threats and challenges are being proactively observed and mitigated
- New leaders are being actively developed and decision making is promulgated down the organisation
- Activity is aligned towards achieving the organisational purpose; organisational purpose is widely known and talked about
- There is time and space for new opportunities and ideas to come from leaders and managers; new ideas are discussed and there is a system for selecting and adopting new ideas in achieving purpose and priorities

Sustainability

- Good
- You may survive
- Leadership is being used for its purpose - to envision and achieve change
- Managers are managing effectively and processes and systems are being innovated

Adaptability

Organisational State

What does Adaptability feel like?

- There is clear differentiation between managed, efficient business activities and those engaged in innovation

- There may be more than one or two business models in active use

- People and teams collaborate and work together seamlessly; silos and divisions have disappeared

- Presenteeism and clock-watching have disappeared; trust and delivery are all that's required

- Time is set aside for everyone to think and innovate in their own function and/or role

- Change processes are widely known and used; change is a by-word for making the most of opportunities

- All activity is pointed towards achieving an uplifting and audacious organisational vision

Leadership Bandwidth

Are my leaders in Adaptability?

- Leaders are adept at both telling the vision narrative and organising activity towards achieving it

- Leadership is collaborative and inclusive

- Hierarchy has all but disappeared with a recognition that everyone brings unique strengths and talents

- Growth and learning, and the allowance of a certain amount of mistakes, are the daily experience, as well as stretch and challenge

- Horizon-scanning, thinking and reading are commonplace and different fora exist to support those activities

- New and disruptive ideas are generated and taken on within the organisation or implemented as white label brands

- Diversity of thought is encouraged

Sustainability

- High
- You are becoming a disrupter
- Higher order leadership is both enabled and promoted
- Personal purpose and meaning is created
- You may be leading your market
- The challenge is staying here

From the Fix perspective, it may be hard to see what Adaptability truly looks like, and one could be forgiven for calling Adaptive characteristics idealistic. However they are based in fact; seven out of the top ten largest companies in the world by market capitalisation in 2018, have intentional and adaptable cultures. If you are a senior leader determined not to preside over the decline and closure of your company, these principles are highly relevant to your continued success and the ongoing health of your organisation.

If you disagree with or feel no need for higher Perspective in your company, or if you dislike or are put off by the spiritual dimension to integral leadership, you are rather painting yourself into a corner. You simply cannot achieve Adaptability through total rule or high degrees of control. Adaptability means a distributed leadership culture - a flotilla, not a supertanker.

As a species, we can no longer choose to be either spiritually integral or materially reliable. We must be both, and.

"Hell is other people."

Jean-Paul Sartre

CHAPTER 5

AUTHENTIC LEADERSHIP

We have considered Perspective and Sustained Success as key aspects of surviving and thriving in the constant change context. In this chapter, we will explore a number of different lived experiences we all have of leadership, and frame them inside the experiential leadership structure we have already defined: Reach, Perspective, and Motivation. We will explode the myth that the Boss style of leadership is essential, and want to encourage anyone reading this to reach for their Authentic leadership power.

Mark and Neil were working with the top leadership team at a Middle Eastern energy utility. The business was in significant trouble with costs exceeding income and pressure coming from stakeholders. The top team had been in the job for a long time, with several close to retirement. After years of successfully managing the business in a stable commercial environment, they were struggling with the disruptions caused by decarbonisation and digitisation.

Because of a distracted internal focus, there was an inherent acceptance of the cultural dysfunction. For example, both of us waited hours for meeting appointments. On one occasion, after a wait of two hours, the executive Mark was due to meet eventually appeared and apologetically conducted a brief interview. As Mark was leaving, the executive drew a canvas bag from his bureau drawer, with a flourish, and handed it to Mark saying, "I give one of these to everyone who has the courtesy to wait more than 30 minutes for a meeting with me". He was proud to have a system for this extraordinary, dysfunctional practice!

In fact, he himself had been detained in an unscheduled 7-hour meeting with his CEO, who had normalised lateness and disrespect for time. The gift was a way of hiding his inherent shame, because his own values had been compromised. Imagine: Cost of delay + cost of reputation + cost of frustration + actual cost of goody bag x number of people x time...

Yet this crazy situation was born out of a genuine desire to improve: the CEO wanted his team to step up and lead the business through their challenging context. However, once we actually conducted our interviews with the top team it became clear that they were all, more or less, frightened of the CEO and reluctant to expose their true feelings for fear of rebuke or humiliation. The CEO for his part explained his theory of motivation; it was to put the team on an emotional "burning platform". The result was a broken team, most of whom would avoid the CEO whenever possible, and a frustrated CEO at a loss to explain why he needed to spend 7 hours haranguing them for non-performance.

The CEO's idea of what was actually happening in the business was inaccurate because none of his team could, or would, tell him the truth.

After self-awareness, the second requirement of leadership is followers.

Transformational (Change) Leadership
Although there is no single definition of leadership, it is possible to identify a group of qualities and behaviours consistent across many highly-researched and validated approaches (such as those of Kouzes and Posner, Bass and Avolio, Covey and Covey, Goffee and Jones, Sinek, Collins, Buckingham, and others). This research, conducted across time, geography, sectors, ages, genders, and cultures, validates a small number of distinct, identifiable human values and behaviours in transformational, or change leadership:

- Shows vision, scans the horizon, thinks about the future, and includes others in that thinking;

- Role models the right behaviours to achieve the vision and is generally perceived to be both ethical and moral in personal conduct;

- Is capable of inspiring others to do and be their best, and shows how this is possible - including working through vulnerabilities;

- Generates ideas or creates fora where ideas can happen, allowing innovation and iterative experimentation;

- Creates the space for others to grow and develop, becoming personally involved in the development of others according to their personal needs;

- Takes on and role models accountability in both job role, and personal standards and discipline;

- Executes effectively and reliably.

All of these attributes would be found in what our model calls skilful Authentic Leaders. We would amplify a few additional attributes such as:

- Highly self- and other-aware;

- Creates an inclusive space where everyone else also feels safe to be authentic;

- Puts themselves in the heart of any crisis;

- Sees success and failure as systemic issues;

- Demonstrably takes greater risk than they ask of others;

- Articulates the vision and culture in life-changing ways and is the embodiment of it.

This sounds like a tall order, but these leadership attributes are critical to generate willing followers. And yet there remains a doubt. Surely these attributes are also often descriptive of despots and tyrants? In its early stages, the transformation of Weimar to Nazi Germany captured the attention and admiration of most of Europe. Was Hitler a transformational leader? Are there modern examples we might also look to, relevant to our context, such as Trump, Erdogan, and Xi Jinping? And is their leadership not also transformative in nature?

We say no. Our explanation brings us back to mythologies. These are not Authentic Leaders, but Rulers. Charismatic Rulers are adept at telling the stories that people, at a dependent/independent level of maturity, want to hear, and delivering the policies they want. The populist handbook starts with: "The reason you are suffering is because of [insert 'out group' here]. I am strong and I alone can eradicate them. Then your life will be good" (more on this later).

Rulers are also skilled at high profile, feel-good activities that bestow a sense of status on their followers, for example, Nazi parades and the entertainments and propagandised military victories of the Roman era.

Once a myth is accepted, it is fantastically difficult to shift. To paraphrase Mark Twain, "It is far easier to fool people than to convince people they have been fooled."

The fundamental problem for the sustainability of despots and tyrants is that any project based on status will rarely outlive the influence of its leader. From Nero's Domus Aurea to Franco's Spain, the egotist's fantasy tends to die with the egotist. In examples like North Korea, the personality cult may last a few generations, but it too will fail. The same is true in business. The problem is that the pursuit of status breeds competitors faster than it breeds collaborators. You can demand loyalty and delay the demise with fear or bribery, but ultimately collaboration wins out.

For those who allow tyrants to rule over us, the cost is much, much higher. Whatever Rulers achieve comes about by stealing from the future. The cost, from Julius Caesar to Donald Trump is borne by those who outlive them, and the generations that follow.

However, In elective systems, followers swiftly become leaders.

Lived Experience

We all experience different kinds of leadership in different situations, such as family, schools, sports teams, organisational life, etc. The quality and outcomes of that leadership vary because a leader's intention may differ from their impact on people. This is the 'lived experience' of leadership and the reason two-thirds of any business bookshelf is all about people.

Leadership ability is neither fixed nor a genetic trait. How we behave is largely a combination of Perspective and skill. I am more or less conscious of my behaviour and its impact, or I am unconscious. I am somewhere on a continuum between being skilled in relating with or directing others, or unskilled. Therefore, leadership can be learned through deliberate and sustained practice.

> "I do not fear [the person] who has practised 10,000 kicks, but [the person] who has practised the same kick 10,000 times."
>
> Bruce Lee
>
> "We are what we repeatedly do. Excellence, then, is not an act but a habit."
>
> Aristotle

Desire, Awareness, Understanding, and Application may be the only step-model required to exercise outstanding leadership. The other question we need to answer is what do we truly want to lead for? Because if we aspire to lead, we must be prepared to take on the consequences of that power, privilege and influence.

If leadership is a choice rather than an appointment, it will not be the right choice for all contributors. At its best in a team, leadership is dynamic, allowing anyone to lead, with leadership flowing to the right places at the right times. For some, the role of "Expert' is generally far more appropriate than leadership.

Being a skilled (and possibly expert) follower is every bit as valuable to change as being a skilled leader; and being able to switch nimbly into following is often a very effective demonstration of leadership, and certainly sets a positive leadership tone.

Leadership only exists in tandem with following. As Derek Sivers said, "Without followers you are just a lone nut".

So, let us start at the beginning of the leadership journey.

Exercising Leadership

The very instant we decide to take responsibility for some sort of change, and someone chooses to follow, or is influenced by us, we are leading. We have all done this at some point in our lives, at least during a childhood game. When we do it repeatedly, on an increasing scale and with some wider strategic intent, we are developing our leadership.

Just because you show leadership, you may not be 'a leader'. And even when you have the hierarchical responsibility, you can and should switch roles to manage, follow, learn or be a team player when relevant. What makes leadership behaviour consistent is a disciplined focus on standards in the pursuit of a shared Cause (the vision, purpose and mission we are pursuing) and Conditions (the values, behaviours and habits required to achieve the Cause, more on this later).

There is an almost universal challenge in the way organisations appoint 'leaders'. In most organisations, management and leadership are the only routes to promotion. It is exceptional to offer a pure expert route, where people can be promoted for their technical skill without having oversight of and responsibility for other people. Universities, some manufacturing, and a small number of engineering businesses promote experts, but it is unusual. In addition, expert routes rarely offer equivalent remuneration and status to leadership routes. Yet our organisations habitually intertwine expertise with leadership.

In business, people are generally promoted because they become expert at something, like design or accounting. Once expert enough, that individual is promoted to lead teams of designers or accountants. So far so good. But deep in our limbic brain we need to feel a sense of self-worth and inclusion. So when our role requires an expertise we don't really have, such as leadership, and we are poorly supported to learn and develop, we tend to retreat and spend our time on the expertise that got us promoted; the design or accountancy skills that give us that sense of self-worth. As a result, leadership activity is pushed to the side of our desk and we typically feel very stretched, and risk micromanaging the expertise and under-performing on leadership.

Leadership is full-time work and a skill that needs to be built into expertise.

"What got you here, won't get you there."

Marshall Goldsmith

There is a crucial mantra at the heart of leadership: "everything that can be delegated, must be". This means that we have to delegate the expert activity that previously gave us our sense of self-worth and focus on an activity that initially fills us with self-doubt. If we seek to lead, we must invest all the time we can in learning and practising the art of leadership. No construction firm would ask a team of obstetricians to build a suspension bridge, and yet we ask financial experts, or subsea engineers, or visual merchandisers to become leaders all the time. Thinking of the supertanker, this is a little like asking the helm, who is used to steering the ship by pressing buttons and programming course corrections into a computer, to suddenly steer a 32-foot yacht by handling a wooden tiller. In organisations, the 'captains' who promote people into leadership are regularly asking for this degree of behaviour change from managers and experts.

These principles were at the heart of one of our coaching assignments with a technology leader at a universal bank. The leader had proven himself a great technical strategist and accordingly had been promoted to head a very large department of technologists and coders during a time of radical change. He was ambitious, but inexperienced in leadership. His personal values didn't allow him to mimic the culturally common Boss-type leadership he saw around him. As a result, he was taking on far too much work, trying to lead the department and create the technical strategies himself.

The first step was for him to delegate, decline and defer work, in order to create the psychological and emotional bandwidth to lead. With the space he created he was then able to define himself differently and accept the accountabilities of his leadership.

One of the very few institutions in our society to take leadership seriously is the military. In the military, leadership is trained and practiced from a young age and throughout your career, with a focus on the qualities and disciplines needed to maintain sight of the bigger picture and build the respect of followers. As a military leader's Reach gets wider, skillsets are developed in tandem with Perspective, using a continuous education approach involving Staff College or special-to-arm training at different career stages. Motivation is rarely addressed directly, although service is a fundamental to military leadership, with everyday maxims like 'Leaders eat last', and 'Serve to Lead' underpinning the theory that leadership activity is driven by purpose and not status.

As a military officer, at 21 years old, Mark was responsible for a Troop of soldiers (Troop is Royal Artillery nomenclature for a Platoon) on active service. Many of the soldiers were older men who had been on active service two, three and four times before. Mark's youth and inexperience counted against him, but his leadership position was not at issue because he showed essential competence plus an ability to listen to the wider experience around him in order to make better decisions. On active service, decision-making is always contextual and situational. For Mark, effective leadership meant he did not need to be the best soldier, but he did need to be agile at understanding the big picture, co-ordinating ideas, and re-shaping tactics in service to the vision.

Mark was taught to appreciate any given situation and problem-solve from that place. Often his were not the ideas implemented, and some of his decisions were wrong. Sometimes discussion was possible and sometimes command decisions had to be made quickly and alone. However, his general approach of listening and examining experience created a depth in relationships, so that when diktat was necessary, or the decision proved wrong, there was still willingness to move, follow and operate. Boss-style leaders would likely have felt it incumbent upon them to (appear to) know everything, becoming the fount of all control. Young officers of that style failed frequently and were left by all to hang in the wind, cheeks burning. In the words of Mark's sergeant major, "Sir, there's a reason why the blokes listen to you. It's because you listen to them."

Unlike the military, organisations tend to expect experts to succeed in leadership simply because they are the best in accounting or design. If you are the best expert, they seem to believe, you are ready to lead others in that expertise.

There is very little evidence that this approach works.

Lived Experience Manifests as Impact

All this thinking coalesces into quite a dense model. Any model is going to have to deal in generalities and stereotypes. Reality is much more nuanced than any generalised model, but creating a high-level view of our discussion allows for shared definitions, and helps you identify the leadership style you want for yourself. It may be, for example, that you yearn to lead in a different way, but the culture you work in is the opposite of who you feel you are. It may be you are already leading or on a Management Team, but your natural preferences for interdependence and authenticity are being overwhelmed by fear, social pressure or business imperative.

If so, now is the opportunity for you to lead change in that culture.

The descriptors in the model below can apply to anyone, in any position, in any organisation. Attitude is not hierarchical. So too, values and behaviours - where anyone can show leadership. Some say that true leadership occurs when positional authority is irrelevant to the ability to garner followers. Leadership is gifted to us by others.

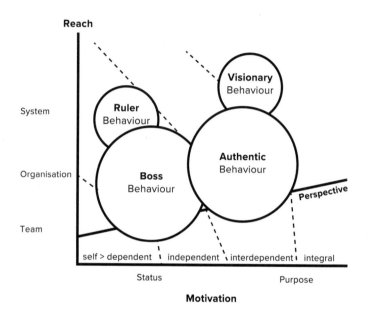

How leadership behaviours occur across the Reach, Perspective, and Motivation axes.

Holos Authentic Leadership

Holos have developed this triple-axis approach to leadership in order to differentiate the Visionary from the despotic Ruler and link the model to vertical development. We happily acknowledge a conscious bias: the diagonal axis (Perspective) promotes purpose-driven, integral leadership as preferable to hierarchical power (the Reach axis) that steals from the future.

There is a clear left/right distinction between Boss/Ruler, and Authentic/Visionary. Bosses and Rulers are primarily motivated by their own status and by their perception of what success means. Authentics and Visionaries are primarily motivated by purpose and a shared consensus that changes should be as equitable as possible for all in the system.

The Boss/Ruler style is far more common in human history and will be what many people associate with the term 'leader'. This gives us a mental model that often triggers cynicism in us. Boss and Ruler leaders do not seek to change things for the good of all, but usually for either themselves, their Ruler, or their elites. In business today, Visionaries and Authentics are in the ascendant because they embody the practice of 'leadership' and, broadly, seek change that addresses the needs of humanity and nature. For Rulers to stay in power they continually have to outrun the cost of their own legacy, building ever more elaborate reward and control systems to keep the damage at bay. Ruler and Boss style leaders tend to be more effective with people with a Dependent or Independent perspective. Authentic and Visionary leaders work better with those at an Interdependent perspective. Ruler and Boss style leaders will create a stressed culture that keeps those with an Interdependent perspective triggered to lower levels to retain their status. Visionaries and Authentics tend by nature to be investors who play more for the long term. Because they often struggle to make headway against legacy (Ruler) power systems, you often see them outside the mainstream.

Nothing is fixed. The future is neither inevitable, nor predicted by the past.

Definitions

Rulers

Ruler leadership has status, power and control as key personal drivers. The role of Ruler has at its core a resistance to change, except where change creates and maintains the Ruler's worldview, and can be supported by an established hierarchy and way of doing things that preserves control or order as defined by the Ruler. Rulers tend not to rise through the ranks in the way that most people do. There is an inherent extractive impulse at the heart of the Ruler style of leadership, which treats resources (including people), as existing purely for exploitation by the organisation, or (in extreme cases) the Ruler. Ruler leadership originates in an I-centric worldview often associated with high levels of personal ego, or 'divine right'.

Who follows Rulers?

To an extent, we all have to. Our history books are studies in the impact of Rulers: it is social governance by Chiefdoms, Oligarchies, Monarchies, Theocracies, Autocracies and Dictatorships. There is a huge disparity between the proportion of social structures led by Rulers and the number of Rulers in the general population. In fact, Rulers are rare, but their fixed world view, which always has them at the top, means they will move rapidly (and sometimes brutally) to the top, if they are not there already.

Rulers know that they cannot have the power they crave without followers, and so they are adept at recruiting and motivating a cadre of close followers, typically Boss types who value the status conferred on them by the Ruler. This is very much a gang dynamic, made of loyalty, status and threat. Rulers and Bosses value loyalty over competence and will punish disloyalty more harshly than incompetence. Thus, a Ruler will usually control through an elite.

For the wider population who may elect, select or promote a Ruler, the attraction lies in the idea of a 'parent' taking responsibility for their problems. The most likely to follow a Ruler is population, at a Dependent or Independent level of perspective or maturity, facing complex problems and unwelcome change. Those people want someone else to take responsibility for them and are willing to trade infantilisation for the illusion of security. The Ruler accepts such responsibility in exchange for power, adulation and status.

Visionaries

Visionaries see themselves as responsible for some significant cause that is greater than them. Visionary leadership is driven by a perceived necessity for 'change': change is the vehicle to disrupt and create different definitions of success. Visionary leader behaviour embraces power in order to drive change, although Visionary leaders tend to use power with others rather than over them. There is an inherent investing heart within the Visionary style. Visionary leaders are willing to give opportunity and decision-making to those seen as having the talent to deliver. Visionary leadership operates from a We-centric worldview and, at its best, can transform whole systems, society and the human experience.

Who follows Visionaries?

Visionaries are as rare as Rulers. Because of their impact on society, we can all probably name a dozen easily, but Visionary leaders do not always seek positional power or status. Their priority is the achievement of their purpose or vision. Gandhi, for example, never held public office. However, if their vision requires a large organisation or political power, Visionaries will create the structures needed in order to make the vision real.

Visionary leaders often inspire cult-like relationships within their organisations; a group of passionate true believers who are willing to work extremely hard. Typically, Visionaries also have a high moral code and standards, and these can be hard for followers to match. However, Visionaries and their followers have such motivation to enrich the future that they have no need of Ruler-style fear, although there are parallels such as the controlling behaviour in the early years of Steve Jobs' leadership.

When the wider population elects, selects or promotes a Visionary as leader, the attraction lies in the vision and the future they believe it will create. The cult-like nature of a Visionary-led organisation can flow beyond the organisation itself, out to customers and other stakeholders.

For readers who aspire to leave a legacy, look to history: more Visionaries than Rulers live on in our collective memory.

Bosses

Status and power through relationship are key drivers for the Boss. A Boss leader is usually relying on the formal authority or positional power of the role in order to get things done. Boss behaviours emphasise control and order, often by diktat or direction. Boss leaders pay attention to operational necessity, the task or project to be completed, rather than the values or emotional dimensions of working together. Efficiency, results and outcomes are important because reputation is important. Boss leaders can be attractive in a system because of their ability to deliver results quickly. However, these results are generated by stealing from the future: often this theft is through damage to the cultural dynamic of the team or organisation. It can also be through failure to innovate or maintain, or the manipulation of data, or physical in the form of such things as deforestation to create palm oil plantations.

It is important to state that Bosses and Rulers are not necessarily 'evil', but they place more importance on the short term than the long and gravitate to status and power above all else. The Boss mindset can be either I-centric or We-centric, depending on the status drivers in their system.

Who follows Bosses?

The Boss leader can be found throughout most organisations. It is the dominant concept of what a leader is. Because of this, many individuals with great authentic leadership potential never even consider themselves as possible leaders.

People generally follow Boss leaders for one of two reasons: a perceived lack of choice, or because they themselves aspire to status and the Boss can confer it. A key weakness of the Boss and Ruler styles is that followers are rarely honest with them. Understanding accurately what is going on is critical to successful leadership; the sycophantic or fearful relationship between Boss leaders and followers tends to corrupt the data. Like Rulers, Bosses value loyalty over competence.

Visionaries and Authentics often feel morally superior to Bosses and Rulers, whom they judge to be limited or immoral. That sense of superiority has left some sections of society feeling belittled and looked down on. These individuals are making themselves heard in societies across the world by rejecting the prevailing Visionary and Authentic liberalism of the last fifty years and returning to nationalism, led by Bosses and Rulers, who tend to see Authentic leaders as weak, and Visionaries as destructive of the status quo they value.

Authentics

Purpose, values, ethics and morals are key drivers for the Authentic style. Diverse and free-thinking inventiveness is valued by Authentics, while Rulers and Bosses would see it as risky or threatening. Authentics are confident and secure in their own identity and seek to enable and empower those around them. The Authentic leader is humanist, permissive and open to personal reinvention, seeing life (and work) as an individual quest for learning and development, both for themselves and for others. Authentic leaders see teaching and enabling others as a welcome responsibility, but do not demand compliance as a Boss leader might. Authentic leaders may deliver results more slowly than Bosses, but they always deliver more sustainably. Authentic leaders may be directive when the situation demands it, rather than in the reflexive way of a Boss leader. There is a tendency to support group benefits and be We-centric in the Authentic style.

Who follows Authentics?

Authentic leaders are everywhere, and nowhere. Of the tens of thousands of leaders (at all levels) we have worked with, by far the majority are predisposed to the Authentic style. However, because of the myth of leadership as an appointed position, and the preponderance of Boss and Ruler models at senior levels in organisations (and throughout history), very few Authentics perceive themselves as having leadership potential. For those who see the potential, and would like to accelerate their progress, the right kind of leadership development and training is not always available. Authentics often find themselves engaging in deep and reflective learning activities seen as 'fringe' (retreats, a spiritual search) in order to find validation.

People love to follow skilled Authentic leaders. If you have ever worked for a brilliant leader, who really understood and got the very best out of you, it is highly likely they were Authentic. Authentic leaders create space for others to be authentic and show Authentic leadership. Since leaders are defined by having followers, if each of us becomes more discriminating about who we follow, we can help to create more Authentic leaders.

A caveat: we do not believe that authenticity requires endless navel-gazing, nor does it justify bringing unwelcome 'shadow' aspects of our personalities to work. Authenticity is not 'warts and all' behaviour, heedless of those we work alongside. Authenticity is about cleaving to the interdependent, inclusive ideals and values cherished by many. A 'take me as I am' self-validation would tip into Boss behaviour.

Warning: Batteries Not Included

One key characteristic of the Boss/Ruler style is the use of the "Us vs Them" approach to creating loyalty by identifying a common enemy (a 'them') to demonise. This could be a competitor or another department in the same organisation, or it could be a sector of society. In organisations this leads to destructive silo thinking, while in society it can lead to segregation, violence, racism, and genocide.

Steve Bannon and Breitbart News in the US tended to demonise 'globalisers' and 'immigrants' as detrimental to the interests of US citizens, for example. This has been retrograde for liberal humanism in the US, and has contributed to an increase in conflict and division. This has a status-driven motivation because it is based on one segment 'losing out' to another; their suggested remedy is to reverse the see-saw. This mindset is in direct opposition to the work of Trump's predecessor, President Obama, who sought to effect systemic change in order to protect the future. We would categorise Bannon and Trump as short-term Rulers, and they are on record dismissing Obama, a long-term Authentic, as not a real leader.

In June 2010, Neil was working with a team from a tech company that was suffering from a period of Boss leadership. The team chose to go to Rome for an offsite, to learn from history. The first stop was near the Colosseum, where we searched for evidence of Emperor Nero's magnificent Domus Aurea, the vast palace he built to demonstrate and cement his status and power. The palace was demolished or buried less than 70 years after Nero's death, its only obvious legacy today is the name of the Colosseum itself, which references the colossal statue of Nero that was sited nearby (and that was converted to a statue of the god Helios after Nero's death, and has now vanished entirely).

After admiring the smaller palaces of the Palatine Hill, the Circus Maximus and the Forum, we made our way to the Pantheon, the remarkable temple that is still intact after more than 2,000 years. We remember who built the Domus Aurea, but Nero's name is not remembered fondly. Few among us can state who built the Pantheon. We do not know who built the Taj Mahal, only that it is a pure and monumental expression of grief; its massive dome a white teardrop in the sky. The glaring lesson is that when our edifices are built to glorify an individual, they are far less durable than when they are built to the glory of all, or a shared human experience.

Us vs Them abuses evolutionary psychology that says 'same' means safe and "different" meant dangerous. It creates false loyalty and belonging by identifying the tribe, team or organisation as 'us' (an in-group) and creating a sense of opposition to 'them' (a specific out-group). There is also the implied threat that those on the inside could at any time be cast out. Does your organisation treat losing your job as akin to excommunication, expulsion or banishment? If so, you may be in a Ruler/Boss-led environment.

Working with one of the major banks in the wake of the LIBOR rigging scandal, we came across a leader who was reputed to bring a baseball bat into meetings and slam it on the table for emphasis. Like any effective Ruler, he had a loyal cadre of followers who were dependent on his patronage and carried out his orders to boost/maintain their own status. When he left in the post-LIBOR clear-out it became obvious that the whole business, which he had run as a separate empire within the bank, needed rebuilding because all of its systems, processes and culture had become dysfunctional under his leadership.

Authentic/Visionary leaders use shared Cause and Conditions as the key driver of genuine loyalty. The Authentic/Visionary will seek to enrol all stakeholders (including competitors) in pursuit of the Cause, which is precisely why Tesla made all of their electric car patents available to all. Leaving your job in these organisations is treated as an opportunity to expand the network ("Let's keep in touch!"), and organisations that pursue this model often have a thriving alumni community.

Working both in corporations and private businesses, we see the tremendous levels of personal loyalty and even love that followers have for Authentic and Visionary leadership. Rulers and Bosses find the personal loyalty given to Authentics and Visionaries both incomprehensible and threatening.

In two cases - at a global technology company and at a global bank - we have seen brilliant authentic leadership ousted from the company because of these dynamics. We have helped Authentics to navigate this situation by working with them to enrol Bosses and Rulers on their own terms and reduce the threat level that they feel. Within the political environment in many corporates, Authentics have to find alternative ways to operate in order to be successful, or simply to manage their own conscience. For most organisations, Authentic leadership is by far the most effective style for delivering sustained success in a disrupted environment.

The Boss/Authentic schism basically comes down to differing Perspective/Maturity levels. Bosses operate at an Independent level of Perspective, while Authentics operate at an Interdependent level. However Interdependent Authentic leadership won't be able to heal the rift with Boss leaders. To do that we need to look to Integral Authentic or Visionary leadership: Perspective, married to Motivation, matched to Reach. Such leaders can embrace all others to truly act in the interests of the wider cause or for the good of all, from the integral perspective. 'I' becomes 'we' and ultimately, the 'we' motivation encompasses not just the planet and its ecosystems today, but the planet and ecosystems in perpetuity.

It is incumbent on all who aspire to lead to spread and foster purpose-driven leadership because it is longer lasting, more sustainable, and less reliant on ego, status or personal success. We must reject the myth that leaders have to be appointed and accept our own talent for, and influence in, leadership.

In Part II of this book we look in detail at how these behaviours and systems manifest, and what they feel like. This will certainly help you diagnose where you stand as a leader, clarify your thoughts on your role in leadership, and offer you more food for thought about the culture you work inside, or want to create.

"It's my daily mood that makes the weather."

Haim Ginott

Leaders have an effect. The tone, texture and intention immanent in our leaders creates outcomes in the culture. In the next chapter, we will examine how culture impacts performance.

"Culture eats strategy for breakfast."

Peter Drucker

CHAPTER 6

CULTURE IS THE STRATEGY

The idea that there is a 'right' culture has been seized on by Authentics because it indicates that beliefs, and therefore the ways we work together, show up in our behaviour to the degree that they predict performance. But how true is that in reality?

Whenever we put a group of people together over a period of time, culture happens. They will tell stories and establish ways of being. Without any other curation, that culture will be defined by the dominant mythologies and characters in the group - the formal and informal leadership.

In an unconscious culture, the mythologies are framed by gossip and the rumour mill, a chaotic series of perceptions, assumptions, and experiences amalgamates into some kind of reflection of dominant individuals. In a conscious culture, an intentional mythology is established. People can align within a framework for collaborative working in order to perform in ways that are agreed, to achieve the shared vision.

When the dominant individuals are Bosses or Rulers they will create a culture of subservience where people wait to be told what to do, and manage the messages they send upwards. More skilled Bosses and Rulers will be focused on delivering results that enhance their status, then moving on before the consequences of stealing from the future manifest. Less skilled Bosses and Rulers have less interest in performance, and focus more directly on symbols of status: getting the prime parking space or corner office, wearing monogrammed shirts and so on.

If the dominant individuals are unskilled Visionaries and Authentics the culture is likely to be values-driven, but vague, procrastinating and changeable. There may be a tendency to judge ("My values are better than your values"). The organisation may become too inward-facing. Skilled Authentics and Visionaries will create a conscious, reliable and empowered culture of distributed leadership focused on a common cause.

Most 'conventional' organisations have accidental cultures; the culture has not been deliberately designed and is not consciously curated. These cultures will often be in flux because they depend on the current leaders. There are organisations, especially the new breed of 'post-conventional' tech companies like Google, Valve and Netflix, that are extremely intentional about their culture. From an early stage, they codified the required mindset/behaviour, and actively curated it. These organisations recruit, on-board, develop and reward strictly in line with their culture. These cultures are so well-embedded that they outlast a change of leadership.

A culture delivers whatever it is. A culture that is internally unreliable will deliver unreliability. A culture that lacks trust will deliver mistrust. A culture that is collaborative will deliver support. If we want results that are profitable, innovative, investing and adaptable, we have to work out how to create a culture that consists of and delivers all of those things.

A simple definition of culture is **'the combined impacts of all behaviour'**. On this basis, performance is the outcome of culture. It follows, therefore, that the role of leadership is the creation and curation of culture to effect change, and directly impact performance. It also follows that the culture created will be the sum of the habits of leaders, and the behaviours attached to them.

Some critical research around this occurred in the late 1980s, started by David McLelland of the Harvard Business Review, and continued by Beckhard, Schein and Davies. Their combined studies began in the psychology of motivation, and quickly diversified into understanding team motivation and performance. Their research indicated that there is a deep correlation between leadership, culture, and performance. They discovered that 70% of culture is created by the preferences, attention and scrutinies of leadership, and 30% by other factors such as policies, processes, efficiency and so on.

In turn, 70% of performance is created by culture. This means that through culture, leadership directly impacts approximately 50% of performance. It has taken almost 40 years for this data to become accepted wisdom.

Most CEOs would want to have a very firm grip on a lever so powerful that it could affect 50% of their company's performance. Since culture is created by leadership, those CEOs should be very clear about who, how and why they promote people into influential senior positions.

Yet culture is not an easy lever to grasp; it can seem as slippery as a fish. As a means to drive performance, it wriggles and evades, bites back and betrays. It is not executable in a straight line, like a project plan. Many senior executives would rather change their job than embark on a culture change/ development programme. The conventional wisdom says: "Culture change is hard and takes years".

Values and Behaviour
Business likes a straightforward approach. It has become accepted wisdom that an explicit focus on the right kinds of behaviour will make an ailing organisation successful. Therefore, it has become popular to run organisational programmes on 'Values & Behaviours'. Yet in recent years there have been a number of significant failures with this kind of approach. In fact, only about 25% of 'Grand Launch' values programmes succeed. This makes them an expensive and risky way to try and achieve culture change.

It is no good expecting your employees, teams and other contributors to be 'reliable', 'responsible', 'excellent', 'disciplined', etc, if those qualities are not either present in the leadership, or role modelled by senior figures. If it is OK for the leader to turn up late, it is OK for everyone else. If it is OK for a leader to be disrespectful, we give the nod for everyone to be disrespectful to each other. If it is OK for you to get angry when you hear bad news, it is OK for them not to tell it to you.

If you want to change the results of a team or organisation by changing its culture, leaders have to start with their own behaviour and habits, and the behaviour and habits of other leaders. Change leadership first, and you create a firm foundation for a change in culture.

For many years Mark and Neil worked with a global energy company to strengthen the safety culture in the business. One of the cultural habits developed in the business was that every meeting started with a safety briefing and also, very often, a safety moment where participants would discuss any near-misses or safety issues anyone had experienced, including safety at home, driving and so on. Visitors to any of their offices would receive a safety briefing on the building, before they came in, and could expect to be reminded to hold the handrail when walking up or down stairs, or to put a lid on a hot drink.

It is easy to see such behaviours cynically, but there is no doubt that it helped to create a culture where safety was front-of-mind for most people. One example of this was a story we heard from the Head of Country in a Middle Eastern office. There had been a high number of injuries and fatalities among employees in the country due to a culture of not wearing seat belts while travelling by car. The Head of Country and a number of his executive team had taken to standing by the exit of the car park each evening and asking people to put their seat belts on before they left the carpark. Some might see this as overbearing and nannying, but in some ways that was the intention. One of the things these leaders were communicating was: "If you are not prepared to take your personal safety as seriously as we do, this may not be the right place for you."

We also worked with senior leaders in more administrative roles such as legal, finance and strategy to help them understand how decisions that they made about budgets, repairs or procurement very often had safety implications, so they should incorporate safety considerations into support function activities. Over time the culture became much safer, particularly as people at the front line began to believe that they really could question the safety implications of leaders' decisions and processes.

The main precondition for a culture development programme is humility. There is an implication inherent in culture change that the current leadership has in some way got it wrong. If the current leadership is made up of Bosses and Rulers, a culture change project would be either be an attack on their ego, or taken to mean that other people should change. When changing a culture, people look to leadership; leadership must therefore first show the new attributes required. To change also needs high levels of self-awareness, help and new habits. All three of these things are Interdependent activities, and so may not be attractive to Bosses and Rulers.

Working separately with the chief executives of two private companies who felt they were overburdened, Neil was asked to get the leadership team to step up and take more responsibility. Through workshops and coaching sessions, the leadership team began to take more initiative. However, the Boss style CEOs both hated it. They didn't want to be so busy, but they also didn't want to give up any of their status or control.

When crisis is the propellant for change, there is much more power behind the need to change behaviour. It is obvious that change is required when an oil tanker has exploded, a whole department of an organisation has been acting illegally or fraudulently, or our workforce is out on strike. 'Never waste a good crisis', in other words. In recognition of the power of adversity to re-shape mindsets and behaviours, some leaders even say: 'If there is no crisis, create one'.

We do not need to go that far.

Psychologically Safe Culture

For most, safety is pretty boring. However, safety is not just a procedural issue, it is also cultural. It is an aspect of Sustained Success.

In 2015, the People Operations (HR) team at Google set out to understand what makes teams effective. They wanted to discover, without a shadow of doubt, the behaviours critical to effective teamworking, and created 'Project Aristotle'. The intention was to understand, template and replicate these behaviours across all leaders and teams, to create universal high performance. The rather frustrating conclusion the researchers came to, was that there is no formula for high performing teams, but there is a culture that will produce them.

People are people, and they operate subtly and differently in different groups. Julia Rozovsky, an Analyst at Google who conducted this research, explains:

> "Over two years we conducted 200+ interviews with Googlers and looked at more than 250 attributes of 180+ active Google teams. We were pretty confident that we'd find the perfect mix of individual traits and skills necessary for a stellar team -- take one Rhodes Scholar, two extroverts, one engineer who rocks at AngularJS, and a PhD. Et voila! Dream team assembled, right? We were dead wrong. Who is on a team matters less than how the team members interact, structure their work, and view their contributions. So much for that magical algorithm.
>
> We learned that there are five key dynamics that set successful teams apart from other teams at Google:
>
> 1. *Psychological safety: Can we take risks on this team without feeling insecure or embarrassed?*
>
> 2. *Dependability: Can we count on each other to do high quality work on time?*
>
> 3. *Structure & clarity: Are goals, roles and execution plans on our team clear?*
>
> 4. *Meaning of work: Are we working on something that is personally important for each of us?*
>
> 5. *Impact of work: Do we fundamentally believe that the work we're doing matters?"*

Of these five elements, Psychological Safety was by far the most important in enabling teams to perform at their very best (there are parallels in this research with the work of Marcus Buckingham and Gallup Q12).

The relevance of this data is profound. What it means is that organisations who slavishly control the dissemination of values and behaviours, (even if the espoused values and behaviours are innovation or autonomy, for example), are probably doomed to fail. Humans are messy, complex and chaotic, and our response to behavioural direction, even ideal and aspirational behaviours, is unpredictable.

We certainly need some principles and suggestions for what constitutes the right kind of behaviour to achieve our vision. Being so prescriptive, that we impose a 7x9 behavioural competency matrix over it, deadens the whole endeavour; we disengage when it is reduced to a series of rat-mazes.

Our leadership of culture needs to be infinitely more creative. Rather than a stick-on solution, we need to move more into the realm of the shared stories and beliefs that we need to *succeed around* here, plus our positive day-to-day experience. It is not the posters or the expectations but the actual habits and observed behaviours of MY leader that define my experience of the culture and, therefore, my level of enrolment in it.

And that, we recognise, is vague, nebulous, and may require challenging upwards and thus is unattractive to managers who love measures, reports, conformity and results and don't want to have to challenge the behaviour of their line manager.

And yet it is the leadership way.

Mindset and Identity Logics

Ruler or Boss leadership can achieve high performance and fast results by creating a culture of obedience and conformity. However, these cultures are always vulnerable to the Ruler or Boss being wrong, to low levels of challenge or ideas, to silos and internal conflict, and to an unwillingness or inability by the front line to accurately feed back to the higher levels. They do not get you to the Ownership and Adaptability needed for sustainable business success. (Ownership and Adaptability reference the Sustained Success model discussed in Chapter 4).

If you examine the background for any corporate crisis, from Andersen Consulting to VW, you will find a common factor: some people knew in advance about the coming crisis, were concerned, and almost certainly expressed that concern... But they were not listened to and their concerns were not acted upon. Why not? Because the culturally dominant mindset made the organisation blind and deaf to other psychological and physical risks.

In oil production accidents the logic **'production at all costs'** contributes to errors. In the banking crisis it was **'pass on the debt'**. These fundamental behavioural commandments or logics are the primary factor in creating 'cultural risk'.

The frustration in organisational safety (for both human and economic risks), is that when you do it right, nothing happens! There is no opportunity to save people from danger or be a hero, by narrowly averting disaster. When organisations achieve cultural (and psychological) safety, even near-misses don't happen.

Mark worked with a number of Fire & Rescue Services across the UK during their modernisation in the mid-2000s. Part of this work involved establishing fire and rescue prevention, rather than response. There was considerable resistance from many of the firefighters who saw their role as saving people from fires and driving big red trucks fast with the sirens wailing. Driving slowly in a transit van, handing out leaflets and installing smoke alarms - while much less sexy - was actually more effective at saving lives. A more productive and effective definition of their job such as 'Keep People Safe', required a tough mindset change. The early adopters had to fight to make their case against a surprising headwind. In the end, the *prevention* 'logic' won out over *heroics*.

When Neil was at Razorfish in the late '90s, it became clear that client projects were not always delivering the intended value. After researching the problem, it became clear that many client cultures did not have the digital mindset and habits to successfully integrate the tools and technologies Razorfish was selling them. This logic was one of *process* taking precedence over *behaviour*.

Neil and Mark had an experience working with a team of healthcare professionals whose regional wellness campaign had floundered for years. Only a minority of the leadership team were proactively and visibly pursuing a healthy lifestyle themselves. Not surprisingly, they had little credibility around health and therefore could not talk about it convincingly. The foundation of their cultural logic was *'Just manage the risks'*. The system needed a different form of leadership inspired by the logic *'Be a healthy population'*. The leaders would not change their view of their own role, and so could not stir up enough passion in their followers to change the business outcome. The project did not move forward.

When Steve Jobs returned to Apple in 1997, the company was in financial trouble, the product lines were a mess and the culture demoralised. Steve Jobs rapidly called a meeting with some of his senior managers and walked in unshaven, wearing shorts and sandals. He took care to point out that he had been working all night and had been flat-out since he got back. He also said it was worth it. This is important because it demonstrated his commitment to and belief in the company.

He took care to praise the company, the brand and the people, while also critiquing the confused product line and emphasising the urgency of action. Then he announced what our leadership approach calls 'significant symbolic acts': visible commitments to the new way of doing things. He announced that Apple would rationalise the product line, and then shared the new "Think Different" advertising campaign designed primarily to restore confidence and pride in the workforce.

The cultural logic behind this was a switch in mindset from *Marginalised Microsoft Competitor* to *Home of the Think Different Elite*.

From 2009-2016 Neil and Mark worked on the global transformation of an oil super-major. The company worked relentlessly to change the identity logics around taking action. The company modelled 'virtuous cycles' (in place of 'vicious cycles'), as the basis for cultural and behavioural changes. These were buttressed by an ethical leadership initiative and extensive cultural inductions and on-boarding programmes for new hires.

In this clever piece of ethical insight, the organisation recognised it had been making decisions based on faulty logics that could seriously disrupt performance or even lead to catastrophe. Therefore, a safer culture (both psychologically and physically) required the right thinking to drive decisions, and the expression of personal identity was critical in that equation.

The Vicious Cycle

In the vicious cycle every team member knows that production is the priority (an ill-conceived goal in the model below) and would worry about stopping production on safety grounds because of negative consequences if they turned out to be wrong.

So team members would decide to do nothing, and retrofit thinking to justify those decisions. Mostly, nothing would happen, so they would get away with it... But the same problems of equipment, behaviour or process would still exist a week, a month or a year later. They would continue to decide to do nothing, and keep production up, because nothing went wrong last time. This vicious cycle corrupts or changes who we are at the level of values and human care. And then, on the next shift, the machine fails or the behaviour impacts negatively, and a colleague is injured - or worse. It is easy to see how this logic steals from the future.

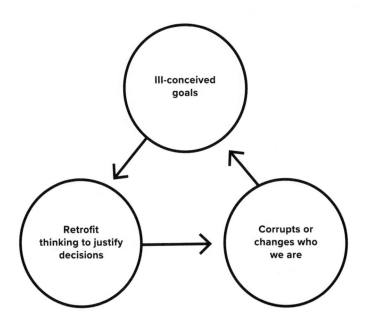

The Virtuous Cycle

In the virtuous cycle the team member would have stopped production and the machine would have been checked. When nothing was found to be wrong, the team member would be praised anyway - for their vigilance and courage.

With the virtuous circle the logic changed to *safety first,* because getting safety wrong was terminal and expensive.

The organisation had recognised that mindset and behaviour are critical in deciding what to do in high-risk environments, and that personal autonomy and identity were major factors in safe performance. If the organisational values, logics and culture supported the expression of individual identity in better decision-making there would be a natural and improved version of what we do. This is because *we care for ourselves and each other and act from that place.*

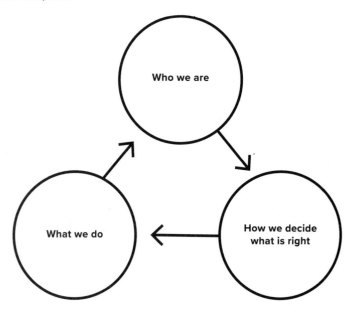

It was an idea that was impossible to argue against and gained instant currency in the business, inspiring new joiners and re-energising many middle managers.

Examine Your Beliefs
In 2002, Mark worked for Nokia in its special projects division, an innovative new business that would become the Vertu brand - the world's first luxury mobile phone. At that time, Nokia was a household name and a virtuoso business with a status similar to Apple's in 2018. Nokia then enjoyed almost 40% market share, with 60,000 employees and a massive hegemony over nearest rival Motorola, which had 15% market share and 100,000 employees.

To work inside Nokia was something of a dream job: forward-thinking, energetic talent in an open culture where anyone could approach senior staff with ideas. Innovation mattered, presenteeism was a joke, our aim was simply to achieve our objectives 'the Nokia Way'. Business practice was underpinned by a great purpose: 'Connecting People'. And 'Human' was a corporate value, chosen to ensure the right culture connected the products to the consumer. The future looked amazing from a fantastic platform.

Yet Nokia held fast to a single logic about the future. Stated almost daily in meetings, was the belief that people would only ever want to use mobile handsets to make/receive telephone calls and send/receive texts. It was this profoundly mistaken assumption that enabled Apple, in 2007, to completely blindside Nokia - the market leader - with the smartphone. Three years after that, Nokia was on a terminal trajectory, frantically scrambling to recover lost ground with the Lumia, but it was too late.

In reality, the cultural logic or belief around 'innovation' simply meant *Continuously Improve* what we've got, not *Invent Amazing New Ways to Connect People*. Apple had foreseen the coming 3G technology, which opened up broadband internet in a mobile handset, whereas Nokia stayed fixed within the slower data limitations of 2.5G.

Horizon scanning by Apple reshaped the whole industry... While Nokia lived its Human value to extinction.

Intentional and Authentic Culture

Intentional and authentic cultures are still relatively unusual, largely because the Authentic leaders who define them are rare in very senior positions and tend to be less well-known.

Barack Obama is one high-profile example. During, and since, his tenure as President, his leadership style has been criticised for taking time, espousing values-led thinking and moderation, and for seeking collaborative, long-term solutions. Mr Obama sought to heal, unify and move forward together, while attempting to stop the economy from stealing from the future. He was opposed by many less conscious contemporaries, still caught up in a dog-eat-dog system that is profoundly territorial and short term. Their perspective and maturity level made them incapable of seeing life as a long-term collaboration.

Intentional collaboration as a winning mentality takes much more committed resolve than competition. It is far easier to hate the immigrant next door and seek to defeat her, than to empathise, collaborate and integrate.
Yet Authentic leader motivations are stronger and more resolute than those of the Boss leader. The arc of history supports authenticity, the pursuit of which (though currently experiencing a setback), seeks personal freedom and self-expression. Control systems eventually fall by the wayside: men-only voting, apartheid and legal slavery are examples. They are contrary to our essential nature.

An intentional culture in business is one where the culture is designed, planned and curated as part of the overall strategy. It is embraced as a critical C-suite issue and accepted as the responsibility of top executives. Adding authenticity to this intentionality encourages and enables people to be themselves, skilfully in all situations. Business purpose is served by people bringing their unrestricted talents and strengths to their role. The upside is that we avoid catastrophes (such as those at VW, Tesco, Olympus, BP, Andersen Consulting, etc) and we promote a more effective, long-term culture. At the same time, we promote the importance of leadership bandwidth and permanent horizon-scanning in order to avoid a Blockbuster or Nokia scenario.

Organisations that enable authenticity in their population attract more people who are already aligned with their culture. They also get the very best out of employees because their personal purpose and organisational purpose are in sync. When people have a deep sense of meaning and purpose through their work, it's easy to motivate them - and oneself - because work takes us towards something that is affirming.

In one of their current projects, Mark and Neil are observing first-hand as a historically 'toxic' business is moving into authenticity. This is a very effective business, offering great remuneration and working environment. Employees tend to stay for decades. And yet the products it sells have been a deep source of unease for its talent for many years.

In recent developments, a far-sighted CEO has persuaded shareholders and stakeholders alike that its 150-year legacy business is doomed, and that it must find new ways to sell products and make profit. The vision he has espoused has created an immediate wave of support and relief across ranks of dedicated employees who now see a way forward that eases the tension between their personal values and the previously demoralising business purpose. As individuals, they can now be more authentic, and this is releasing trapped potential in the system. The best ideas are now coming from within, and change is happening fast.

Both Yes and No
Intentional and authentic organisations are explicit about their culture, detailing not just their vision, purpose, mission, behaviours and goals, but going into signifiant detail about what kind of behaviours and beliefs work in their organisation (as well as *what not to do*).

When human behaviour is unregulated, many of us 'misbehave'. The acid test of any culture is what people do when no one is looking. Conformist cultures have sub-cultures where people do things they wouldn't do in front of the leaders. They toe the line in public, but behind the scenes all manner of things may be going on. In authentic cultures however, the rebellious sub-cultures begin to die out because there is a shared pull towards our better natures.

Positive behaviour in teams is best achieved when we have a set of aspirational values or principles that we hold up as ideal - the 'target' culture. *And*, critically, underneath that sit regulated codes of conduct specifying unacceptable behaviours: the red lines. Both of these sets of behaviours are public, role-modelled by leaders and enforced. Great behaviour is rewarded, bad behaviour is punished. We head towards the Yes, and avoid the explicit No. Environments where these principles are applied equitably create psychological safety.

Mark was assisting one of the UK's prominent sugar companies in the early 2000s. They were suffering from a culture of cynicism in its long-standing employees and unions and were underperforming badly. The CEO wanted to rejuvenate the culture towards a more respectful climate, where behaviour became 50% of how employees would be measured. In the ensuing changes to their values, behaviours, and annual appraisal cycle, employees complained that they had 'seen all this before' and that nothing would change. When one of the highest performing salespeople was fired because the way they achieved their figures was consistently against company values, everyone suddenly took notice. Being measured on *how* to behave as well as *what* to deliver became a critical red line that assisted in shifting bad behaviour into good.

Support for the chosen mythology needs to be found throughout the organisational narrative, not simply as a list of behaviours in a company handbook and a once-a-year appraisal. Supportive structures and systems that make the destination culture inevitable, include things like office environments, collaboration policies, evaluation and reward systems, and fair and equitable HR policies. It is easy to accuse such organisations of cultishness or elitism, but as an organisational model it is supremely effective.

Nassim Nicholas Taleb writes about "anti-fragile" as the opposite of fragile. Anti-fragile is more than being robust; anti-fragile actually becomes stronger and more resilient under pressure. Muscles are a good example. A good, intentional culture becomes anti-fragile, responding well to crisis and pressure, by learning, bonding and improving.

All of the above flows from consistent Authentic leadership.

In spite of their relative rarity overall, 7 of the largest 10 companies in the world (in Spring 2018) are intentional about their culture and are on the authentic journey: Apple, Alphabet (Google), Microsoft, Facebook, Berkshire Hathaway, General Electric and Johnson & Johnson. Of the others, Exxon Mobil and Amazon are intentional, but probably not Authentic, in that they prioritise conformity over authenticity.

So if it's not through a nice and neat Values and Behaviours programme, how can leaders inculcate something as nebulous as culture?

Context, Cause and Conditions
We have mentioned Cause and Conditions above. Now we need to go into their essential components in more detail.

Effective leadership does not ignore either global or local contexts. Horizon-scanning is the study of what is going on in the world and how it may be impacting your own sector. This discipline is now more important than strategy.

Constant change is the **Context**, and no organisation can either ignore it or do nothing about it. How the context manifests will change from sector to sector and company to company, but the fact of disruption and change will not. Leadership is the only superpower available to mitigate this.

Cause and **Conditions** are the foundational elements for any cultural change project, outlining the destination of the change and the principles and habits which, when lived, will help bring about the change as envisioned. Usually there will be an organisation-wide statement of Cause and Conditions, with different parts of the organisation needing to understand in a relevant way how they should behave to support that narrative.

Many organisations use the terms 'Vision', 'Purpose', 'Mission' and 'Objectives/ Goals' interchangeably, and they are widely misunderstood. In Part II below, we will outline some common definitions. We have collected all these terms together and named them the organisational 'Cause'. The Cause is why you do what you do, where you are going, and how you will get there.

Millions of organisations work and exist without Cause. Or, they say that their Cause is to make profit, and their daily occupation is essentially cranking a handle to make more of it.

However, when we look at the finest examples of organisational achievement such as Apple, Google and Novo Nordisk, we notice that they are really purposeful about what they want to do and where they are going. Those organisations excel at achieving sustained success, weathering disruption (in many cases they themselves are the disruptors), and leading their markets. Organisations that lack Cause rarely initiate change. Instead they are forced to respond to changes others are making, which makes them vulnerable. The companies that succeed sustainably no longer compete with others, but with themselves. Self-improvement becomes the cause of individuals, and self-improvement the goal of the organisation.

Other organisations have a stated Cause and Conditions, but something about how they conduct themselves prevents us from believing in it. Enron, for example, had a vision "To become the world's leading Energy Company - creating innovative and efficient energy solutions for growing economies and a better environment worldwide" and had the values of Respect, Integrity, Communication and Excellence.

Often the Cause and Conditions may have been adopted in a naked attempt to generate commitment and will, or it is not role-modelled by leaders. Or it is, but other priorities are allowed to obstruct its delivery. It can be demotivating and chaotic to work in organisations like this and they often lose talent. They also remain exposed to cultural risks.

All of this points to a simple, but critical, point: only create a meaningful Cause and Conditions if you intend to follow through and deliver it. Inevitably, this delivery must be more than a tick-box exercise. Specifically, it requires the leaders' behaviour to be aligned to both Cause and Conditions.

There is no 'right' way to articulate Cause. Sometimes the components are separated and sometimes woven together. What matters is that they are all there.

Below are the elements captured in the best Cause (Vision, Purpose and Mission) and Conditions (Values, Behaviours and Habits):

Great vision
A vision that inspires is:

- Scarily exciting

- Stirring to the soul

- Something we are willing to fight for

- Something we willingly push the boundaries on

- Something we are dedicated to

- A definable destination

- Motivating to all stakeholders – not just employees

Engaging with a well-written or conceptualised Cause is easy because it has a universal quality that appeals to almost everyone. Some are relatively easy to buy into, such as NASA's vision to land a man on the Moon, or Elon Musk's intention to colonise Mars. But what about if you sell paint? Or make toilets? Or supply electricity?

Creating an energising Cause is not about emulating SpaceX. It is about defining a clear and distinct future that you currently do not know exactly how to achieve, and then aligning adaptive and innovative activity towards it. The crucial aspect to this is not necessarily the destination itself, but the actions, creativity, and alignment (and hence changes to culture) – that it inspires.

A great Cause sets a clear direction. It assists in protecting the organisation against the threat of change because the focus is about creating the future, not aimlessly fixing the present. What is more, if we remember our statistics about the adoption of energising change from Chapter 4, research tell us that up to 87% of the workforce come along with you when the Cause is inspiring.

Setting a vision, one of the components of the overall Cause, can be challenging. In November 2009, Neil was running a vision session for a non-profit in Berlin. One of the participants protested that "we must be realistic". We disagree: a vision is future-focused and the one thing we cannot predict is what will or won't be realistic in the future.

At lunchtime that same day, while in search of a sandwich, Neil had stumbled on U2 practicing for the evening's concert at the Brandenburg Gate, celebrating 20 years since the fall of the Berlin Wall.

At the beginning of 1989, East Germany's leader, Erich Honecker, had made a speech predicting that the wall would last for 50 or 100 years. By August that year, Hungary had opened its border and by September thousands of East Germans were escaping through Hungary and Czechoslovakia to Austria. On November 9th, the East German government decided to allow limited travel to West Germany through selected checkpoints, starting the next day. The task of communicating the new rules at a press conference was given to an individual who had not been present when the rules were made. The spokesperson said, "This 9 November is a historic day. The GDR has announced that, starting immediately, its borders are open to everyone. The gates in the Wall stand open wide." Very quickly thousands of people gathered at the wall demanding to be let through and after some frantic phone calls, the authorities had to relent. So fell the Berlin Wall, followed swiftly by the collapse of the USSR.

In late 2015, David Cameron, then Prime Minster of the United Kingdom of Great Britain and Northern Ireland fulfilled a Tory Party manifesto promise by calling the population to a referendum on membership of the European Union. Mr Cameron fully expected the result to state: "the British people want to be part of the EU". By June 2016, this had proved a highly risky miscalculation.

In early 2017, against the odds and (apparently) the calculations of his own campaign team, Donald John Trump was elected President of the United States.

All these examples go to show that visions can be plausible without - at the time – needing to be realistic.

The pre-requisites of a robust Cause (Vision, Purpose, Mission, Goals and Measures) are discussed in Chapter 12.

Defining 'Conditions'

Organisational Conditions are how we need to be in order to pursue the Cause most effectively. Many organisations spend lots of time working on this because they accept that culture predicts performance, which predicts results. Not all of them get it right because an effective culture requires effective leadership (and after years of prioritising management as a skill, leadership can be in short supply).

Typically, an organisation will promote certain beliefs or values above others, believing those values will create the best culture to achieve the stated Cause. There are several levels to this hierarchy:

1. Values/Principles: a high level articulation of the cultural boundaries, using perennial human aspirations

2. Behaviours: how chosen values translate into how we act, make decisions, or treat each other

3. Habits: the day-to-day rituals and routines we expect to see around here

4. Measures: how we calibrate behaviour to know we are on track.

This approach can lead to Sisyphean attempts to sell a set of words no-one really believes in because leaders sponsor them, but do not role-model them.

Our observation and careful working with levels of change within systems has brought our thinking on change to a more emergent approach. It is useful to land a few behavioural concepts and champion them, but we have to be aware that these efforts are likely to be received cynically. We find it far more productive to begin the conversation with a series of real questions across the organisation and to involve as many people as possible:

- What behaviours will get us to our vision?

- What is wrong now?

- What is right now?

- How do we need to work differently in order to release your trapped potential?

Executives find this approach hard at first, as they must give up the illusion of control. (They believe they have control but in fact have usually achieved only some degree of obedience). We have worked on many initiatives where employees, given autonomy, have easily created the open culture they long for, much to the surprise and delight of the Executives who feared such an open approach.

Try it. You will be surprised.

Adaptive, constant change means we initially need to work hard for our leadership coin. But longer term it pays dividends in terms of both results and our own workload.

We must also have our finger on the pulse of a few slightly more vague concepts:

1. Living what the vision asks of us - role-modelling the standards and disciplines to make it stick

2. Articulating and living a core narrative (both the ideal aspects and the no-go areas - the 'yes' and the 'no')

3. Working on relationships and habits

4. Seeking constant feedback about the lived experience of working here

5. Measuring and rewarding the right behaviours.

Give Values Teeth
Create the right narrative for the vision. This works for individual as well as business change. Work out what the behaviour looks like that will embody the vision. Then start living it - every day in every small way. Forget the 'Grand Launch' of your Conditions, even at team level. Instead, discuss and work daily with the right principles and behaviours to create the mythology or support the beliefs until they are broadly there and observed habitually in a

particular team. Once people around you are satisfactorily embodying that story, you and they can work with the next layer of the organisation. Repeat this process with ever-widening circles, or by cherry-picking influential teams or business areas, until the Conditions are widely recognised and people start saying, "Yes, I see a change in how we do things round here", "Yes, the story makes sense to me".

You then have the basis to talk about Cause and Conditions, because they are already present: "See how such-and-such a team has progressed - fantastic work". The evidence is there and can be used to create the 'flywheel' of behavioural change because it is a pull energy, not an exhausting push.

In the same way, establish what we will not do in our story. Again, though, the same qualification applies. Rules - and values - must be lived and enforced at all levels. Leadership must be prepared to do something with them and about them. They are not posters, but people in action. So, bullying must be banished, sexism stopped, racism removed, corruption cleansed and tardiness terminated. Values and beliefs in tension with one another can create world wars, as we know, so if your changes are profound, there may well be periods of conflict and turnover in key positions.

One company we worked with sought to introduce a new Cause and Conditions (they called it a vision and purpose, together with a new set of detailed values and behaviours). The whole project was launched with a great deal of fanfare and large plinths in the Head Office lobby extolling the values. Our job was to train internal 'values leaders' to run values sessions for their colleagues. In under four months they achieved the remarkable feat of running a half-day values session for over 100,000 people globally. There were also special leadership ethics sessions for all of the senior leaders in the business and the CEO attended every one and had a frank conversation with his top people.

The excellent values and purpose were gratefully embraced by the vast majority of staff, but most found the vision vague and confusing. The real problem was that many people were embracing the words of the values, but neither the mid-level leaders nor the executives at the very top of the company were behaving remotely in line with them. Over time, the vision and, to a lesser extent the purpose, were quietly dropped. Although a lot of people privately appreciated and wanted the values, they knew them to be ineffective in the event of any complaint against a line manager.

This organisation's culture undoubtedly changed for the better in this process; it is a more psychologically safe place today than it was in the past. But the cultural transformation did not achieve its higher aims, largely because leaders at the top level were not role-modelling their own Cause and Conditions.

They aspired to an autonomous, agile, safe culture. But the concept was being forced on everyone by an elite who still played political games and fundamentally misunderstood leadership. Four years after it started, the Chief Executive was fired, even though he had materially improved the overall lot of the organisation's employees and customers, and delivered exactly the same amount of profit as had the previous CEO.

One of the natural barriers to effective change is employees and leaders waiting for visible signs of change 'from above'. While understandable, this is ultimately the wrong approach for anyone who aspires to authentic leadership. The reality is that changing organisational culture requires the involvement of all who aspire to leadership, not just the appointed leaders. Anyone can lead through behaviour and role-model their values, without waiting for an appointed leader to do it first. If you believe in it, act according to your own integrity and take up the mantle yourself.

This can, and often does, make individuals unpopular. Those showing leadership risk being marked out, scorned for a 'career limiting move', or for upsetting the behavioural paradigm. When no-one will thank us for making a stand for who we are and becoming more authentic, it can be tempting to go with the flow; that is an easy option available to us at any time.

These are decisions we can only make individually. A little like accepting feedback as a potentially life-changing gift, deciding to raise our own standards can change our life for the better.

Mid-career, Mark worked in a small business consultancy with ten employees. Its leader, an entrepreneur, was by turns extremely inspirational and extremely toxic. Within a couple of years he had succeeded in creating a successful small business with several million dollars in turnover. There was an energising vision and the team was working on uplifting new change and leadership material to bring to its clients. However, the internal culture was pure chaos. You never knew what you were going to get.

The owner's presence dominated the office and clients, and he was nicknamed the 'mood Hoover'. Staff constantly had to navigate his changeable moods and pick exactly the right moment to give him feedback, which he either accepted or was upset by. Sinister sides to his personality also emerged over time and no senior person succeeded in working with him sustainably. Sometimes there were direct personality clashes through disagreement, and sometimes there were more malign moves against people. He was a bit like a mercurial 'dad' who would beat you one day and buy you a pony the next.

In terms of Perspective, this leader saw himself as Integral, but he behaved more in ways that were a mixture of Self and Independent, setting colleagues against each other to create a culture of Ruler-style Dependency - on him. He claimed to be Visionary, but ruled with an iron fist. He publicly proclaimed to want Authenticity for and from the team, but responded as a Boss if it exercised autonomy.

With growth came the appointment of an Operations Director who ended up being a bit like 'mum'. He supervised the 'kids' who ran client projects, and had a different value set to dad. The team looked to dad when he was there, and complained to mum when he wasn't. Then concerns emerged around the treatment of female employees, and someone was paid off and promptly left. This small business became a hotbed of gossip, rumour and, probably, illicit behaviour.

Disgruntled and unsettled, Mark realised he was in a 'red lines' situation. The company had a clear Code of Conduct but the culture prohibited its enforcement with a single owner-MD. Any challenge to his status and authority was met with excommunication. Mark realised this was now a question of personal values and courage. He had reached his own red line, and was no longer prepared to tolerate that culture. Without directly challenging the owner, he resigned.

Working as an independent, Mark's first main client was his previous employer. The owner grew upset as Mark tried to develop alternative new clients and, sure enough, the excommunication occurred. This led to a period of hardship for Mark's family as he built up new business.

In the end, that values-led stand carried long-lasting and damaging consequences. Was it worth it? Certainly, there was no recognition of the validity of the stand. His former colleagues thought badly of him. But a stand on values is a stand on values, and its meaning can only be measured by the person making it. Mark acknowledges that he could have been more skilled, influenced differently, and made people aware of the basis for his decisions. But the answer is: of course it was worth it, and authenticity can have a cost.

If a stand is necessary, you may have to make it alone, because people have fear and will throw out cherished ideals one by one until they reach their own red lines.

You cannot have integrity if you compromise yourself, and the longer term consequences to Mark of compromising his integrity, at that stage in his life and development, would have been more grave than the effort of finding new clients.

Values must have teeth. Principles are not fluffy hugs, but razors for sharp decision-making. Without standards in adversity, we cannot shape who we are; instead the adversity will shape us.

In many ways the generic corporate approach to values has devalued them. But personal values are real and highly significant to each of us. We often ask participants in sessions if they have tried working in a place that went against their own values, as Mark did. Usually a few hands go up. The second question is, "how long did you last?" To which the answer is, "usually less than six months". The third question is, "How was it?" The answers vary on a scale from awful to unbearable.

Even those of us who have never articulated our values are very clear when we or someone else goes against them. By contrast, working somewhere that is actively aligned to our values is uplifting, energising, motivating and generates all sorts of discretionary effort.

Organisations are complex, but cultural cause and effect is, ultimately, pretty simple.

Understand How Power Works

One of the most valuable pieces of leadership research is the work of Barry Oshry. He has devoted decades to understand how systems behave, calling it Power Lab.

The simplicity of 'cause and effect' behaviour discussed above manifests instantly across systems. Oshry has codified his observation of behaviour into a language for discussing it, noticing that there are predictable stages and characteristics in how we behave and perform when we work in an unconscious way. It is a blend of how we behave as animals, and our modern, rational overlay of consciousness. It exposes individual perspective and the inherent assumptions that lie within the current culture/s of your organisation. It then extends these habits into an observation of how the true potential beneficiaries of your culture (your stakeholders and customers) get sidelined or ignored.

The language of "Tops", "Middles" and "Bottoms" in the examples below is Oshry's, and he chose this language deliberately to describe the actual condition, not the ideal.

Burdened Tops

Tops have power, but often wield it unconsciously. The very instant we become a 'Top', we feel burdened by the position and begin to act in predictable ways. We feel the latent gravity of the organisation beneath us and become conscious that our every action casts a long shadow. We want to do our best and make great decisions, and yet we also like to confer on ourselves some special privileges in order to mark us out as Top. Boardroom lunches, reserved parking spaces, and so on.

Tops instantly become less accessible, usually develop a distance between themselves and their organisation, and every word is interpreted and re-interpreted with special meaning by others.

Tops also super-segment, into Top of the Tops (the main core of decision makers and power brokers who 'get things done'). Tops rely on Middles to work as a conduit between them and the organisation as a whole. If Tops lose faith in that Middle tier, they will work around it. Ruler or Boss Tops expect their instructions to be carried out, and will rely on loyal Bosses to do so faithfully and without interpretation. Visionary Tops will expect everyone to be giving their absolute best and bringing all of their talents. They will look to promote meritorious Middles and Bottoms. Visionary Tops willingly give trust and autonomy, but do not really understand when individuals do not take power for themselves or fail to meet high standards.

The objective of the Tops is to execute organisational purpose.

Torn Middles

Middles can become unanchored in organisations, because they spend a lot of time serving two masters. The first master, the Tops, must be listened to and their orders carried out. The second master, the Bottoms (who may well be mission-critical), must be protected against the perceived changeability of the Tops. Consequently, Middles are torn, running between - and often interpreting and sanitising messages from - both sides in order to minimise conflict and preserve the relative efficiency of the system. To the Bottoms, Middles appear to be in control and taking care of things; to the Tops they may appear objectionable and resistant. Middles feel they have expertise that is not listened to by the Tops, and that they may well be able to execute better than the Bottoms due to their higher levels of experience. Middles feel their experience and expertise is unappreciated by anyone. Depending on their Perspective, Boss Middles may micro-manage Bottoms and only give good news to Tops. Authentic Middles will protect Bottoms from the harshness of Top decisions, and possibly appear to drag their feet or make unnecessary demands of the Tops.

The objective of the Middles is to preserve their own sanity and run either an efficient system, or a healthy system, depending on their Perspective.

Oppressed Bottoms

Bottoms await instruction and to be included, in that order. They feel they have talents to offer and that their talents are often wasted. Many Bottoms spend their lives giving lip service to a job they do not especially enjoy, awaiting the moment when they are recognised for their efforts, or can leave to pursue their dreams.

Bottoms are hyper-sensitive to the messages they hear from Middles and Tops, and will often create their own myths and assumptions in order to justify their views of the world. In unconscious systems, this can lead to breakdowns between levels of hierarchy, and Bottoms can and will self-organise to protect themselves from what they perceive to be bad decisions. Unions, strikes, pressure groups and lobbying movements all grow out of these conditions.

Status-driven Bottoms aspire to become Middles so that they can wrest some degree of control from the system, or at least receive some approval. Purpose-driven Bottoms either abdicate their attention, giving it to their own meaningful pursuits, or become extremely vocal and resistant to the culture in order to socialise what they see as the right kinds of change.

The objective of Bottoms is to be able to bring their talents to what they do, and be appreciated for it. The overall culture will determine whether they do that to obtain status or meaning.

Neglected Customers

All of the above is rather absorbing, if we remain inward-facing. The net effect of many of these disruptions is that our customers are neglected. A neglected Customer is a power that usually votes with its feet. Even neglected Customers who stay with you tend to tell, on average, 20 people of their bad experiences.

Neglected Customers have been the demise of many businesses. In his book 'Customer What?' Ian Golding recounts a myriad of examples and situations in which customers have punished those who consistently get it wrong, and the list is eye-watering: BHS, Woolworths, Motorola, and many others. In a social media-driven world, these impacts come faster and more furiously than ever before, and standards are rising all the time. Ten years ago, a poorly performing company would get poor results. Now, a poorly performing company is at risk of being out of business entirely.

The objective of Customers is to get value for money and to feel that their custom is appreciated.

Ignored Consultants
Pity the Consultants. There are only two reasons to contract an outside agency to help your business:

1. You do not have a specific capability or best practice internally, and/or

2. You need a level of objectivity that is otherwise unavailable to you.

Some consulting models do not lead to good customer experiences, and some consultancies have a reputation for consuming time and organisational bandwidth just to tell you what you already know. However, only some of that loss in performance edge is down to the consultants. There is no point contracting a consultancy for a piece of work and then not using their findings.

The real benefit of effective consulting is in providing a researched worldview that incorporates best practice, competitive edge and internal profiling. The real challenge with the outputs from consulting is integration into the organisation's day-to-day. Again, this is a form of agility that is learned. Systemically ignoring consulting advice is neither rational nor reasonable.

The objective of Consultants is to be allowed to do their best work in order to assist their client.

The other, fascinating observation Oshry codified is how behaviour changes the very instant our personal context does. In a conversation with subordinates, you are the Top. In the next conversation, simply by moving into the corridor and meeting a group of more senior colleagues, you have become a Middle. Then you are asked to present at a Board meeting and suddenly you are a Bottom. Our behaviour constantly shifts along with our personal context. This is one of the most powerful arguments for authenticity.

Someone who is fully Authentic is more likely to be consistent across all of these levels and groups, and much better able to navigate differing conditions with the same degree of motivation.

In order to mitigate the effects of these unconscious patterns, it is incumbent on senior leaders not to take on assumed or unconscious Top-like behaviours, but to consciously curate a culture that distributes autonomy and decision-making power as widely as possible across the organisation. We have worked with teams who began a task under conditions absolutely as Oshry described. When they became conscious of this cause and effect, they very consciously and quickly (within a few hours!) break the patterns, relate to each other differently, come out of their offices, establish working groups and clear ways of working, and completely reshape their understanding of how culture performs. Chief in this change is their ability to laugh at themselves by using the language. "Ah, I see, I'm being a burdened Top", or "Sorry for being an Oppressed Bottom, I didn't mean it that way", and so on.

To help clients understand these dynamics, we often use Oshry's wisdom in a simulation-based workshop. Typically, we ask clients to undertake a real business task and then set the team up with two Tops, two Middles, two teams of Bottoms (one run by each Middle), two Consultants and sometimes a Customer or two. We give the Tops an 'office' and the Bottoms a space for each team. We give the Middles a corridor and put the Consultants in a café nearby. We give all of them the same cultural brief, which sets out some hierarchical norms and traditions, but which also says that anyone can challenge the system at any time. What is remarkable about this exercise is just how quickly - almost instantly - people fall into the roles Oshry describes.

Part way through the simulation we bring everyone together for what Oshry calls a "Time out of Time". We ask everyone how they feel. The Tops say they feel burdened. The Middles say they feel torn. The Bottoms say they feel oppressed or confused, and the Consultants feel ignored. Having shared all of this, we restart the simulation and 9 times out of 10, it continues exactly as before. Zero value is delivered on the real project, as everyone focuses on the 'political and emotional' drama.

What's the Alternative?

The alternative to the unconscious hierarchical system is the conscious adaptable system. In the conscious adaptable system, the titles are the same, but responsibility is distributed and leadership is dynamic, flowing to where it is most relevant.

Culture Change Is Easy. Really.

The power of culture is the link to our limbic centre in the brain - the one responsible for social structures and fitting in. We know from our own personal experience, and from many researched psychological experiments, that most people will quickly conform socially, even if what is being asked of them seems pretty weird.

Extreme cultures can normalise the practice of belittling others and verbal violence, as well as intimidation, harassment, institutional racism, and other evils. When we find ourselves in an environment where everyone else seems to be behaving in a particular way, it is very hard for us individually to challenge that behaviour, even if those behaviours are ineffective or harmful. This is precisely because we are programmed to fit in or to respect authority in order to fit in. New leadership, brought in especially to change the culture, can suffer tissue rejection because of this.

However, 'Corporate Evil' is largely another myth. Corporations in the last twenty years have done more to advance conscious inclusion, diversity, co-operation, learning and more moral decision-making than many other sectors. There are high-profile exceptions, but they serve to prove the rule: increased transparency is working to create much more conscious and integral approaches to collaboration right across the world.

For any leader or organisation seeking to change and become more intentional about their culture, there is both a challenge and a key. Cultures can change quickly and easily when we experience a compelling enough message, together with consistent role-modelling of behaviour from enough respected peers. When leadership is conscious and intentional, behaviour changes rapidly.

Finally a word about different national cultures. Between us we have worked in at least 40 different countries on six continents. Many times we have been carefully briefed about how different a culture is, or how special are the conditions. It is true that there are some differences, but national culture differences are far smaller than organisational culture differences.

There are national cultural differences around deference to or respect for hierarchy. Typically - but not universally - Northern European countries (Nordic plus Netherlands) have the least respect for hierarchy, while Middle Eastern countries have the most respect for hierarchy (according to Hofstede and Trompenaars). It is also fair to say that some national cultures are more relaxed about time-keeping than others. Working in Angola we found ourselves very un-relaxed as we tried in vain to bring participants back from coffee and lunch breaks on time. In desperation we tried playing music which, in the UK, would attract people's attention and bring them back to the room. In Angola, on the very first beat, everyone just started dancing.

Other cultural challenges to pre-conceptions exist. We generally work with a relatively well-educated and affluent slice of the professional sector in a country. In our experience, the country where people show the greatest hunger for learning is India, probably because education is widely seen as a route out of poverty. This is compelling, considering their age demographics compared to the rest of the world, (see Chapter 2 on Ageing).

Finally, it is also worth commenting from our experience not about what makes us different, such as national or regional culture, but what we share. If we were to measure what it is to be human as a depth of one metre, we would estimate that national or regional cultural differences would only be about one centimetre of that metre.

The remaining ninety-nine centimetres would be about the values we have in common, such as love, family, community, safety, peace, fulfilment, meaning, purpose, legacy, memory, feeling, progressing and learning. We may also share ego, which can lead to many catastrophes. However, it is in the practice of being Interdependent and Integral in Perspective that we learn to let go of that.

Regardless of national culture, it is entirely possible to run the same leadership development in Manchester or Manila, Zagreb or Zanzibar and appeal to exactly the same human impulses. The session logistics might differ, but the learning towards ideal outcomes remains very, very similar.

The best Cause is plausible without being limited by what is currently thought to be possible.

YOU CAN'T HAVE CHANGE WITHOUT CHANGE

"Change is good. You go first."

Anon

CHAPTER 7

CHANGE IS EASY

The essential nature of the world is change. All of its systems and effects are based on constantly moving, ever-changing adaptation. Evolution, plate tectonics, and even the orbit of the earth around the sun, create the paradigm for our natural state. Consequently we are superbly set up for change; it is healthy, ever-present and inevitable. As a result, our brains are designed to learn, perpetually enabling us to find new ways to succeed in new contexts. In the preceding chapters we looked at personal and professional change, whether caused by crisis, opportunity, or enforcement.

Though change is the fact of life, we all experience change differently. Change is seen by some as positive, some as easy, some as hard, and some as negative, all set up by our own predisposition towards change and the changes on offer. What we have not yet fully discussed are the emotional transitions needed to deal with change in adult, adaptive and positive ways. Evidence suggests that as human beings during change, we travel an emotional trajectory before we can accept a new reality and adjust our behaviours and habits accordingly. Unless we are one of a relatively small group of people who live for change and love it no matter what, that series of transitions impacts most people negatively, at least at first.

It could be argued that many of the conflicts in the world are caused by poorly handled or ill-conceived change. Many organisations attempt cultural and operational change and fail. Many organisations need organisational change and don't even try. Some cultural change efforts succeed a little, a few succeed a lot. Many personal change efforts start with good intentions, but slip very quickly from a strong internal narrative inspiring habit change into permanent indecision and lost opportunities.

Why?

As we know from our explorations above, the critical components in any cultural change are Interdependent and Integral leadership, along with commitment and skill. For incumbent leaders to lead culture change they first have to adopt and integrate the new habits and behaviours, and do it visibly. For individual change, there are two factors only: decision and commitment.

Research and experience predict that there will always be change resistance of some sort, and this resistance can derail, stop, delay, intensify, or make the change conditions worse. That is because we have to deal with people (including ourselves!), and people are complex beings with needs, emotions and unpredictable responses.

In this chapter we explore the emotional aspects of personal and organisational change.

Learning Change From Experience
Much of the material we use to help people and organisations to grow and change is widely researched and recognised, coming from a variety of thinkers and leaders. From business and the military, to government, politics, philosophy and psychology, the global body of work on change is wide, deep and varied. Most of it is useful depending on shifting context, in contrast to the problems, which tend to be perennial. Some of the material is too theoretical and does not really stand up in the face of reality.

The experience of working in change for three decades has also created our own new thinking. Time spent working with organisations has deepened and enriched our appreciation of how change really works. Lastly, as we know from Chapter 2, the personal and global context for change is radically different from anything any theorist has anticipated before: **change itself has changed.**

Nevertheless, wherever you are and whatever you do, you already know quite a lot about change: you have been doing it all your life.

Chief within our refreshed change approach is our determination to blow the myth (which is perhaps only really present in organisations), that things are supposed to stay the same. They don't, and never have, so we're mystified as to why many people expect or want them to!

Next is to encourage all of us to shift our mindset and approach to one of *personal* agility. The prevailing message is that change is hard and takes years. Obama is widely quoted as saying "Change is hard, but always possible."

We suggest that change is *easy* precisely because we want to challenge all that thinking. We accept that some change is extremely challenging, but the reality is that change is essential and ever-present. So, change is not difficult; it is our attitude to change that we must address. Change is experienced as easy when it's a change we want or have elected for ourselves, and it is well planned and executed.

An example of just how quickly a culture change can happen came from our work with a marketing team at an international consumer goods brand. The brand had a very clear and inspiring Cause and Conditions, but the team felt their cautious and inhibited culture was getting in their way. Through a workshop we explored their vision and values statements and it seemed to tick all of the boxes.

However, on further discussion we found that one team member, who worked in another location, had a very different cultural experience (more dynamic, more enjoyable) in her normal office from the one that the rest of the team worked at. We discovered that in the main office all of the business' top executives shared the same large, open-plan floor with the marketing team and others.

There was no suggestion that those executives had asked anyone not to have fun or to keep the noise down. However, they tended to be quiet themselves, and so the 200 people on the floor did the same. We came up with a plan, which was for this team of six simply to greet each other in the mornings and talk without inhibition during the day. Almost immediately the tension was broken, and the whole office, including the senior executives, became more relaxed. What is interesting here was that this was an entirely unintentional and unconscious imposition of an unhelpful culture on a large number of people, by a very small number of people.

In a nightclub in Amsterdam, cleaners complained daily to management about the amount of urine they had to clean off the floor in the men's toilets. The problem was that drunk men could not aim especially well. In a flash of inspiration, management commissioned urinals that had a realistic-looking fly painted onto the urinal porcelain. This cleared up the problem almost entirely.

In a manufacturing business, they were experiencing issues with teams not wanted to wear safety goggles to protect their eyes. Near-misses and actual incidents to do with eye safety were constantly being reported. However, it was noted that all of the workers wore sunglasses to drive home when it was sunny outside. They commissioned Ray Ban to create cool-looking protective eyewear, and the problem disappeared.

Your mission, should you choose to accept it, is to find, enable, and accelerate equivalent transitional, adaptive, easy change moments, whether they be personal, organisational or societal.

Change and Transition
Change is experienced as difference in our external environment. When things change externally, we also undergo transition internally: the emotional impact of the difference. When circumstances change, we need to understand and integrate their meaning. Often, change takes place in organisational life without addressing the psychological and emotional transition that people experience. We can visualise this with the 'change curve', an extension of the grief-related work of Elizabeth Kubler-Ross.

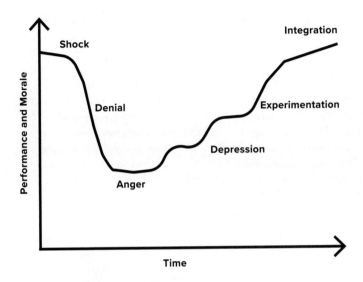

The change curve identifies a predictable series of emotional stages we transition through when we experience change. Having our project cancelled or getting a higher tax bill than we thought, are minor examples relative to a bereavement, yet they trigger the same predictable stages of shock, denial, anger, depression, experimentation and integration. The change is also resisted, in some cases more deeply, if it is perceived as contrary to what we ourselves believe. We will prefer to continue to believe the old thing than take on something new, even if the new thing has the potential to improve our own circumstances.

We know that change is an emotional journey. Whatever the change is, we will travel this curve; our confidence and performance will dip before we are able to integrate the change and raise our level of motivation and performance in the new state. However, our own experience observes that populations that have been socialised and prepared for change adapt extremely quickly to new conditions. Rapid and constant change reframes our perception of our own change capabilities. So, where constant change has been normalised, the population becomes change-agile.

Although change-agile individuals may still experience the curve, they can travel from start point to end point over the course of a coffee break, rather than the two years the unions are on strike.

In addition to the emotional change journey, we each sit somewhere on a continuum that describes our personal preference for change. At one end are those who prefer order and stability; deep change affects them profoundly. At the other end are those who love change and build their lives around novelty, making frequent significant life or career changes. There is also a large section of people in the middle who may lean one way or another depending on their personal views or the level of persuasion around the change.

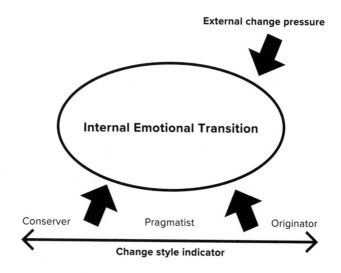

The language and ideas illustrated above are based on the work of William Bridges and the Change Style Indicator from Discovery Learning, as well as our own research conducted in major multinationals over the last ten years.

The leadership of change - especially to succeed at constant, adaptive change - must take account of and give importance to these emotional cues and preferences. This is why successful business change is not a process or procedural issue, but human. In the constant change environment, business leadership must also let go of the need for perfection at the start and completion at the end, but instead adopt new ways of looking at and dealing with the processes of change. The digital mantra of 'permanent beta' is helpful here. Finally, adaptive change leadership must constantly take account of how people feel in an environment of constant change. Perhaps it is this dimension that causes many of us to say change is hard.

Over the last few years, general business language has absorbed some helpful phrases: being 'comfortable with ambiguity', 'sitting with not knowing', being 'mindful' and 'receptive', and the practice of 'resilience'. These are all useful in dealing with constant change. But they are also passive coping strategies.

Businesses are now fond of talking about resilience as a preferred skill to deal with the chaos of constant change. Of course we must be resilient and able to bounce back, but to put a resilience practice into our organisations in preference to fostering excellent change leadership is to risk accepting that change will be reactive and poorly done.

The first principles of personal adaptability are:

- Horizon-scanning and trend identification
- Thinking, reading and idea generation
- Consciously moving through and integrating our own emotional transitions

The first principles of organisational adaptability are:

- Creating and ring-fencing leadership bandwidth
- Collaborative leadership and inter-team integration
- Experimentation, based on a design-thinking approach, targeted around critical groups such as employees and customers

Notice how similar these principles are to those of transformational leadership. In this case, we are leading and transforming ourselves.

These are not rarified attributes unique to leadership heroes. They are essential prerequisites for any person seeking to take greater responsibility for their own thoughts, actions and life. They are all vital if we want to make or lead a change, or become personally or professionally adaptive in approach. They also abandon any pretence of *control*.

The Four Pitfalls

There are four common mistakes that leaders make when dealing with the emotional, psychological and cultural dynamics of a change they have initiated. These dynamics apply at all levels from a partnership or marriage, right up to national systems. Even a well-led change cannot avoid the change curve completely, but it can flatten and shorten it, or turn it into a series of manageable waves. A poorly-led change will make the curve deep and long - sometimes so deep that we cannot climb out before the change initiative fails.

1 - Shock

We all know the scenario. Everyone is quietly getting on with their work when, seemingly out of the blue, a major change is announced and everyone is shocked. In this situation our neurological response centre is the medulla, triggering fight, flight or freeze. Thus, when an organisation or team is shocked many individuals just stop, for an hour or a day or a week, depending on the nature of the shock, and the strength of the leadership.

Working with a global financial services organisation we experienced multiple occasions when announcements from the top froze the company. Whatever projects or conversations were supposed to be going on, they were wholly or partly displaced by people discussing their shock. After a succession of shocking, poorly led changes, people became numb and major new announcements were more or less ignored.

There are two main reasons people might be shocked by an announcement. The first is that they are not sufficiently aware of the context (no horizon-scanning). The second is that announcements are made (deliberately or recklessly) in a shocking way. If leaders want to avoid announcements causing shocks in the system they have to take responsibility for pre-socialising the change. Even if that is done only in the most general terms, skilled leaders can ensure that people understand the local and global context for change, for example by sharing the relevant narrative from the Megatrends earlier in this book.

If you work in the energy sector, understanding the pressure that decarbonisation will put on previous business models is critical to the ability of workers to understand why change is happening. The same is true of the effects of digitisation on financial or legal services, or ageing on health services.

2 - Anger

Once the change has been announced and people emerge from shock, some might be angered by the implications of the change, or by unhelpful rumours spread about it.

The mistake that leaders make at this point is to back down in the face of the anger. Often, the change is stopped or watered down. This shows that the leaders themselves were not sufficiently bought into the change, or lacked adequately thought-through responses to the potential anger.

When the vision and the change plan are inadequate, or when the context is poorly understood, people will fill in the blanks themselves. Rumours will start, typically focusing on negative examples, and people will become angry.

It is far easier to avoid this anger with skilful communication from the start, than to recover from a situation where too many people have become angry. However, if anger is unavoidable, leaders must have the courage, skill, commitment and compassion to push and support people through it. If the leader of the change does not have the commitment, it is because of investing insufficient time and effort to overcome their own doubts.

To paraphrase Winston Churchill, "Leadership is the ability to tell someone to go to hell in such a way that they look forward to the trip."

We don't advocate riding roughshod over people's legitimate anger. Clearly, the best time for feedback is in the planning stage, before any announcements take place, but there is still room for listening and compromise throughout the process. The problem comes when listening and compromise in the face of anger derails the whole project.

At a national level it could be argued that the failure of successive governments to adequately explain the positive and negative effects of globalisation, digitisation and ageing has allowed populist anger to target immigrants. With better, more candid leadership, people might have reconciled without entrenchment to the more nuanced reality.

Another way to fail at the anger stage of change is to restrict opportunities to vent.

In one memorable change project where the initial announcement of the change had effectively been through the media, we ran what became known as 'venting sessions' as part of a wider leadership event. In these sessions we just allowed people to complain and express their anger, so that they could be open to learn and change afterwards. Sometimes these sessions felt a bit scary, but eventually the participants would start to talk each other down. We ran a number of these sessions over a six-month period and the level of venting subsided as the organisation slowly came to terms with the new realities.

In another example, we were part of a team managing the merger of two ancient competitors of 100 years or more, who were also creating a new, joint head office. To make matters worse, the two old head offices were based in Liverpool and Manchester in the UK, which, if you know anything about the football landscape, is not ideal. No one was looking forward to it and everyone was expecting trouble. It was an extremely ambitious decision on the part of the leadership. Running venting sessions was a revelation, as it emerged that it was not the move that people feared, nor their old competitors, but how leadership was handling it. Leadership anticipated trouble around local biases; employees were simply angry at the leadership for being infantilised.

Emotions are legitimate in change, and suppressing them just means they escape in another way. If anger is unavoidable, creating fora for venting, where the anger can be expressed legitimately and safely, allows colleagues to help each other move on.

Anger is predictable in almost every change scenario. Failing to plan for it is a failure of leadership. Once you are clear about the change needed, it is time to work with stakeholders, especially those most affected by the change, to understand what aspects of the change are likely to trigger the strongest emotional reaction. At that stage it may still be possible to make adjustments to reduce the reaction. Where there are aspects that cannot change the leadership team will need to make a judgement: either add mitigating language into the announcement, or to have a prepared response to the predictable angry reaction. It is also useful for leadership to examine how they took their own journey into the proposed changes, pinpointing what about their own beliefs had to modify, and to work these stories into how the changes are presented more widely. Admission of difficulty humanises leadership and unites through shared adversity.

3 - Depression

Here we are not talking about clinical depression but a state of helplessness. Helplessness can lead to giving up or the emotional condition of believing that trying anything new is pointless. This can be brought about through personal experience of having tried and failed at several new approaches, or it can be because of the influence of gossip and rumour, which spreads resistance like the plague when working against a change. Even in a well-led change, people struggle to understand new processes, structures or technology.

We all get our sense of self-worth from doing things well, so an abrupt, enforced adjustment, such as moving from expertise with an old toolset to beginner status in a new one, will diminish our confidence and self-worth. Just think about your reaction to a new phone or computer, or moving house or job. There may well have been moments when you questioned your decision. That moment may pass quickly or be extended.

What gets us out of our funk is experimentation, or asking, "What if I just try this?". Keeping an open, flexible approach also enables resistance against the pressures of the rumour-mill or those around us who say it won't work. Experimentation is the antidote to helplessness.

In his book *Managing Transitions*, William Bridges calls this the Neutral Zone. In it, a person may move one way or another way, towards or away from. In that space people are ineffective and risk giving up and leaving.

4 - Experimentation

Even when people find their way through the Neutral Zone, leaders are still not entirely safe from mistakes that could lead to failure. The way forward requires experimentation, trying out the new system, process or technology and seeking feedback for improvement. When we experiment with anything there is a heightened probability of failure, but also a heightened probability of success, provided we learn together what not to do, as well as what to do.

The mistake that leaders make here is to be critical or blame people for failure. While failure may not be desirable, experimentation is; if we slam people for failure they are likely to shoot straight back to helplessness, or even be triggered back into anger. They will be far harder to move forwards thereafter: "Don't try that", they will have learned, "for no good deed goes unpunished."

Leaders have to find ways to encourage and support experimentation by valuing the learning that comes from failure, rather than worrying about the failure itself. It can take great skill and emotional self-regulation to cultivate the habit of celebrating learning, rather than stressing about failure, but it is the only way to progress towards full integration of a constant change agility.

Adaptive Change Modelling

If we can flatten and shorten the emotional response to change, we are beginning to lead in more human and adaptive ways. These leadership approaches may take more time than decision-makers prefer, but investment at this point will guard against backlash and failure later on.

Yet even in the face of carefully laid plans, the biggest single barrier to change is often the entirely human and understandable desire for others to demonstrate change before we opt in: "You go first". This approach is often self-limiting: (s)he who hesitates will experience more resistance and more unhelpful gossip and misperception, meaning hesitaters will delay doing the things necessary to fully evaluate the change. To be clear, we are not suggesting you should automatically and unquestioningly jump on board with all change, but we do argue that if you are not skilfully and deliberately role-modelling effective change yourself, you have no right to expect it of anyone else; even your senior leadership. The solution is to approach each change with positive intent, seeking out the clarity that will enable you to engage. When we are clear and inspired ourselves, we breathe life into others.

Of course, other work may need to accompany a cultural change in order to enable and accelerate it. This might include the design or redesign of organisational processes and procedures, or the alignment or realignment of working practices. It can be extremely helpful to tag the cultural change on to a necessary business change such as a digital transformation, which gives more cause and weight to the need for behavioural changes. The adaptive approach enables leadership to think about and proactively deal with these most challenging of organisational problems.

There are many change models. Most of them have something true and essential at their core, but no single model contains all of what you may need to do or consider. However, trying to make a change without a model will increase the likelihood that change will fail. Using a linear or outdated change model unsuitable for achieving adaptability in a constant change environment, may also doom the effort.

Choose a model that aims to create agility; educate all leadership in its use and language, and create significant symbolic acts that demonstrate progress down that path. Then celebrate steps forward, praise those that do well, and focus on sustaining success.

... And never declare victory.

The Role of Data

There is a paradox in the use of data when describing vision and change. Data is the science of understanding what is or has been. Vision is the projection of effort into the future. Data may not predict the outcome of vision, and vision is certainly not data-based in any reliable way. As Henry Ford once said, "If I had asked my customers what they wanted, they would have said faster horses."

It is unlikely that we can use data to describe constant change in the same way we might explore a business sector to see if this or that market will expand or contract. Those calculations are useful, to yield small-scale goals or continuous improvement actions.

There is a larger body of evidence that indicates that many day-to-day strategies and business decisions are not data-led at all, but informed by in-the-moment bias, business 'instinct', and learned experience. Even if we exclude the imaginative leaps required of vision-based opportunity change, we are still, in the second decade of the 21st Century, not leaning very heavily on data for our decision-making.

A woman goes to the doctor, and the doctor says very clearly, "Unless you change your habits, you will die within ten years." The woman is unsatisfied with this prognosis, and decides to get a second opinion. She goes to a second, more specialised doctor, and receives the same evaluation. "You have acute levels of dysfunction in your behaviour and unless you change your habits, your overall ill-health means that you will die within ten years." The woman is again unsatisfied and decides to see as many doctors as possible. In the end, she sees 100 doctors. 97 of those doctors give her the ten-year maximum prognosis. Only 3 say there is no evidence to support death within 10 years and she can continue to use her body as a rubbish dump if she likes.

What does she do?

Evidence suggests that this very human woman will choose to believe the three doctors, even though the overwhelming evidence is against her x32. Why? Because she does not wish to change her habits.

The example above reflects the proportion of scientists who have presented evidence and predictions about our global climate. Overall, 97% of climate scientists - specialists in the field - support the doomsday view if we humans do not change our habits. Yet, because 3% disagree, somehow there are many who continue to ignore the overwhelming data and choose not to act. So, rational facts alone can be used selectively to support any outcome. Perhaps this is why we are resistant to data.

As we explored in the Megatrends chapter, there is a massive move towards Big Data and automated learning through machines. What machine-learning can tell us with pinpoint accuracy (subject to the purity and volume of data) is the current state of things. Over time this can also give us indicators for behavioural trends into the future. Many organisations, including Facebook, Google and many large banks, are currently monetising these vast amounts of data in order to help 'those who know' to conceive, design and market either the data itself or new products. The 2018 Facebook/Cambridge Analytica scandal proved that data about how humans behave is extremely valuable to business, and can be used in ways that are sinister as well as inspiring.

Machine learning and behavioural algorithms are now used in many specialist change-related areas such as propensity for change, change readiness, how culture operates, and even diagnosing levels of leadership and change capability.

We can use this kind of data, to a degree, to predict the likelihood of an outcome. Government and business leaders would do well to understand and utilise these new technologies. And the general public needs much higher awareness of their causes, effects, and exposure. New areas of law are developing to define and protect rights around data capture and transparency, and new ethical boundaries are being set around the role of large corporations and how they drive behaviours. Facebook went on public record in 2018 to express regret for some of the dimensions of its social media platform and to acknowledge some unhelpful and unhealthy ways in which it has used customer data.

Though the right data can give us predictive abilities, we cannot be prophetic. No data can assess with certainty the success of an endeavour. So data is necessary and useful, but only gets you so far *in an environment of constant change.*

In this new environment, our change methods must be iterative, experimental, and excellent in design so they obtain the right feedback at the right time. We then need the right processes and the right ways of working to act nimbly in alignment with the speed and regularity of information received. In other words, the best use of data is as feedback, iteratively and often, to provide real-time information to assist our daily decision-making.

We are not talking here about Employee Engagement surveys or team profiles. They are useful data sets, but only as annual metrics for specific purposes. Using these tools to move culture is a little like spitting into a hurricane.

We are advocating for 'fast' teamworking and learning, where ideas are mooted, tested, and proven or disproven in small, limited-risk ways. This then informs the product or service taken forward, or perhaps indicates how we might nudge culture on to the next stage.

And, whatever the data says, the future is not fixed. The future is always created by those with a vision and the determination to make it happen.

Change Process - the Flotilla

Constant change is all about holding paradox lightly. Just as we cannot really trust all the data and yet we still require it, we also cannot fully trust any process, and yet we need it. In a constant change context we need just enough process to manage the flotilla, while avoiding the slavish processes that hinder the supertanker. We need to create a shared basis, language and approach to change that enables leaders and teams to understand where they are. We then need to give latitude and autonomy in order for iterative experimentation to take place across the system.

Thus, the formula is:

- A shared direction and destination - very clearly outlined and articulated with a story formed around it; with clear examples and significant acts that demonstrate it.

- Common understanding and collaboration role-modelled by the leadership.

- Leadership that supports the right culture and behaviour to achieve the vision; no need to hold on to status and ego by being a classic Top.

- Diversified meaning across the change context - for some it means little change for now, for others, much more change more quickly. Those change proportions will flex with time, so each team must clarify its own 'From>To' journey to become adaptive over time, sustain the existing business, and extend into the new.

- Long-term horizons, short-term actions - we can only ever act in the short term because we execute what is actually in front of us. But those actions must align towards the Cause. Imagine a conveyor belt of planned action coming towards you. The actions move from long, to medium, to short term as the execution machine delivers them to you in the present. Simultaneously there is a constant supply of new actions in the long-term horizon. The Cause feeds the conveyor belt.

- Permanent beta - forget the perfect answer, it never existed anyway. Resist the 80-slide briefing pack for the Board. Instead, work to the 80/20 rule, try important stuff out in a limited context, receive feedback, iterate and then experiment again in a wider catchment. Digital developers call this 'permanent beta'. Agile practitioners call it 'scrums and sprints'. Leadership experts call this Interdependent Authentic leadership in pursuit of a Cause.

The Constant Change Cycle

Many conventional businesses have enjoyed a period of relative stability over the last few decades. The job was to keep 'cranking the handle'. At some point they may have added machinery that cranked the handle overnight, and around the year 2000 they might have added a website to tell people about whatever was produced by cranking the handle. But the business model was essentially the same. There have always been a few outlier businesses like 3M whose whole business model was built around innovation, but for most businesses, innovation was separate from cranking that handle.

If change happened in conventional businesses it was a change between steady state A and steady state B, perhaps as a result of an office move, a merger or acquisition, or a new product, tool or restructure.

Post-conventional businesses have normalised what had previously been the outlier approach: focus on leadership to create and curate an intentional culture to simultaneously deliver both innovation and handle-cranking. For some, the innovation extends to intentional disruption of the business model; the constant change cycle.

Apple is the past master at intentional disruption. It was Apple who invented the desktop computer and then disrupted it with the Laptop. It was Apple that disrupted the Laptop with the iPhone and the iPad and it is Apple who are disrupting the Smartphone with the Apple Watch.

For conventional businesses to catch up requires a culture change from hierarchy, obedience and conformity, to collaboration, empowerment and creativity. In such a business, overall objectives are set and teams work to create new ideas rapidly while reliably cranking the handle where it is relevant. And they do these two things without creating cultural tensions between them.

Leadership for these activities also generates the organisational culture to support such approaches.

An organisation we work with has a global presence and 135,000 employees. It has created an agile change process, using a phased 'Transformation Academy' approach, in which a central team of agile-trained experts visits each market for 12 weeks and educates leadership and management in the skills required for the new world. The sequence of market visits is designed according to market location, size and the rollout of new products. The Transformation Academy uses agile technologies and methods to completely reframe the business model, and educates leaders in the new way. Simultaneously, the leadership continues 'cranking the handle' so that the old, but expiring, business model can support the new until it is self-sustaining.

"We are now far too clever to be able to survive
without wisdom."

E. F. Schumacher

CHAPTER 8

AGAPE

Where are we going? How will our civilisation manifest in years to come? Are we doomed to continue the Greek tragedies of the past, and simply spin around in an accelerating blur of destructive cycles, purposeless, meaningless, and without end? Or perhaps we will face some kind of great rebalancing, where a large part of our species is laid waste, limiting our ambition and proliferation? Maybe we will be surpassed by our own creations, fading from evolution like Neanderthals as we are assimilated into a new race of higher functioning beings? Or will we finally learn how to cohabit and collaborate in this world, somehow finding a step-change in Perspective and compassion, and through that, learning to live sustainably, in health and well-being?

It's probably too early to say. What is true is that we now need to come of age. E.F. Schumacher said in the 1970s: "We are now far too clever to survive without wisdom", but who is to say which wisdom is the correct one? Are the Liberals right, or the Greens? Or the feminists? The Neo-Cons? The indigenous peoples of the Amazon? The Buddhists? A Bhutanese approach or some other, less-inclusive extreme?

The most sustainable examples seem to indicate that a positive future will be diverse and plural. If we can change sufficiently to limit the damage done by an increasingly irascible climate, (a very big if), the trajectory of history suggests the most likely future is one where there is more equitability. If the planet allows us, the only remaining question is whether that equitability extends to all other life forms, and so enables a future for everything else too.

In the world of the Megatrends, how might an equitable future look? So many of the ideas and innovations breaking upon us are radical, so assuming that life won't change much from the post-War model, feels a little like wishful thinking. So then what does a radical vision of the future look like? What would the future look like if we lead the way through the Megatrends, rather than simply being wrong-footed and upset by them?

We'll now take some of the specific issues that are emerging from these huge forces and look at them in more detail, imagining how they might affect the social fabric.

In deciding how to address the Megatrends, there are two questions we at Holos ask ourselves:

- Do I have a role in helping to influence this trend?

- How could Integral Authentic leadership help steer this trend to serve, rather than rule, our future?

We ask that you keep these questions in mind as you read.

Jobs, the Role of Humans and Citizen Salaries
Digitisation means that repetitive and process-oriented tasks, analytical and data-based roles will be replaced by machines. This means that the nature of jobs will change beyond recognition.

To succeed in this environment we will have to let go of many of our preconceptions about work, wealth, and income. We will have to let go of the belief that hard work and income are directly related. It has been clear for some time that the richest people in the world are not the hardest workers and also that the poorest are not the laziest. We now need to accept that work and income need to be decoupled; not just for the rich. We also need to accept that sustained success will be based on renewable resources like sun, wind and tide, and infinite resources like human creativity rather than finite resources like oil, gas and time.

Digitisation opens up immense creative opportunities for people. It could enable the long-held dream of choice around free time, but only if we can also pay for a reasonable lifestyle. If we are to keep the paradigm of money, two of the key questions for us to answer as a global society are around the nature of personal taxation, and a 'citizen's salary'. It may be that it is more profitable for companies to pay people to be consumers than producers (but this may not be good for the world itself, which is already stretched as a finite resource).

In 2016, Finland, Switzerland and Ontario in Canada debated a citizen's salary, and there have been a number of trials and experiments. In the UK a universal basic wage is part of Green Party policy and has not been ruled out by the Labour Party.

It may be that a citizen's salary is not unconditional, but asks in return that people contribute to the community, environmentally and socially. We may want to form a system of local organisers who maintain public spaces and look after those who need help, in a wider scale update of a traditional village model, perhaps using digital currencies to pay them.

Unless our ageing population want to be cared for by robots (as they already are to some extent in Japan), we may also need to find ways to make caring professions far more attractive with better pay and leadership.

Direct selling of products or services has never been easier, thanks to digitisation. This Megatrend also opens up tremendous opportunities for people to fulfil their dreams with creative and craft-based activities such as making movies or publishing books. There are many who would welcome the chance to trade a monotonous job for doing something they love. Ironically there is emerging evidence that successful YouTubers, doing something they love, can suffer from high levels of stress as they try to satisfy the expectations of millions of subscribers often on their own.

There have been, and are currently, societies where a large part of the population does not really have to work. There is much to learn from these societies before the robots occupy too many roles in our current world. In Rome (and other societies where slavery was common), the slave-owning elite did not work. Today some of the oil-rich states employ migrant workers and foreign contractors to do much of the work.

We are not arguing in favour of either of these models; because they are often abusive and not wholly successful even for the apparent beneficiaries, however it is important to learn from them. The evidence of these societies is that people can be sucked into apathetic lives of competitive excess and politicking.

We need to find other ways to encourage us as citizens to engage purposefully, guard against apathy, and fill our lives instead with valuable purpose and meaning.

Let's not rush to fear. If robots do much of the work, we can be more free to pursue our dreams of creativity, health, connection, family, self-expression, love and contributing to the benefit of all living things.

Education

In order to realise the social potential of digitisation, we have to reinvent education. We have to move away from industrial conformity and the obedience-based model. We need to replace it with a model based on purpose, self-leadership and personal responsibility. Instead of learning to wait for instructions and do what they are told, students will learn self-awareness and how to take responsibility and initiative. Education is moving in this direction but may need to accelerate; students who started their formal education from 2016 will be entering a very different adulthood in 2032 and beyond.

Excessive obedience leads to an unwillingness to speak up, even about serious issues. Little is questioned. Large companies in particular, currently have a preference for recruiting those who were most successful at school. One of the key skills cultivated by those who succeeded at conventional schools was 'not challenging the teacher'. As a result, that same unwillingness to push the boundaries on how (and why) things are done, inhibits innovation and stymies the prospects of those self-same businesses.

Few of us leave school with a profound sense of understanding the world as it is, a personal purpose, vision, life plan, or the skills to create one later on. Without these basic components of self-knowledge, people are vulnerable to the plans and visions of others, which nearly always place them in a subordinate or exploited role.

Those who are invested at a young age (usually by parents) with the means and insight to do so, are stigmatised as 'privileged' or 'maverick' or 'eccentric' by those who have not had such advantages. The proper role of education is to create those opportunities for every single person, so that each of us feels we had a privileged upbringing, not just by studying Isaac Newton and Jane Austin, but also by being prepared to live inside and succeed in social systems, explore our own personal potential, and discover ideas, creativity, and leadership.

We need an education system for the digital age, teaching the core skills of communication, numeracy, self and other-awareness, influence, relationships and context (history, future and sciences). Such a curriculum should encourage students to explore and experiment collaboratively with others, guiding them towards a rewarding and purposeful future. The old, secure careers are no longer so safe. In the future, safe careers might well be in the environment, tech, entertainment and sports, as well as teaching and healthcare.

As Jack Ma, founder of Alibaba said at the 2018 World Economic Forum: "We cannot teach our kids to compete with the machines, which are smarter - we have to teach our kids something unique. In this way, 30 years later, kids will have a chance."

Government, Politics and Democracy
Given the challenges of the future, we need to have systems of government that attract those with an integral leadership perspective. We have said above that the overall trajectory of human development has been towards greater freedom and transparency. In many ways digitisation is accelerating such ideals. However, digitisation has its dark side and the ideal is not guaranteed. 'Fake news' and 'alternative facts' create a worrying new paradigm around perception and reality. So many debates are fraught with claims and counter-claims because those who have mastered digital communication

can easily manipulate perceptions if they choose to. There is precedent for this in the 1930s, when populations were susceptible to manipulation by the first mass medium of radio, before they developed the perceptual 'antibodies'. Without a reliable platform of truth and integrity from which to operate, democracy and the rule of law are under threat.

Part of the reason for this state of affairs (whatever your point of view and however welcome or unwelcome), is the 'first past the post' voting system. Used in the UK, USA and Canada (and no other developed countries), it has proven over and over again that it delivers success to candidates who can get people to vote for them, rather than candidates defined by a service mindset, or who are good at collaboration, leadership and government. There are very few who would claim that the British or American electoral system had delivered more than one or two genuinely good leaders to the top job since 1945. And those on opposite sides of the spectrum would disagree about who was which.

Some say that is the nature and the risk of the democratic majority, and that all other systems have been proven even more fallible or less desirable. But the real question is, "is the risk of electing poor leaders ultimately acceptable to us or not?"

For example, in the US and the UK there are no prerequisite qualifications to become a Representative or Member of Parliament. There are no educational or experience thresholds required, only the ability to attract votes. Standing for election is, of course, an act of leadership, but what worries us is the motivation towards that bid for leadership. How and by whom, should these motivations be assessed? The only approval methods we currently possess are the Party political processes, the propaganda of those seeking election, the filters of the media, and the court of public opinion. Is that sufficient in a diverse, plural, digitised world? To become a warehouse supervisor currently requires more qualification than to become a U.S. President.

The Chinese government system requires that candidates start at the local government level and work their way up to national leadership. This means that all Chinese politicians have deep experience of social service and responsibility before they get into high office, and those who do not have that capability are weeded out along the way. Even then the results are far from perfect, there are still many opportunities for improvement in the ways in which we govern ourselves globally.

The Liberal Party in the UK has for a long time promoted the idea of proportional representation as an alternative to 'first past the post'. In Europe, countries such as Germany and the Netherlands have long traditions of coalition government where collaboration and horse-trading are the norm. There are powerful arguments to support such interdependent approaches: the tendency of the UK to regard itself as not just geographically but also socially separate to the mainland of Europe has reoccurred multiple times across its history. Sometimes this independence has served its citizens and those of the world, such as during World War II, and at others it has resulted in a globally dominant white supremacist Empire, and in 2016 a bid for independence out of step with its nearest neighbours. The USA, possibly because it is a composite of old European mindsets, follows the same pattern. Would a different, less binary system of government in both countries serve their populations better? Would a method of representing all of the people, rather than the views of its largest voting segment, succeed in promoting interdependence over competition?

The Constitutional monarchy of Bhutan has chosen to measure progress and success not by GDP but by GDH - Gross Domestic Happiness. Happiness, not volume of transactions, is their definition of success and drives substantially different policies.

The challenge is not democracy itself, but the party system which inevitably promotes ideology over pragmatism, and self over public service. In the new world, these motivations can only bring us more and more chaotic outcomes.

Climate Change and Decarbonisation

Our fossil fuel addiction impacts negatively in two ways: first by adding carbon to our atmosphere, and second by creating a huge amount of work to mitigate that.

At the least, we will continue to experience impacts such as disruption and damage from changing weather patterns, climate refugees, interruptions to food and water supplies, wildfires, severe drought and flood, significant cost, and loss of life. At worst - if left unchecked - runaway warming will cause the extinction of all species on the planet. Venus, close to the sun, has an average temperature at its surface of 462 degrees Celsius. It is not hot because of its closeness. Mercury is closer to the sun than Venus and yet has an average temperature of 167 Celsius at its surface. Venus is hot because of the carbon dioxide in its atmosphere.

There are no sustainable upsides to climate change, but there are temporary upsides for a few powerful people with vested interests, intent on stealing from the future.

We will all experience these changes regardless of whether or not we are carbon polluters: increasing costs, new legislation, changing regulation, and disruption to both supply chains and our daily habits. Those risks escalate with every passing decade, giving our descendants even more of a problem than we currently face.

Regulation to tackle increased carbon in the atmosphere may also mean some of the most dramatic reversals to freedom since the liberalisation of the world at societal, governmental, organisational, business, household and personal levels. The faster we are able to decarbonise our homes, businesses and societies, the quicker we will be able to take the edge off these impacts and accelerate new, liberating ways of being. The irony of climate change denial is that it increases both the risk and the costs of solving it, and protects nothing.

When we act as a species, we succeed. In the 1980s and 1990s ozone depletion was a pressing threat. The preventative changes the world put into place to eliminate chlorofluorocarbons (CFCs) from aerosols and industry were both unprecedented and successful. The threat that we would all fry without the protective ozone layer meant that we took concerted action.

It took that single threat - the clear 'burning platform' - to inspire change. What is the shared and united vision we can all get behind to tackle decarbonisation?

Technology and Mindset

We often hear that the answers to many of these problems will come from technology. This or that new technology will be invented just in time to save the day. This does seem to be happening in the case of renewable energy, although the window for preventative change is extremely narrow, and closing fast.

However, to pin our hopes on 'just-in-time' invention is far too passive an approach. It also ignores the underlying destructive behaviours of our species. Humans are now too numerous, too industrious, and too tempted by the line of least resistance. We must advocate active, simple behavioural change. New technology drives new behaviour, but often in unwanted and antisocial ways. Just the small, day-to-day example of the how the smartphone is not always beneficial demonstrates this.

The best change initiatives anticipate and address human mindset and behaviour, designing them into the new form and function. For example, creating new zero-carbon vehicles should necessitate no new behavioural change. To be adopted by the general public, such vehicles must have long range, be easy to replenish, and have large carrying capacity, etc. In the same way, central power generation of renewable energies will need to enable the same standard of living (while doing so with much less risk).

However, some aspects of the coming changes will require a shift in mindset and approach. For example, a future where we consume the same levels of red meat is not sustainable (something consumers in the US and Western Europe will struggle to come to terms with). Consuming goods at current levels is excessive and damaging: for 7 billion people to live the way UAE citizens do, would require resources equivalent to 5x planet Earth. For France and Germany, 2.5 planets. The USA, 4 planets. Clearly, we are storing up problems (stealing from the future) because successive national governments do not wish to tackle behaviours that are ingrained in our modern mindset. What is the 'one planet' (sustainable) global level of consumption for 7 billion people? What is the 'one planet' global level of consumption for 11 billion people, which is the predicted world population by 2050?

Technology will be helpful, but not enough on its own. If our children are to enjoy anything like the Golden Age we have lived through, and if we wish to safeguard it for subsequent generations, we must swiftly act for the good of all. Ignoring the need for sustainable change cannot be dismissed as a natural human trait, as there are many examples of tribes and peoples living in perfect harmony with their environment. Our constructed, paternalistic society seems to play to our most childlike and irresponsible needs; we want everything now, we want more than enough, and we want someone else to take our problems away for us.

We are seeing efforts at collaborative leadership from many governments on many of these issues, including climate change. But there remains this deep challenge: our individual mindset remains largely transactional - we experience a problem, allocate blame and tell 'them' to fix it. Due mainly to the lack of leadership education, (and perhaps the perceived lack of time), we rarely revisit why something is occurring or how we need to behave in order to avoid or ameliorate it in the future. We flee from uncomfortable engagement with the problems we've caused. This no longer works.

Success Stories

There are examples of countries that get things spectacularly right:

Finland: education

Finland's school system is consistently at the top of international rankings. They avoid the centralised, evaluation-driven model that most other countries use. Students start school at age seven and are rarely set homework until their mid-teens. Exams don't begin until students are fourteen. Teachers only spend four hours a day in the classroom and have two hours of personal development per week. Teachers must have a Master's degree, only the best are selected and there is a low student to teacher ratio. While this sounds expensive, the costs per student are 30% less than in the US.

Netherlands: prisons

While other countries suffer prison overcrowding, the Netherlands has the opposite situation. They have closed around 24 prisons over recent years and now import prisoners to justify keeping some open. The Netherlands has a number of policies that help keep crime rates low, especially non-criminalisation of some recreational drugs, rehabilitation instead of punishment, and electronic monitors that allow convicts to go out and work. A 2008 study found that monitored and supported convicts were 50% less likely to reoffend than those locked in prison.

The result is a remarkably low imprisonment rate of 69 prisoners per 100,000 people. Out of a population of 17 million, only 11,600 people are in prison. By comparison the US has 716 prisoners per 100,000 of population, the highest in the world.

China: renewable energy

China leads the world in renewable energy generation, producing 1,425,180 GWh (Gigawatt hours) of renewable energy mainly from wind, solar and hydro. This is nearly three times the amount of the second largest renewable energy producer, the USA, and almost enough to power the whole of the UK. China is also the world's largest polluter and has some of the worst air quality in the world, but the commitment to renewables and the levels of growth are significant.

At the start of 2017, China committed to investment of $360bn in renewable energy by 2020, and cancelled construction of 85 coal-fired power stations.

Portugal: drugs

By 1999, 1% of the Portuguese population was addicted to heroin and the country had the EU's highest rate of drug-related AIDS deaths. Criminalisation of drugs was not working, so the country took the bold step of making drug use a public health issue rather than a crime.

The results have been promising: drug-related HIV infections fell by 90% between 2001 and 2016. In 2016, there were 3 overdose deaths per million people (the second lowest in the EU), compared to an EU average of 17.3 per million. Since 2001, the reported number of adults using drugs in the previous 12 months has decreased steadily. Portugal has the lowest 'legal high' use in the EU. Between 1999 and 2012 the percentage of drug-related prisoners fell from 44% to 21%.

Reasons to Be Cheerful

An organisation called *Biomimicry* 3.8 estimates that in 2018 around one million organisations worldwide are acting in the authentic, purpose-driven space. Their causes vary, encompassing every dimension of Interdependent and Integral behaviour, from ocean cleanup to new energy, from tech solutions to social engineering. The global flotilla is alive, well, and growing.

With good leadership, all of these changes can be huge wins for everyone. No one needs to do a job they don't like anymore. We can clean up the air and halt climate change. We can all live long, healthy and happy lives.

We face a choice between the dystopian future so commonly depicted in movies about zombie apocalypse and robot domination, and a more utopian option. As in any change situation, the choice we end up making at a global level will come down to two things: the quality of leadership, and our individual commitment to make changes in our daily lives and habits.

Unconscious leadership by Bosses and Rulers who continue to steal from the future, will lead us to the dystopian nightmare. Collaboration and creativity through Authentic and Visionary leadership creates the possibility of the shared ideal. This utopian version of the future is possible but will require some radical choices, and really bold leadership and change, to enable it. We have to make this challenge about more than hope. It must be about *purpose*.

It would be helpful if that purpose were to be embodied in some kind of supra-national organisation like the UN or the EU. In some ways both those bodies look as if they could perform that function, but both are poor at vision and engagement, and so have sunk to become transactional, rules-based, sprawling bureaucracies, under attack from the simplifiers and the nationalists. Plus, divesting our personal accountabilities into a bureaucracy is once again to pass the problem on.

We currently find individual countries such as the USA and the UK backing away from these supranational ideals. Independence and marginalisation are popular with Bosses and Rulers who are really only motivated by their own status and the pleasure of being in charge; they wield power *over*, not power *with*. Nationalism is not a lasting antidote. Ultimately, it brings only more division and a regression to practices that separate, pollute, destroy and deny.

Investing in the Future
Collectively, the Megatrends could represent the ultimate challenge to humanity, to prove that we are worthy of being sustained on Earth. There are many who would prefer to believe that climate change is a hoax and social liberalism an abomination, and will protest too against the "Uberisation" of the workplace. These are all valid and inevitable responses to poorly-led change that neither describes the destination, nor engages us into the Cause.

Leadership can bring all of this together: profit and planet, old and young, machines and humans, success and humility. We must stop battling "otherness" and collaborate to justify our place and future on this planet. The superpower of outstanding leadership is readily available to us all to inspire better definitions of human success, and inform better choices about our own lives, the lives of our children, the conduct of our organisations, and the impact of our globalised society.

So, in saying 'leadership', we hope that through the process of reading this book, you will understand this does not mean someone else. This means you. It means us.

Perhaps, in the end, becoming our better selves is the only real route to personal and collective redemption. **The #campaignforauthenticleadership** If you are touched by an integral cause, ensure your own happiness and develop your leadership by actively leading it. If you broadly agree with the principles of freedom, transparency, diversity and pluralism, role model that integrity and contribute to those ideals.

Your positive intent and the desire to make a difference will carry you through your chosen course of action. What you end up with will likely be manifestly different from what you started out doing, but that is the nature of change and agility. By definition, change means that we must leave something behind; that something might be both cherished and holding you back. Hard personal choices may lie ahead.

In the second half of this book we present a space for you to profile and reflect on yourself and your leadership. You can use this as a platform or pause in the development of your own Perspective, or a chance to gain some clarity and purpose around how you go about growing your leadership skills.

Everyone has leadership skill and leadership opportunities. Not everyone can be the leader of a country or a movement, but every individual contribution we make towards the human ideals, to which we all hopefully aspire, is a gesture of faith in our species and a powerful contribution to the leadership of change.

The theme of 'World Peace' may seem too large; that doesn't matter. It is easy to be overwhelmed with a sense of our own insignificance in the face of such forces as a global banking crash or 110m tonnes of carbon ejected into the atmosphere every day.

"How can I possibly affect that?" we ask. The world is an integral place, and thoughts become things, so these doubts are ultimately unhelpful, and can only stop you from becoming (and doing) something more. We all have an array of thoughts in our heads; the positive and negative, the sacred and profane, the virtuous and vicious. What matters is how we channel and corral those thoughts into how we act; the deeds we do in relationship with others.

If we do nothing:

1. we are complicit, and

2. nothing will change. So do something positive, no matter how small.

The simple question for you to answer is: "Who am I?". Its answer lies not in the values and ideals we hold in our hearts, but in the actions we take in the world, especially when no one is looking.

As a result, and separately to the contents of this book, Holos has launched the #campaignforauthenticleadership. The campaign is a call to action for Authentic leadership in service to integral principles. Our experience is that many people emulate Boss style leadership because it is their only model for how to lead. They might in fact be Authentic by nature but lack the permission or opportunity to be so. Bosses and Rulers tend to organise together to exercise status and control; Authentics, because they are permissive and plural, do not.

The Reverend Charles F. Aked said in 1916, "It has been said that for evil men to accomplish their purpose it is only necessary that good men should do nothing." For 'good men' (people) to succeed in gaining power to make sustainable change therefore, they must share some kind of platform that contradicts the work of the Rulers and Bosses - or better still shows such leaders an inclusive, purpose-driven alternative they can join.

We see this platform not as one where another dogma is created, but one where Authentic leadership can find sustenance, resilience, purpose, and a community. It resides both online and in every Authentic and Visionary leadership act. Events, articles, examples, learning, and evidence of better outcomes through such leadership will be built by the community. We hope it will be an Authentic interchange, where one may join Causes, create other movements and platforms, and share successes with like-minded people, all intent on creating the world we long for.

www.holoschange.com/campaignforauthenticleadership

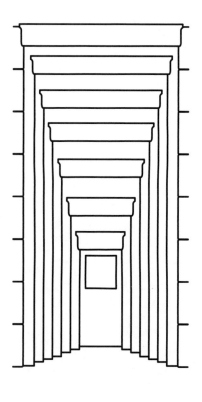

PART 2

GATEWAYS

"Inanna opened her ear to the great below."

Ancient Sumerian text

"It is not the mountain we conquer, but ourselves."

Sir Edmund Hillary

CHAPTER 9

SKILLS 1: LEARNING, THRESHOLDS AND TRIGGERS

Going beyond what we have previously thought possible can be a scary prospect. It needs support, encouragement and coaching of the type no book can adequately offer or sustain. This process of development is often called 'self-help', which is quite a good term, but self-help alone is not enough for our purposes, because the craft of leadership also relies on views beyond your own.

It is probably not possible for a person to go through experiences, learn from them, integrate their meaning and monitor the ongoing expansion of their consciousness, alone. We need to be in touch with others in order to sense-check and socialise meaning from new experiences. We need feedback on our impact and level of skill.

The commitment to a lifelong process of stretch, pushing personal boundaries and learning better leadership skills can be very rewarding. But it can also be full of pitfalls, disappointments, retrograde steps and loneliness. We may believe we have finally made it, and the very next day find ourselves back down the trail in a worse condition than before. Deciding to pursue your personal purpose in the world means you will need to speak up for yourself in one way or another, which means you need to be self-aware, and constantly pushing your own boundaries. Given that public speaking is #3 on the general list of 'scariest things to do', this is a skill you are likely to need to become comfortable with.

Only new thinking, different perspectives, empathy, collaboration and support can guarantee upward progress in your vertical development. The upside is: these things are their own reward. A significant body of research says that on our deathbed we focus not on material success, but on relationships and personal legacy.

In this arena, learning is a little like going to the gym: we have a muscle we need to exercise, and exercise makes it stronger while non-use makes it atrophy.

There are thousands of ways we can upgrade our consciousness and skill. They include:

- Study of theoretical subjects such as psychology or neuroscience to take on new ideas and research

- Reflective practice, giving time and space to consider subjects that hold meaning for us and integrate them into our personal worldview

- Therapy or Counselling that helps us look at our current or past problems in an attempt to understand and move past limiting factors, beliefs or trauma

- Teaching and Mentoring to help us receive and share new information and advice to build skill and practice methods others have previously learned

- Coaching, a future-facing technique that encourages us to bring into focus what we want to achieve, and helps us to develop our own insights, and devise and execute our own strategies

Out of all of these approaches, many report significant positive progress from coaching because it is self-generated, dynamic and focused on taking action to change our present reality. Like change, coaching and its processes rely on iterative trial and error in order to progress.

The practice and awareness of *self-leadership* is only recently gathering momentum, probably because we are used to conferring the idea of leadership on to titles and positions, and generally not on to those who self-regulate and role model behaviour. In 2018, even the term self-leadership remains relatively unknown outside the leadership development industry.

In order to reach Interdependent and Integral forms of leadership and self-leadership, daily personal learning and growth must be valued and practiced as important and lifelong.

Self-Leadership
The leadership of oneself operates outside of position or level of authority, beyond extroversion or introversion, and without direct correlation to our formal education or sphere of knowledge. Self-leadership is not attached to qualifications, to expertise, or to personality traits.

Self-leadership is determined by our personal standards and disciplines, and can be learned. Even if you have had the very worst life and experiences, had no education, have been assaulted, abused, severely injured or suffer any other manner of difficulty, you can still be a self-leader, because it is about the choices and decisions we make individually from moment to moment.
It is really a very simple thing, because it is a choice.

Leadership Moments
Let's say you have decided to become physically fitter. You make a good start and over a couple of weeks you learn to stretch and do some moderate exercise, and have even gone for a couple of jogs after work. You determine that you will start a practice of going for a 1-mile jog every morning at 6am just before you start your day. The first run goes okay, but the second day starts badly. The alarm clock goes off and you groan. It is raining outside, still dark, your feet are aching, and the last thing you want to do is to get out of bed. What do you do?

This is a self-leadership moment. It is a test of your commitment to yourself. No one else is involved. It is just you, and your power of choice.

The first decision is not to hit 'snooze'. Sighing, you get up. You get dressed. You stretch in the hallway, and then open the front door. The rain is still pouring down, and cold floods over you. You really don't fancy getting wet. This is the second test. Do you go outside? Reluctantly, you do. You close the door behind you and start jogging down the road. A couple of hundred metres in, you are already wet. The first hill beckons. You start up it. Your tiredness has not yet worn off, your legs are freezing and you are straining with effort. Do you stop and walk? Do you go back? Do you carry on? All are choices.

This is the nature of self-leadership. It is a continual process of moments in which there is always the invitation (or demand) not to do the thing you intend. Each time you stay true to the best version of yourself, you put one small deposit into your self-respect bank account, and the sum grows with each affirming decision.

In contrast, not following through makes a small withdrawal.
Every negative decision you take, no matter how small, diminishes your level of self-respect. The more self-respect you have, the more powerful the potential of your self-leadership.

If you have high self-respect, you will feel much better able to have that difficult conversation you have been avoiding with a colleague. With high self-respect, you will feel able to make that YouTube video and blog about what you are doing, or go to that networking meeting and talk about your activities. If you do these things consistently and in line with your intentions for yourself, you are becoming a self-leader.

These techniques also work with Interdependent principles. For example, we have worked with many Bosses who demonstrated high personal confidence, but were competitive and aggressive in their behaviour to others. Their self-leadership challenge is to make the leap into Interdependence by practising empathy; their moments of opportunity involve reaching out to others to know and connect with them more deeply. Every time they were overbearing or dismissed another's response, they were withdrawing funds from their Interdependent bank balance. Every time they made an empathetic connection and saw other perspectives, they were making deposits and building their self-leadership practice.

In both cases we may feel we are 'faking it' at first. That's okay! Aristotle said, "Men acquire a particular quality by constantly acting a certain way." This has become famous in acting circles as: "Fake it 'til you feel it." The limbic brain does not know the difference between real and fake (which is why adrenaline pumps through your body when you play a violent computer game). Military training relies on the same principle: you drill yourself in certain procedures so that when real bullets start to fly there is a higher likelihood that you will conduct the same practised drills and be effective under fire. Self-leadership uses these principles, we train ourselves to make the right choices; we act in aligned ways, using deep intentions to influence our behaviour.

Being a good self-leader does not guarantee you can lead others, but it is a very good start.

Self-leadership becomes especially powerful when we act in alignment with our most deeply held purpose and values. It stands to reason, therefore, that unless we know what our purpose and deeply held values are, even in a vague way, we will be unable to fully self-lead.

Self-leadership also occurs when we face adversity, conflict and derailment, and will have a deep correlation with our ability to regulate our emotions.

If we cannot regulate or lead ourselves, we cannot really expect to lead others. We can Boss them and Rule them, but not lead them. If we cannot self-lead very well, but still have the position and responsibility to lead others, we may experience 'imposter syndrome', or feel that we do not really deserve the credit or faith we receive. In those circumstances, our leadership may well become unsustainable.

Achieving Next-Level Perspective

We have said that horizontal development is about the acquisition of a new skill or ability. Vertical development is about stretching our Motivation, Perspective and Reach. We cannot exceed our own consciousness, and we cannot act from a level of Perspective, we have not attained. Research by the Centre for Creative Leadership suggests that just 31% of the population achieve long-lasting Interdependent and Integral Perspectives.

You may have heard the term 'comfort zone', now commonly used to describe the range of activities with which we are familiar and at which we are practiced. This zone comprises the experience, knowledge and skill we use daily to pursue our regular patterns of life. In order to make personal change and grow our Reach, Motivation and Perspective, we need to expand our comfort zone so that it incorporates additional experience, insight, knowledge and skill, through applied learning and reflection.

Two zones sit beyond the comfort zone: the 'learning zone', and the 'panic zone'. The learning zone lies just outside comfort and describes an arena into which we can stretch and expand without breaking. If we stretch the learning zone too far or too fast, we take on more than we are able to withstand, which causes panic and causes us to snap back into the comfort zone.

Habitual learners tend to have a very wide learning zone and seldom panic. If we have not learned for a while, we are likely to have a narrow learning zone and may feel pushed by relatively small stretches. Hitting the panic zone too often or too soon may slow down or even stop our thirst for learning because we perceive it to be too risky.

However, like a muscle, if we do not exercise and grow the edges of our comfort zone, it shrinks. While we remain increasingly attached to what we are used to, the world moves on. So, at the static, tiny centre of the comfort zone is not ultimate comfort, but despair.

'Sweet Spot' Learning

If vertical development and moving towards an Integral Perspective is your desire, there are tried and tested ways to get there. You will need help, but it can take many forms. Talking and weeping with a friend might be just as useful as being profiled by a qualified Psychiatrist, as long as the outcomes from both are applied and used: the learning 'sweet spot' (shown in the model below). It is unlikely that learning can sustain and be fully integrated into our body and actions if we do not access that sweet spot.

As we move through the model below, keep in mind the four stages of learning we discussed earlier: Desire, Awareness, Understanding, and Application.

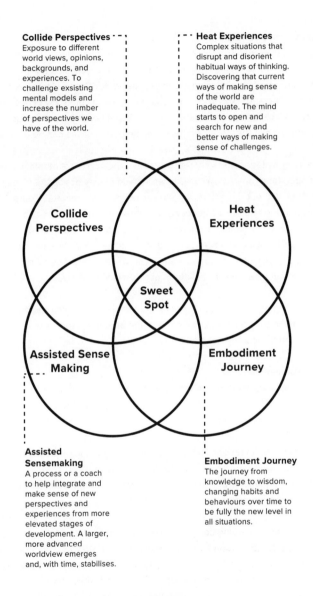

Collide Perspectives
Exposure to different
world views, opinions,
backgrounds, and
experiences. To
challenge exsisting
mental models and
increase the number
of perspectives we
have of the world.

Heat Experiences
Complex situations that
disrupt and disorient
habitual ways of thinking.
Discovering that current
ways of making sense
of the world are
inadequate. The mind
starts to open and
search for new and
better ways of making
sense of challenges.

Collide
Perspectives

Heat
Experiences

Sweet
Spot

Assisted Sense
Making

Embodiment
Journey

**Assisted
Sensemaking**
A process or a coach
to help integrate and
make sense of new
perspectives and
experiences from more
elevated stages of
development. A larger,
more advanced
worldview emerges
and, with time, stabilises.

Embodiment Journey
The journey from
knowledge to wisdom,
changing habits and
behaviours over time to
be fully the new level in
all situations.

Based on work by the Centre for
Creative Leadership

Colliding Perspectives

If you have ever met a seasoned, lifelong traveller, or perhaps an executive who has worked for some of their career as an ex-pat, the first thing they will talk about is how enriching it is to see the world. They will reference the 'collision of perspectives' they encountered, through contact with people who see things differently. Meeting new, different people expands our understanding of the world and how multiple perspectives can be useful.

Travel is a privileged and very real way to see the validity of others' views, and understand that our own cherished viewpoint may not be the ultimate truth. Even without the gift of world travel, however, we can force ourselves to collide our perspectives curiously with those of others. This need not be confrontational or traumatising. By asking questions to understand how and why others think a certain way, and listening to their response, we create incredibly powerful learning experiences in which we practice being more open, accepting, and insightful about our own life and impact.

Just colliding perspectives may not be enough, however. We need to go beyond the purely rational level, and engage our bodies for learning to become integrated and habitual.

Heat Experiences

Once we have collided different perspectives, had the debate and wondered aloud about what it might be like to live in a different worldview, we need to have some 'heat experiences' and feel, in a visceral way, how it is to live in that different world. A heat experience is any experience that stretches our limbic system beyond the rational into physical form. This could be eating food from another culture, spending time on assignment with a different team, role playing an unfamiliar situation or behaviour, or doing team activities in adverse conditions.

Heat experience learning converts rational understanding into lived experience. The developmental outcomes occur in two ways: through our relationship with ourself (we have stretched in different ways and learned something about who we are and what we do in different conditions); and in our relationship with others, with the best outcomes driven by our sympathy and empathy through shared experience. Interdependent human connection occurs when we go through something tough and have to work together to succeed. In contrast, Independent action uses a heat experience and its learnings to take advantage of or win over another person or group.

Just colliding perspectives and undergoing heat experiences are not enough on their own. If our desired outcome is sustainable personal growth or an increase in Perspective, there are a couple more stages to go through before we can declare real advancement.

Assisted Sense-Making
Assisted sense-making for an individual is similar to facilitation for a group. The role of great facilitation is to provide a forum where all views are equal. If all views can be equal, we create space to look more objectively at what we are studying, to learn or apply lessons from it, and integrate its meaning.

Assisted sense-making can occur in many forms. It is a process by which we cross-compare sets of experiences and adjust our mental models in order to incorporate the new learning. Sometimes this takes place as a build in learning, and adds to what we already understand. Sometimes we face the more challenging prospect of undoing something we have learned previously and realising we have been holding some illusion or misperception.

People who grew up in cults or who suffered brainwashing, often report the depth and long-lasting impact of 'wrong' programming. Illusions can hold on to us for a long time, because they served us in the past and we have built neural pathways around them. Aristotle is quoted as saying, "Give me the boy until he is 7 and I will show you the man." This principle was adopted by the Jesuit Order of the Roman Catholic faith, and is also used widely in Africa in training child soldiers.

Teachers of this type have understood the brain is plastic and can be trained (and retrained) in any direction. Recent research into neuroscience has proven beyond any doubt that brain plasticity can overcome the most severe of handicaps or accidents. In his book, 'The Brain that Changes Itself', Norman Doidge explores the ramifications of this research into areas such as severe stroke and even a response to Alzheimer's disease. In one example, a University Professor who experienced a severe stroke, taught himself over the course of years to by-pass the neurological damage he had experienced. He re-learned how to walk, talk, wash dishes, and, eventually, resume lecturing.

This research even brings into question the nature of identity being fixed or values being endemic to our 'essential nature'. Framed positively, what it shows is that any kind of re-programming is possible, and damaging neuroses that create unhelpful behaviours can change.

If we are able to sense-make (often together with a coach) towards an integral viewpoint, no matter where our start point, we are building our Reach, Perspective and Motivation. The use of a coach can be very helpful in this process, because effective coaches do not provide their own viewpoint, but assist you in integrating different perspectives towards developing your own.

The Embodiment Journey
Here we return to the realm of practice; the place that elite athletes, artists and musicians inhabit. Here, we do not talk simply about trying or embedding; here we must talk about embodiment. Once learning has moved from the mind reliably into the body, it has become a habit. Becoming integral in Reach, Perspective and Motivation can be a lifelong journey, and so embodiment often takes years.

However, if we continue to use self-leadership to repeat the process of colliding perspectives, having heat experiences, and seeking out assisted sense making, we can class ourselves in the 'permanent beta' of conscious learning. That places us firmly on the path of an embodiment journey: try something out, take what works and repeat ad *infinitum.*

Many call this the 'perpetual novice' state, in which we lose the hubris attached to expertise, without losing what we know. Once we have become advanced, the temptation may be to think that we are becoming a guru in something. Accepting guru status is a blind alley that leads back to ego and Independence.

Embodiment means that we must stay humble as we become more practised and integral in Perspective.

Triggers

One of the central tenets of Buddhism is that desire is the source of all suffering. The more we desire a thing, the more we suffer without it. What we desire is perhaps less important than the desire itself. It could be that we long for a deep relationship, or a million dollars, or our own business, or an Aston Martin Vanquish - it does not really matter what the object of my desire is, it matters simply that the desire is there. Let's call such desires the 'shoulds'. They manifest as "I should have an Aston Martin", "I deserve a deep relationship", "I am worth a million dollars".

'Should' is a prison. It creates a false construct in our minds that is very hard to break out of. Trying to fit a chaotic world into the neat way you believe it ought to be is a little like King Canute's followers believing he was divine enough to be able to hold back the tide. It was Canute who knew he was not, in demonstrating that he could not.

If I believe that my senior leaders 'should' act in ways that demonstrate authentic leadership, I am pouring that energy into railing against them when it would be far more fruitful to role model authentic leadership myself.

If I believe that my country 'should' have a more equitable trade balance with the rest of the world, but only work towards delivering that by forcing the world to pay higher taxes on my goods and services, it is highly unlikely to produce the effect I believe it 'should'. Instead, I could decide to state that things are inequitable and work towards equitability through collaborative means. This is far more likely to get people to rally around that cause and come along with me. (It may be quicker for our purposes to say Trump and tariffs...)

'Should' is a motivation from the Self and Dependent Perspectives. 'Should' has no bearing on what actually is, or can be acceptable to others. Even if your motivation is integral, behaving as if things 'should' be that way will guarantee that you make no progress. It will trigger your noble intent back into an adversarial mindset and stimulate your desire to win... And when someone wins, someone else loses (which is an Independent Perspective).

Having others foist their 'shoulds' on to us can also be very distressing. Of any transformation in our lives, moving from Independent to Interdependent is likely to be the most profound. It is also the most prone to failure. It is easier to believe that other people are idiots and wrong, than it is to move towards them and understand their point of view. It is easier to mock a decision made in good faith and blame others from a place of moral superiority, than to empathise, and seek to understand their system and worldview.

We are human, which means that we will always be vulnerable to being triggered. Even the most calm and authentic people are still stimulated by situations that remind them of past abuses or a hand raised in anger. Regulating our own triggers is the most demanding (and unfair?) aspect of self-leadership. It requires us to regulate our emotions so that we will do something when no one else is prepared to; so that we keep silent when everyone else is venting; so that we have a voice when no one else is speaking up.

These are things we may never be thanked for, and may even be criticised for. They are all leadership moments and choices.

"It is not in the stars to hold our destiny,
but in ourselves.."

William Shakespeare

CHAPTER 10

SKILLS 2:
PERSONAL PURPOSE

The previous chapter gave some sense of the importance of understanding your own personal, or life, purpose. If you have ever let yourself down by giving in to a particular emotion you will understand how difficult, yet critical, it is to live up to your own set of values.

Purpose and self-regulation are fundamental to your leadership practice. They are not taught in school and there is no forum, except perhaps the self-help forum, in which you have permission to navel-gaze, experiment and understand yourself. Some see this as the most critical aspect of their lives, while for others it is a foolish waste of time. Your perspective on this was likely formed in childhood, and depends on the importance others gave it. If self-development has become an issue for you now, you have already in some way progressed your vertical development and are in need of some assisted sense-making.

Everyone Has Somewhere New to Go

How do we start a leadership practice? If we have started, how do we get to the next stage? If advanced, how do I influence for the better and improve my legacy? How do I become more change-agile? If I'm already great at change, how can I pass that on?

Over the next few pages we have included a simple, no-nonsense profile for you to think about where you are in your leadership journey, and where you would like to go. It will assist you in understanding your current levels of Perspective and Motivation, and in shaping your ambitions around Reach. There are no judgements in this: no level of influence is too low, no Reach ineffectual. If you have even one good relationship with another person in the world, this matters, and can make a difference to you and to them.

Leadership is about change, so the first thing we must become skilled at changing is ourselves.

Purpose

Our purpose is not simply a choice we make, it is the sum of who we are: our DNA plus our experience. Some people tell us they have no purpose, or no way of determining what it is. This is fine, to an extent, and for a time. But long-term lack of purpose makes you a ship in full sail, without a keel or rudder. You are likely to be blown here and there by the wind; full of potential, yet getting nowhere.

What is a purpose, then? Why does it even matter?

Purpose is the direction our life wants to go in; the energies and pulls we feel towards particular activities or states. It is not a rational thing but something felt. There is no level of purpose that is not important. You may feel it is your destiny to be the first President of the World, or you may believe you are on this planet to be a mother, father, homeowner, farmer or poet; all are valid and useful. In all cases, you are more likely to achieve your purpose if you have explored it, know it, and are working towards it.

The more aligned we are with our purpose, the more confident and energetic we can be. The more misaligned we are with our purpose, the more stressed and tired we will feel. If we are confused we will flounder, running from one thing to the next without ever really focusing, simply accepting the opportunities offered by others who are more purposeful.

Our purpose provides the spiritual, inspirational energy for our life.

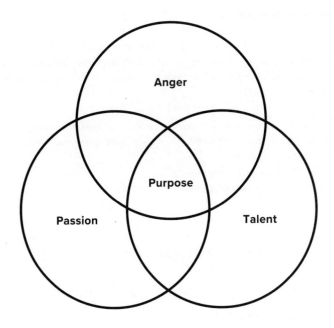

We can use the map above to help us find our purpose. Anger and passion are two sides of motivation. Talent is about ability. If we focus our life on the space where all three overlap, we are likely to be at our most motivated and capable. Working in that space, it is also reasonable to expect that we will be at our most successful and fulfilled.

Our purpose is already influencing our life and our work. Everyone's purpose is already influencing how they work and what they do. Purpose is a little like magnetism, whether you can describe it or not, it already exerts an influence on much of your life. If you don't understand it, the influence of purpose can be hard to manage and might take you by surprise.

Articulating your purpose turns it from an invisible force into a powerful tool that, like magnetism, can be used to power your life and your organisation into the future.

Three Simple Questions

We have done this exercise with over 10,000 people, from students to pensioners. It is amazingly powerful. In some cases, it is transformative (it has been described as an 'awakening' or 'epiphany'), but for most it facilitates an adjustment that helps people feel more confident in what they do and more centred in themselves.

Connection to your purpose is down to you and your own authenticity. To articulate your purpose you need to answer three questions:

1. Anger: What are you angry about?

Some people, especially those who have done a lot of personal development, say that they don't get angry. This is a shame. Anger is a powerful emotion with a lot of energy in it and there are certainly plenty of things in our world to be angry about. Anger is evidence of life, of your values, of what motivates you. Flipped to the positive, anger reveals our ideals.

If you are not outraged, you are not paying attention.

There is nothing wrong with anger, it is an emotion and part of your body's way of communicating with you. Being unable to direct your anger productively is a problem; not regulating or inappropriately channelling anger is a problem, but feeling anger is not a problem.

Write a list of things that make you angry at a societal level.
Think about:

- What makes you shout at the television?

- If you felt completely uninhibited, what would make you thump the table during a discussion?

- If you were President of the World, what are the first five or six things you would change?

Things I am angry about!

1

2

3

4

5

6

Now summarise that list. Look for themes; you may find there is one theme or several. For example, in a list that includes bankers, war, lobbying, gang violence and politics, you might conclude that 'greed' and 'conflict' are themes in your anger.

What themes do I notice? - Group into categories.

1

2

3

If there is more than one theme, can you can look to integrate them or keep them as a two word summary. For example, greed and conflict might be summarised as 'ego leadership'.

You are looking for a summary that encapsulates all of your list, that works logically and linguistically, and also feels right. See if you can check it both ways. Ideally it is also short, i.e. two to three words.

Summary

1

Some real examples from people we've worked with: arrogance and brutishness, lack of big picture responsibility, bad communication, wasted potential.

2. Passion: What do you love?
Most people find 'passion' reasonably easy. Think about people, places, activities, things and hobbies that you love. What would you miss if you were somehow prevented from doing it, or what have you already stopped that you miss. Try to be specific. For example, you may be passionate about 'people', but what is the passion really about? Connection? Debate? Curiosity? Cooking together? Be detailed.

If identifying your passions does not come easily, think about things that give you energy, or that you are drawn to without really understanding why. Simply saying 'family and friends' is not all that helpful to articulating your purpose - if you are tempted to include them, say specifically what it is that you get from those relationships.

Things I am passionate about!

1

2

3

4

5

6

If I am passionate about cycling, there are lots of logical reasons to enjoy cycling, such as the outdoors, speed, fitness, etc, but maybe that passion is fundamentally about exploring my personal limits around control of danger...

Look for the same underlying motivations in your own list. Again, summarise by looking for themes.

What themes do I notice? - Group into categories.

1

2

3

Some real examples from people we've worked with: community/ effectiveness, connecting at a higher level, altered states of consciousness, elegant connected solutions.

Keep summarising to articulate a principal passion:

Summary

1

3. Talent: What are you great at?

Talent tends to be the hardest list for most of us to admit to, as we are often brought up to applaud excessive modesty. For this exercise, we have to ban modesty completely. Modesty is a form of dishonesty. Let's start being honest about what we are good at and where we need collaborators.

Most organisations identify teamwork as a desirable thing. The essence of teamwork is for us to play to our strengths and collaborate with others who are strong in areas of weakness for us. True collaboration is so much harder if modesty prevents us from admitting our strengths.

- So, what are you great at?

- What are the things that come easily to you?

- What are the things that you don't really need to be taught, that you can simply do?

Things I am great at!

1
2
3
4
5
6

Think beyond the normal subjects - are you great at connecting with people?
Do you empathise with their feelings? Do you find that animals respond to you,
or that you easily grasp technical things?

Write your list and then summarise it. Again, start by looking for themes.

What themes do I notice? - Group into categories.

1
2
3

Here are some real examples from people we've worked with: deep connection, teaching, leadership, improvement, aligning, challenge.

Reach a summary by articulating your main talent:

Summary

1

Anger = Values

Next, we need to turn your anger into their positive opposites. The anger is actually evidence of your deepest value set; those values that you will not compromise, no matter what. There are likely to be only two or three such values (remember Mark's example from working in a small consultancy. He thought he had a set of values, but slowly compromised them until he reached his own red line and, in that moment, knew what his real values were).

It is **critical** that you do not assume 'nice to have' values, or values you wish you had. Be as absolutely honest with yourself as you can. No one else is involved in doing this - the only person who will know what is real is you.

Creating a value from what you are angry about is a simple process. It will be its opposite, but the opposite to 'social injustice' may not be 'social justice'. Try to find the real motivation or value that sits underneath it. Here are some examples:

The Anger	The Value
• Bullies and those who get their own way simply because they can	• Standing up for my own rights = self respect
• Destruction of our planet, our home	• The health of my children = long-term thinking
• Corporate corruption and tax evasion	• Fair application of the law = equity

The Anger	The Value

My Purpose

Finally, we need to wrap everything up into a single statement. At this stage, and having perhaps done this exercise for the first time, the words might feel clumsy or not quite accurate at present. What matters at this stage is to put all of your findings into one sentence, and try out that sentence for energy. If there is wholehearted energy and a rush of excitement or inspiration, you are likely to be very close to your purpose. If there is a 'not quite there' feeling, it just needs more work. If there is a bit of disappointment, ask yourself if you have been as honest as you need to be? Is there other self-discovery work you need to do first?

Here's a template:

My life's purpose is to use my passion for *(insert the statement about passion)* to *(insert your talent as a verb)* through being *(the thing that makes you angry expressed as a positive)*

My Purpose

My life's purpose is to use my passion for:

To:

Through being:

Your life purpose may not be fixed. We do experience change throughout our lives, and what we thought was essential at the age of 18 may morph over time and experience into something else by the time we are 40. If we are constantly - and consciously - tending and curating our life intentions and Purpose, there is time and space to nurture these changes. So do not be too wedded to a form of words or something very specific. Your life purpose may, in fact, be quite general. What matters is that you know it, are paying attention to it, and curate it as you develop.

Lastly, it may not end up in this format. Play with the words and the form so that it becomes dense, clear, and has the right 'feel' for you. It can have a lot of latitude within it, so that how you go about expressing your purpose may develop over time, but the essential thrust and direction remain. Here are a couple of examples:

"Help others grow and things to change, and so express myself."

"To heal the world through authenticity."

Perspective

Having read all about Perspective throughout this book, are you keen to know in more detail what your own Perspective is?

This is a useful exercise for two reasons:

1. It would be advantageous to understand our peak level of Perspective

2. It is worthwhile understanding how vulnerable we are to being triggered, and our actual operating level in common situations.

Our peak level is the level at which we are our best. To find this, look at how you behave when you are in your element, or those times when you are most in tune with yourself. When you feel that you are 'on purpose'. This might be when you are with those who are closest and most trusted, or when doing a favourite activity. It is likely to be at times of profound psychological safety. See these times as your benchmark.

In the table below, allocate one tick to one statement per question (chosen from the five possible answers, numbered 1-5). You need to end up with just five ticks in the right-hand column.

#	Question	Possible answers	Tick 1 answer
1		To make money and to do important work	
2	Which best describes why go to work?	It gives me a structure and routine in my life	
3		It gives me the freedom to choose	
4		It means I make a contribution	
5		To make a difference in the world	
1		I have a natural understanding of things, I don't need to learn much.	
2	Which best describes your approach to learning?	When someone tells me I need to learn I will apply myself	
3		When I decide I want to learn something I will apply myself	
4		I learn whatever I need to learn to contribute more effectively	
5		I see everything as a learning experience	

1		I expect those I lead to do what I tell them	
2		When senior people decide what to do I get my team to execute their instructions	
3	Which best describes your approach to leading?	I decide on the right path and tell my people what to do	
4		As a team we agree on a vision and then collaborate to work out how best to achieve it	
5		I challenge and support those around me to be the best possible version of themselves	
1		You can only trust those who depend on you	
2		I only really trust my parents	
3	Which best describes your experience of trust?	I only really trust myself	
4		I am willing to be vulnerable and trust others	
5		Once I learned to trust myself I found I could trust anyone	
1		I take care of myself and do not burden others	
2		I will take care of those I am directly responsible for as long as someone is taking care of me	
3	Which best describes your circle of concern?	I have to take care of myself and my team because no one else does	
4		I feel a responsibility for the organisation as a whole and even for the country and region	
5		I feel a sense of global responsibility not just for the present, but also for the future.	

The number of the statement (in the left-hand column) corresponds to the level of Perspective you prefer (see the table below). Add up the number of ticks you have in each corresponding row.

Scoring example:

#	Level of Perspective	Number of answers ticked
1	Self	
2	Dependent	1
3	Independent	2
4	Interdependent	2
5	Integral	

My answers:

#	Level of Perspective	Number of answers ticked
1	Self	
2	Dependent	
3	Independent	
4	Interdependent	
5	Integral	

Please note this is not an exhaustive analysis but a rough rule of thumb; it is a start-point for further reflection. This picture will represent our general 'default' perspective when not under stress, or at our best. Wherever our peak, we are all vulnerable to being triggered downwards by both acute and chronic situations. An acute situation might be an argument or a frightening situation. A chronic situation might be a toxic culture or relationship.

The first skill to develop is our own awareness of state, so that from moment to moment we are aware of the perspective level at which we are operating. Once we can calibrate our state we can start to learn our specific, personal triggers. When we know our triggers we can find ways to mitigate them. This is a constant journey of self-development, always seeking to understand what might reduce our perspective level and what we can do to hold ourselves to the higher level. The more time we can spend at the higher level, the more we will be contributing and at peace with ourselves and the world.

It is also fair to say that there are situations where being triggered might be the better option. For example, if we are attacked in some way physically, and lack the skill to talk our way out of it, we might be better off being triggered to a 'self' level and fighting back without regard for our attacker's wellbeing. So, learning the skills (horizontal development) to deal with trigger situations goes hand-in-hand with vertical development.

The popular psychological experimenter Derren Brown tells a story of being mugged in a town in North Wales; he was able to use his extraordinary skills to talk the mugger down to such an extent that they ended up sitting together on the kerb, with the would-be mugger crying. As remarkable as this story sounds, these are skills that all of us can learn.

One of the main problems we work with in organisational culture is mass, chronic triggering. We encounter entire organisational cultures that are successful at recruiting people with an Interdependent Perspective, but have a culture so toxic that those same people are triggered, all day, every day at work and end up operating at an Independent level. This manifests through the creation of silos, increased competition with colleagues and customers, and can drop to a Dependent level, where they are no longer able to take the initiative and so wait to be told what to do.

In the worst cases we have seen several individuals at the top of a company triggered to a chronic Self Perspective, where their focus was reduced to self-preservation. That led them actively to seek to sabotage those they perceived as a threat, with a complete lack of awareness of the wider and longer-term damage that their own triggering was having across the organisation. Healing this sort of trauma in an organisation (or a relationship) will nearly always require highly skilled intervention.

Living on Purpose

There are no 'pat' answers that enable us to declare victory and remain happy forever. The practice of living true to your purpose is a constantly evolving series of rising waves. It always brings sorrows as well as joys, but it is worthwhile, and certainly preferable to avoidance or drowning sorrows in addiction. If you aspire to make a change, then become a better self-leader. Working on purpose according to your most cherished values enables much more powerful and concerted action, and guarantees higher levels of impact.

Role modelling personal change also equips you to role model change in the public or organisational domain.

"Our deepest fear is not that we are inadequate.
Our deepest fear is that we are powerful beyond
measure. It is our light, not our darkness,
that most frightens us..."

Marianne Williamson

CHAPTER 11

SKILLS 3: INTEGRAL LEADERSHIP

Leadership style

Each person's preferred leadership style is closely related to their level of Perspective. As we saw in the last chapter, it is not possible to lead authentically unless you are operating from an Interdependent or Integral Perspective. No matter how Authentic or Visionary the leader, we are vulnerable during conflict to being triggered back to an Independent level of Perspective and, therefore, operating from Boss or Ruler behaviour.

If we aspire to visionary style leadership we must develop the skills of visioning and inspiring (see Chapter 5), and the ability to articulate a destination in such a way that people are energised and committed to pursuing it. A Visionary leader will be the most powerful embodiment of the vision, pursuing it with extreme levels of commitment and often at personal cost or risk. In pursuit of their vision, Visionaries, like elite athletes, sacrifice much that others would consider abnormal.

We need and venerate visionary leaders, but authentic leadership is a far more rational aspiration. Authentic leaders may never be celebrated by anyone other than their direct followers, but they touch deeply the lives of those who follow them; that impact ripples out through their own work, social and familial circles and across society.

Since Authentic leadership requires an Interdependent Perspective, an essential baseline skill is learning the ability to hold ourselves to that level in most circumstances. The start point is to know the best version of ourselves, and practice how to be that person skilfully, in all situations.

The next stage is to create psychological safety with those who follow us, to enable their authenticity and inspire them to achieve their own highest levels of performance in pursuit of a socially positive vision.

Authentics are not recognised as leaders by Bosses or Rulers, so Authentic leaders also have to be able to engage effectively with those styles - without compromising their authenticity. To gain the support of Bosses and Rulers, the skilful Authentic leader uses language that connects authenticity and vision with the status impulses of the Boss or Ruler.

We advocate against being, becoming, electing, selecting, following or promoting anyone whose single-minded pursuit of their own status guides their behaviour. This holds true even if that behaviour delivers results that are commercially attractive to an organisation. Those results will be discounted hugely by the toxic impact of such behaviour on culture.

If you are sympathetic to the Authentic style and suspect you may have been behaving like a Boss, then change: you will feel much better.

If you can honestly admit that you enjoy the power and status that Ruler and Boss styles give you, only you can change that (and such candid self-awareness is a good place to start!). It helps to be clear about your motivations. All who aspire to leadership must also aspire to have the power to make change (this is a personal threshold with which Authentics often struggle). Accept the attraction of power, but connect it to your legacy. Do you really want to steal from the future? How do you want to be remembered, as a Nero or a Mandela?

If you already have power, you probably do not need more. Use what you have to help change the future for everyone.

What Leadership Styles Succeed in Today's World?

VIICA Leadership for a VUCA World
Authenticity as a leadership skill is a good foundational mindset, but operating effectively through constant change requires some specific behaviours.

That constant change environment and marketplace is captured in the acronym, 'VUCA'. VUCA stands for Volatility, Uncertainty, Complexity and Ambiguity (manifested in the Megatrends). VUCA is now a permanent state, so leaders need to get really good at thinking and acting within that context. They must embody adaptable leadership traits that deal with contextual change and disruption as well as daily management and control.

Holos calls this approach 'VIICA leadership for a VUCA world'. It stands on the shoulders of the giants of leadership research, and calls for key transformational behaviours to create, change and attract followers:

- V - Visionary
- I - Innovative
- I - Inspiring
- C - Collaborative
- A - Accountable.

Visionary
Visioning is a skill most people find challenging. Yet without a vision, decisions are taken in a vacuum and end up being short term, transactional, and vulnerable to the robust visions of others.

A vision is a statement of a future destination that we truly want to achieve; it is not limited by what we believe to be possible; and needs to be inspiring to all contributors. In addition, it must be plausible.

When articulating their vision, most people struggle to come up with something that is sufficiently clear and far-reaching. First attempts might inspire them as individuals but are unlikely to inspire others. Most vision statements are actually a mission (what the organisation already does) dressed in fine language.

A vision needs to feel scarily exciting. It needs to stir the soul, and be something we are willing to fight for. We need to be truly dedicated to a vision to be willing to push the boundaries for it, so, in that sense, it must appeal to our shared authentic state. The current leadership does not have to be author of the organisation's vision, but must ensure that there is one, and that all leaders embody it.

Being strategic is an equal part of visionary behaviour. Strategy defines the best possible route between two points. If our vision is to climb the highest peak in the Himalayas, strategy answers the question: "How shall we achieve the vision in the way we need it to be done?" For example, if we decide that our mountain-climbing endeavour should be environmentally sustainable, we might choose to travel there by bike rather than fly.

Developing a strategy is about making decisions. Decisions are motivated by turning information into an executable plan. The plan in turn is dynamic, adjusting to circumstance. It has more detail in the short term - Who needs to do what, and when? - and becomes progressively high level into the future.

Being strategic is not only about having a plan. It also involves building agility and adaptability into the execution from the outset, and ensuring that the right people have enough autonomy and clarity around the Cause and Conditions to take operational decisions and deal with the realities in their local context.

Inspiring
The word 'inspire', from the Greek, means to 'breathe life into'. When we inspire others we energise them around our shared intent; - our Cause and Conditions. With that inspiration they shift from bystander colleague to engaged follower.

Followers are the essential ingredient in successful change. If no one follows the Cause and Conditions, or if we have compliance rather than true inspiration around them, nothing changes in a sustainable way.

Followers are inspired by understanding that a Cause will make things better, and by seeing plausible strategies to make the Cause happen. Leaders can inspire followers by co-creating strategies and ensuring that each follower feels ownership in their role, finds it fulfilling and can deploy their individual strengths. Inspiring leaders share the overall progress towards the vision frequently, and take time to recognise all contributions. Part of the skill of inspiring is to allow leadership to morph and move, and sit with different individuals so make certain that everyone progresses together towards the vision.

In the best examples of inspiration, we no longer seek to corral individual and group energy in a quasi-paternalistic way, inspiring leaders allow freedom and expression so that we might ultimately achieve the vision through methods the leader had not even conceived of. Inspired success goes beyond the 'I' status of the leader to generate a shared sense of fulfilment across teams and colleagues.

Optimism is a powerful component of Inspiring. As Henry Ford put it: "If you think you can or you think you can't, you are probably right". To lead change effectively a leader must believe in its importance and achievability. Sometimes the work of a leader is to move themselves to a place of commitment; the belief that we too have taken on and embodied a change creates commitment in followers and provides hope that it just might be easier than they thought.

As strategy is executed there will be setbacks and challenges. Leadership must cultivate a habit of realistic optimism mixed with a relentless 'pre-mortem' mentality. That horizon scanning means we constantly accept that what can go wrong in the future, will - unless we avoid or mitigate it now. Leaders must be able to reframe situations to maintain positivity, and collaborate consistently to revise strategies to keep the project on track and belief high.

Experiments with new tools and techniques will often fail. So leadership needs to cultivate the habit of responding positively to failure and and moving directly to iterative learning without considering blame.

At the same time, optimism must remain realistic and strategies plausible. Leaders can certainly stretch people's thinking, but if we fail to deliver more than a couple of times, people will start to lose confidence. Inspiring optimism is the ability to stay positive while adjusting for the reality.

Innovative

Innovation is a continuum, with continuous improvement at one end, and true blue-water originality at the other. The degree of innovation we need is defined by our market (at the continuous improvement end), and our vision and ambition (at the originality end).

If leadership is about change, a true leader must be continually, setting aside time to think, and working out which parts of the business or organisation need to improve or be radically reinvented or renewed.

It is important to state that, as a leader, you do not need to do the innovation thinking yourself. Your role is to safeguard the existence and constant operation of the innovation processes. That said, some companies rest on their laurels in this regard, assuming that because there is an R&D department, innovation is taking care of itself.

Our experience is that the level of focus within R&D is often critical to the amount of innovation in both the organisational structure and the 'products' developed for commercial or public use. A large R-focus directs money into research, so this is the area that produces innovation. A large D-focus directs attention and funding mainly into the development of existing products/ services, possibly to the detriment of the completely new.

By the same token, pursuing originality and novelty without also paying attention to the overall culture will likely reduce results. To lead constant change, it is vital to push both innovation thinking processes and a culture that nurtures/supports both innovators and their innovations through to market.

Many organisations we have worked with have distinct R-cultures and D-cultures. The management-heavy, production focus of the D-culture tends not to support the innovative, leadership focus of the R-culture. They must be developed in tandem and interdependently for an organisation to have true adaptability.

Collaborative

Collaboration is the 'how' of effective leadership in a VUCA world. Collaboration is an attitude and a skill inherent in good transformational leadership. Effective change requires additional unusual amounts of good collaborative behaviour. A leader must consciously and deliberately break down silos and refocus people on the higher Cause. The unifying cause is so important to collaboration; it elevates teams beyond their individual objectives so they are aware of their place in the flotilla, the direction of travel and the need for mutual support.

Collaboration is natural for those who have an Interdependent mindset. It is more difficult for those whose perspective is Self or Dependent: collaboration loves to share fame and glory!

Most leaders understand the need to be Visionary, Inspiring, Innovative and Accountable. It is through Collaboration, however, that the lumbering supertanker really changes into the agile, adaptable flotilla.

Accountable

When building monumental structures across the Roman Empire, senior architects and engineers took responsibility in visceral ways. For example, when building a critical supporting arch in an aqueduct, the lead architect would stand directly underneath as the keystone was lowered into place and its supports removed. Their life was on the line. This ensured that they had done everything possible to guarantee safety, and the accuracy of their engineering calculations. As a result, there are many aqueducts all across Europe that have literally stood the test of time; that Roman cultural attribute of 'accountable' is manifest and visible in the structure.

Leadership means accountability. Practising leadership means that we put our heads above the parapet fully aware that they could be shot off. Leaders do this not to show off or to be different for its own sake, but because leaders consciously assume accountability for what we are doing. Leadership accepts that it is responsible and accountable for performance. Leadership explicitly demonstrates accountability and helps others grow by sharing those responsibilities holistically.

Accepting accountability as a leader helps build personal reliability. An organisation cannot be reliable externally if it is unreliable internally. It may seem nit-picking in the moment, but a crucial role of leadership is to ensure that a granular culture of reliability permeates the organisation. This is an old-fashioned, yet indispensable sense of standards and discipline.

Leadership does not falsely seek to shift ownership of failures or take credit for successes. It does the opposite. Being accountable means explicitly and publicly accepting responsibility for doing everything possible to get things right. Chief of the Australian Army, Lieutenant-General David Morrison put it succinctly: *"The standard you walk past is the standard you accept."*

Blame is not the same as accountability. Leadership knows that all failures and successes are systemic. When things go wrong it is rarely the fault of an individual, because the system permitted the individual to behave the way or get into the situation that caused the failure. Similarly, when things go right it is seldom due to one individual, but can be attributed to the collective effort.

After the cruise ship Costa Concordia sank off the coast of Italy in 2012, there was an extraordinary press conference in which the executive team of Costa Cruises blamed the entire event on the Captain. This individualisation of blame fails to acknowledge the leadership's responsibility for the culture and systems of recruiting, retaining, developing, rewarding and managing the behaviour of the individual. Side-stepping the systemic nature of accountability eliminates the possibility of learning from a failure, creating the opportunity for it to happen again.

Optimised organisations are those in which everyone looks out for and enhances reliability. That culture has to be created and curated by leadership, from discipline around punctuality in meetings to teaching everyone to do the right thing when no one else is looking.

Internal reliability can be measured and evaluated just as much as external reliability. And reliability starts at the top.

Your VIICA Leadership

Any potential leader must first be themselves, and that begins with self-awareness (a vertical leadership development challenge). Building skills and putting them into practice regularly is part of horizontal leadership development. How habitual are each of the VIICA characteristics for you? How skilful are you currently at each of them? How do you know when to deploy these traits? Are you continually practising and enhancing your skill to become a better leader?

As leaders, we cannot ask people to make changes that we do not first make ourselves. If we want a population to take responsibility for their own health and wellbeing by exercising regularly and eating a healthy diet, the team leading the change must be exemplars of effort and change. The same is true of VIICA leadership behaviours: role-modelling means living the change wholeheartedly and full-time.

Formal school education is still largely individualistic. Collaboration is often called cheating while we are students. We all need to unlearn this myth to unleash the power of positive change in our organisations and lives.

Your Leadership Profile

We talked in detail in Chapter 5 about the four different styles of leadership we've identified in looking at the lived experience of leadership. You may be curious to understand what it would be like to live and work inside each of these leadership cultures.

You may also want to profile your own motivations and leadership logics to see where you fit in the model, and where you wish to develop. We have developed the **Holos Authentic Leadership (HAL)** role profile (see www. holoschange.com/HAL for more information), based on the characteristics and experiences set out in the role descriptors below.

A Word on Roles

Below we unpick the HAL roles in more detail, to understand how they manifest. The language in these descriptions attempts to capture the lived experiences of our research subjects.

A role incorporates everything we use to claim and define our personal identity: our shoes, phone, friends, food, what we watch, the conversations we have, the opinions we espouse. All form part of one role or another, and all can be subject to change. Who among us has exactly the same opinions that we held ten years ago? Who dresses the same, or lives the same way?
No matter who you are, how entrenched your views, how 'right' you think you are, and what 'truths' you cling to, it can all change - and sometimes in a heartbeat. Therefore, how we choose to practice leadership as part of our role can also change.

Until now, we have not discussed Management. You could be forgiven for believing that in some way we frown on management. That is not true. Management is essential, noble, and necessary. However, this book is about leadership, and so we have focused there.

At the bottom of this section, as an extension of the leadership roles described earlier, we include Management as essential first stage. However, in a constant change environment it is essential to be clear about the nature of Management, and not to confuse it with the role of Leadership. They are different skills.

The Ruler Role

Impact When Highly Skilled and Conscious:

Conscious Ruler leadership will operate ethically and morally from the point of view of stewardship. It is adept at seeing the existing big picture and prioritising actions that serve that picture. If those actions are sometimes brutal, that may be an acceptable consequence. Ruler behaviour originates from preferred or fixed views about the 'right way' to operate and Rulers often make unilateral decisions based on this code.

Skilled Ruler leadership can be very effective at getting things done and can lead organisations (and countries) to significant success. The downside is that the Ruler style can be exclusive or dismissive of concerns that exist outside that code, and is unlikely to be persuaded to change course. Whatever success Rulers achieve today is achieved by appropriating some form of value from the future to enrich their present status.

Being within a system led by skilled, conscious Ruler leadership may feel:

- Comfortable and secure, as if there is a steady hand at the helm

- Strategic, certain and predictable

- Traditional, and sure of itself

- Hierarchical, and therefore risky to make mistakes

- As if opportunities for career growth can be slow, and you could be superseded by favourites

- Uncertain or prohibitive around speaking up or deviating from what is acceptable

- Polarised: rewarded followers always in support and those who are unrewarded or whose values are challenged constantly in opposition

Impact When Unskilled and Unconscious:

The unconscious Ruler role is motivated by a belief in their right to seniority and authority, and the legitimacy of using those positions largely to serve their personal ambition. In decision-making, unskilled Rulers are unlikely to count the human cost or the cost to the future. Consequently, success is often short-lived, with a substantial cost coming due at some point in the future (often but not always after the Ruler's tenure). Unskilled Rulers can believe themselves in the role of hero, wanting everyone to believe in them as the 'leader' who can cure all ills. Unconscious Ruler leadership can be polarising and wrong-foot followers, who are constantly unsure whether they will encounter the supportive hero or the toxic tyrant.

Being within a system led by unskilled, unconscious Ruler leadership may feel:

- Tactical, insecure and risky

- At times hugely motivational and at times deeply concerning

- Exclusive and indifferent to diversity

- Political, with inconsistent and erratic decision-making

- Amoral or status-focused

- Competitive and lacking in compassion

- Lacking in career development opportunity

- Punitive, rather than supportive, when faced with a lack of confidence

Extreme Rulers:
Extreme Rulers believe their status is their right and that others exist to serve them. In making decisions, the extreme Ruler role will only accept options that meet the needs of their personal agenda. These behaviours are so deeply ingrained that the individual may not be aware of how they choose to prioritise; instead they see personal success and status as their natural prerogative and a just reward for their contribution. The unusually high incidence of psychopathy in business leaders (3%), relative to the general population (1%), is noteworthy here. (Source: Snakes in Suits: When Psychopaths Go to Work, by Paul Babiak, PhD., and Robert Hare, PhD. They also found the rate of psychopathy in prison populations is 15%)..

The Visionary Role

Impact When Highly Skilled and Conscious:
Conscious Visionary leadership blends styles in service to the Cause, creating a culture that empowers others and creates long-term sustainability. Skilled Visionary leadership attracts support by espousing transparent values and beliefs, and attracting others who share those beliefs.

To be consciously Visionary is to be aware of the need to role model ideals, as well as espouse them. The effective Visionary leader guards against hubris in the role and practises remaining humble. Visionary skills acknowledge the potential in others and encourage discretionary effort in contributions towards the shared cause.

Being within a system led by skilled, conscious Visionary style leadership may feel:

- Motivating and inspiring, with work that matters and makes a difference

- Inclusive and meritocratic

- Long term, but evolving and iterative

- Permissive; ideas and mistakes are accepted as the route towards the right answer

- Frustrating and changeable

- Stretching and challenging, with an almost daily feeling of growth and learning

- Demanding and accountable

Impact When Unskilled and Unconscious:
Visionary leadership can be uncompromisingly authentic and, as a result, may feel impatient with those who are not as committed to the vision or who do not yet have the skill to contribute at the desired level. Unconscious Visionary leadership can be chaotic in nature and suffer from a lack of effective processes and systems. Unskilled Visionary leadership will pay less attention to management and the day-to-day, preferring to focus on the big questions and big picture, and may not account for others' preference for a more grounded outlook, more structure or a clear series of tasks. If unskilled, communication of the Cause may feel too nebulous or inaccessible, and can be hard to interpret.

Being within a system led by unskilled, unconscious Visionary leadership may feel:

- Highly creative but sometimes at the cost of process

- Chaotic and changeable; and generally a more disruptive system to work inside

- Judgemental with regard to level commitment to the Cause

- High levels of creative trust and accountability to deliver

- Accepting of creative mistakes, but unresponsive to the need for process to avoid other mistakes

- Personally rewarding but professionally frustrating; it may be hard to deliver best practice and innovation because of process duplication or a lack of shared learning practices

Extreme Visionaries:
Extreme Visionaries see life as equal for all and without any impediment to progress. They make the impossible possible and have seemingly superhuman energy and capacity for ideas, work and networking. They may expect the same of those around them and either attract those who believe and act in similar ways, or burn out lesser individuals. They may have unstable emotional lives, show extreme disregard for those they regard as fools. It is hard for many to keep up with the extreme Visionary.

The Boss Role

Impact When Highly Skilled and Conscious:
Conscious Boss styles can be productive and rewarding to work for. A conscious Boss role will keep a steady eye on the team dynamic because this is the vehicle to increase performance and success. Team members will always know how they stand with a Boss because frequent, direct and uncompromising feedback will be the norm. Daily routines will be highly managed and choreographed, all efficiently aligned towards goal achievement and reputational gain.

Boss leadership styles can be highly competitive and, as such, react situationally to change; embracing it when it is politically driven, and deflecting change when it appears to be a fad or to have no powerful and senior advocacy behind it.

Being within a system led by skilled, conscious Boss leadership may feel:

- Ordered and controlled, possibly highly structured
- High pressure and public
- Judgemental; with high standards and criteria that may not feel authentic to certain individuals
- Rational and unsympathetic
- Target- and goal-driven, with financial rewards
- As though unquestioning loyalty is valued more highly than challenge
- As if career development is offered for functional business reasons only.

Impact When Unskilled and Unconscious:
Many unconscious Bosses have climbed up through the ranks and worked hard to get where they are by obedient grafting and political savvy. Having reached a level of seniority, the unconscious, unskilled Boss may feel exposed and can become insecure, vulnerable to imposter syndrome, needing excessive reassurance and be extremely cautious about taking risks. Like the Ruler, unconscious Boss behaviour may base decisions on personal agenda. In that role, an unconscious Boss could see life as a competition, so the route to win advancement could involve manipulation. In the unconscious Boss style, people are simply a resource to be exploited in pursuit of personal gain.

Because of many organisational cultures, unconscious Boss styles are often simply learned from observation or experience. It is also possible the style is adopted unconsciously because a leader received promotion without adequate development or support, and so is masking doubt or incompetence.

Sometimes morphing from a Boss to an Authentic role is simply a matter of permission, awareness or the availability of a good role model.

Being within a system led by unskilled, unconscious Boss leadership may feel:

- Manipulative and/or political
- Oppressive; obedience is critical, creating a compliance culture
- Overly emotional with outbursts of anger or blaming (because emotions are not accepted or openly discussed)
- As if values and human needs are fluffy and not worth considering
- Exclusive, with teams turning inward to form cliques, silos and fiefdoms
- As though definitions of right and wrong behaviour differ depending on who you are
- Exposed because of the selection of favourites and 'special people'
- Psychologically unsafe and/or violent

Extreme Bosses:
In his book On the *Psychology of Military Incompetence*, Norman F. Dixon describes a time when Boss leadership was the norm in the military. His conclusion is that if you promote for obedience, you risk getting leadership that lacks the ability to think for itself. This supports our view that no organisation can exceed the consciousness of its leaders.

The Authentic Role

Impact When Highly Skilled and Conscious:
The conscious Authentic appreciates that everyone is at different stages in their personal and professional development. As a result, their team can love them (so may seem to be a threat to a Boss).

If many Authentic styles operate with skill and consciousness in an organisation, they can collectively create very safe, very productive working environments which align towards the achievement of bold and inspiring visions. The conscious Authentic role works to achieve goals by tapping into each person's potential and creativity, in a culture where mistakes are 'just one more try on the way to doing it right'. Skilled Authentic leadership is motivated to build high trust environments that become self-regulating, and scorns presenteeism in favour of reliable delivery.

Being within a system led by skilled, conscious Authentic leadership may feel:

- Highly trusting, with delivery and teamwork the vital measures

- Respectful and inclusive

- Energetic, creative and innovative

- Adaptive and responsive to change

- Aligned towards achieving a strong, clear Cause and Conditions

- Confrontational and risky at times, with people speaking their mind and relishing debate

- Stretching because personal accountability is highly valued

- Supportive of both organisational and personal/professional goals (such as career or learning opportunities)

- Rewarding in ways other than financial: fulfilment, meaning, recognition, etc

Impact When Unskilled and Unconscious:
A strong motivation to enrol and include everyone before starting a project may result in being slower off the blocks than a Ruler or Boss. Because unskilled Authentic leadership can be regarded as weak or ineffective, Authentic motivations may be tentative or masked in order to fit in. The unskilled Authentic role may seem highly opinionated, because their view is based in values, they may have blind spots where others' values lead to different viewpoints. When too many Authentic styles blend without a cohesive Cause and Conditions the results can be chaotic or conflicted. Being Authentic without confidence can also be personally damaging if an Authentic individual remains for too long inside an opposite system (e.g. one dominated by Boss culture).

Being within a system led by unskilled, unconscious Authentic leadership may feel:

- Too woolly and discursive to make effective progress
- Conflicting because of too many deeply held values running counter to each other
- Chaotic and too changeable
- Lacking in concrete goals and targets
- Non-collaborative and accusatory
- As if everything is done by committee
- As though decision-making takes too long or does not happen

Extreme Authentic leaders:

Authentic motivations that go too deeply into the 'I' ask others to accept them for who they are, including all their foibles and biases. The personal journey is important, but no individual is more important than any other. Extreme Authentic leaders forget to work on their shadow or dark side of personality in less public arenas. Instead, the Authentic character's shadow and dark sides can be expressed as a 'take me as I am' mentality by individuals in an extreme Authentic leadership role. This can be unhelpful and sometimes damaging.

The Manager Role

Those taking up the Manager role may have been appointed because of their technical competence in some area, but might lack the training or the self-driven learning, to move into leadership. The Manager is confident in technical and managerial strength and can play to that if allowed, but may defer hierarchically on more strategic and creative issues. The future leadership role Managers take up may depend on their role models. Many unconscious Boss leaders result from poor support for a technical contributor. Manager styles may mistakenly apply management behaviour in leadership, with the result that they see people simply as material with which to solve problems.

Impact When Highly Skilled and Conscious:

Skilled Managers typically deliver effectively within established boundaries, in line with strategies determined by others. The motivated Manager role may support or defer to the 'powers that be' and very much see themselves as a cog in the wheel - and hence deliverers - of organisational performance. This feels acceptable to the Manager style, because compliant delivery is a necessary function and must be done well. The conscious Manager style is conscientious and proactive, foreseeing and heading off problems and bottlenecks in processes and systems so that the organisation remains efficient. The conscious, skilled Manager role is a vital asset to any organisation.

Being within a system managed by skilled, conscious Manager styles may feel:

- Task- or project-driven

- Outcome- and goal-focused

- Efficient and productive

- Constrained within a highly managed working day with set times for repeating tasks

- As if people are valued, but pigeon-holed by their competencies or areas of expertise

- As though ideas are acceptable as long as they create process improvements

- Predictable in terms of culture or working environment.

Impact When Unskilled and Unconscious:

Obedience and approval are key drivers for some unconscious Manager styles. The role of Manager is often constrained or enabled by the nature of the hierarchy above it (which cautious Manager styles are unlikely to challenge). Accepting this role can be unsafe in some contexts, such as manufacturing or hydrocarbon extraction/refining. In such contexts, it is necessary for the sake of safety to speak up and offer different views and solutions. No unskilled Manager should have leadership responsibility in such positions. Senior leadership has the responsibility to create a culture where

Managers are active and can contribute. The skills needed to be effective in the Manager style can be taught.

Being within a system managed by unskilled, unconscious Manager styles may feel:

- Directionless and purposeless

- Routine and boring

- Unimaginative, with creative suggestions unwelcome

- Unsafe or incompetent

- Unchanging or where change is executed badly

- Unappreciative of effort or higher skill

- Blaming, or fostering a victim mentality

Extreme Managers:
Highly unconscious Manager roles may be unable to see the benefits of collaboration or the necessity for ideas. In recent working case studies, it has been the failure of culture at the first line/technical manager level that has caused some of the most public and damaging business incidents in recent years.

Part of accountability for such events lies with the senior leadership in setting tone and culture, accepting or ignoring 'how we do things around here'. Another accountability lies with the potentially passive nature of the Manager style. Proactive, involved Managers can create cultures of zero risk, but they need leadership backing to do this successfully.

Who follows Managers?
Managers don't have followers in the same way as leaders, but they can inspire highly loyal contributors. Working with a skilled manager can be fulfilling without being stressful, which suits a lot of people.

Management is an essential task and role, and there will be many situations where an individual needs to flex between managing, leading and contributing. When this flexing is done consciously and explicitly, it is far more effective and less confusing.

So What?

No person is wholly one style or another. Authentic styles will have aspects of Bosses, the Ruler role can also be Visionary, and so on. At our best we are Integral or Interdependent and adaptable, shifting from Authentic leader to Manager to follower according to the situation. When triggered we are all vulnerable to shifting backwards to Independent, Dependent or Self-motivated. No doubt, you will have spotted aspects of yourself and your own leadership impact throughout these definitions. What action differentiates one style from another can be very small; often a seemingly insignificant motivation or thought can re-shape our intent from Boss to Authentic - or back again. What matters is the role we intend to take on, and how proactive we are in adopting the appropriate different behaviour.

In a world of constant change, leadership roles predisposed to experimentation, ideas, iteration and flexible behaviour will be much more likely to be effective. Organisations tend to dub those who are positive and enthusiastic as 'change champions'. While enthusiasm is desirable, it may not always be effective. Neither may those seeking simply to manage or control the process.

In defining a vision and creating adaptive working practices, we may need to recruit (whether appointed as leaders or not) those people who show the desired change leadership characteristics, and can influence with skill.

In terms of leadership development, organisations seeking sustained success need to avoid promoting for the short term. This means careful selection of talent according to mindset and approach. The choice is clear: do we want and need a culture shaped to individual agendas, or the greater purpose of the business or society?

Accurate evaluation of leadership Perspective at the time of promotion to first level leadership is critical. Most organisations place the strongest emphasis on delivery of job role as the key promotion criteria. Results are important, of course, but they are not a sufficient metric on their own; they were always achieved by some behaviour and we need to assess that too. A business that needs to demonstrate interdependent behaviours in the pursuit of a vision should not appoint technical experts and status-driven Bosses as its leaders. A business seeking to complete a digital transformation that requires subtle changes in behaviour should not appoint Bosses, or Managers who can only control processes.

A Word on Power

Leadership is the exercise of personal influence and, therefore, power. Become deadly serious with, and brutally honest about, your own relationship with power. We have seen Authentic, well-intentioned leaders attain heady heights where leading change became possible, only to see their motivations change and the adoption of Ruler/Boss behaviours. This is usually because although they have done sufficient vertical development; they have not thought about or prepared themselves for holding power or operating authentically from a powerful place. They, therefore, become either self-conscious or inexpert. Once power has been achieved, integral leadership seeks to maintain the values and purpose that gave rise to the desire for power; again this is a skill that requires practice.

Power is easy to abuse, and easier still to misunderstand. Every action, word, gesture and grimace is amplified and given a meaning and story by those who do not have power. Leadership casts a long shadow. We have found the easiest way to head off such misunderstandings is to declare your intention at every turn: "My intention is...". Simply say it out loud.

Power is not something to be avoided. While some like power for its own sake, some find their relationship to power changes positively once they achieve it; they are further enhanced by it, holding it gracefully. Integral leadership seeks to use power not for the aggrandisement of the self or the position, but to further the Purpose they serve.

"'Tis so much to be a king, that he only is so by being so."

Michel de Montaigne

"In a world of infinite choice, context
- not content - is king."

Chris Anderson

CHAPTER 12

SKILLS 4:
CONTEXT, CAUSE, CONDITIONS

One of the significant challenges in achieving sustained success in constant change is defining the things that won't change. In the Holos system, the constant is a powerful leadership platform. From this we can contextualise the change, articulate the Cause that we will all need to exhibit to deliver sustained success. So, in constant change, culture is the strategy.

Specific tactics, plans and actions are all important, but they are secondary to the essential ingredients of Context, Cause and Conditions. Tactics and plans are temporary, iterative and mutable ways of achieving the Cause.

Context, Cause and Conditions are the foundation for the leadership platform beneath sustained success and define an organisation from inside to outside. They shape thinking, brand, marketing, sales, innovation, reward, and measurement. In an environment of constant change, they nevertheless need to be reviewed regularly and any essential assumptions rigorously re-examined (remember Nokia's assumptions that we only wanted to text and phone from a mobile handset...?).

The most common way to create an organisational Cause and Conditions is for 8-10 people, usually the Leadership Team, to sit in a room for a day or two and bash out a series of words to which it asks the organisation to adhere. This is the least effective way to create direction. It also leads to false assumptions that the 'job has been completed' and everyone else just needs to deliver it.

Of all the leadership development activities we have ever been involved in, creating Cause and Conditions is the most misunderstood and the most prone to disappointment. It is better never to do this than to treat it as a task to tick off the list.

Designing effective change

Factors behind change can be dealt with in three main blocks: the Context (Megatrends), the organisational state (against Sustained Success), and the complexity of the change at issue. The change enablers are leadership, existing culture, and levels of team performance. The resulting Change model is presented in detail on the following pages.

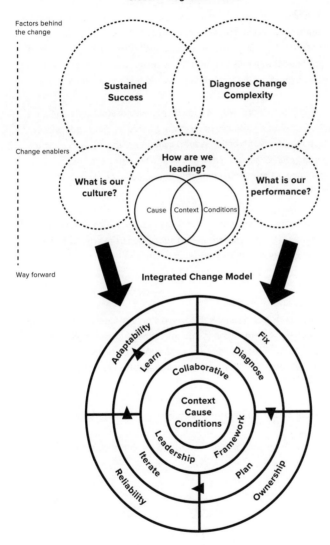

273

Nevertheless, having senior leadership (or a selection of appointed leaders from around the organisation) craft the Context, Cause and Conditions remains a valid choice. It is an act of leadership, after all. As an alternative, we have seen 'bottom-up' vision creation programmes. These can create very powerful messages, but carry inherent risk, as the bottom of the hierarchy may not be plugged into the realities behind future plans, investments, or looming regulations, for example. To succeed, this method takes planning and training.

Truth to tell, there is no 'right' way. We have seen successful Context, Cause and Conditions crafted by a single person; co-created by 300 leaders over four months, through a 50% version issued by leadership; and with a vertical slice of all employees completing it over a year. Therefore, the critical conditions for success are about commitment and believability, rather than just having one.

Through commitment and sincerity, all of these methods successfully created buy-in and momentum. What differentiated successes from equally intentioned failures was the quality and skill of leadership. Trust (rather than control) was key.

Steps to Success
Any organisation considering a new or revised Context, Cause and Conditions should put in place wide education in integral leadership, as a precursor. While that foundational work is done, daily business should be maintained. Even in the face of momentous crisis that needs immediate attention, there is still time to get things right.

1. Focus first on the language and permissions for leadership

2. Select appropriate significant symbolic acts that leadership teams can sponsor

3. Create a unifying language and narrative - your 'mythology'

4. Place accountability for the delivery of the symbolic acts firmly within individual teams, as the unit of organisational performance. Allow each team to interpret how to deliver (with leadership consultation and guidance, not control)

Creating Context
The Context is the landscape of change that your organisation exists inside. There may be elements of crisis, opportunity and enforced change. There may be macro-market forces that do or will affect your context. There may be cherished ambitions of founders to consider. Context is never the same from organisation to organisation, so its examination is critical to understand the shape of both the change and the leadership required.

Useful Context requires a narrative, story or mythology. Precise simplification or some other memorable form for expressing the Context can be helpful. For example, the Nokia outcome may have been different if their Context was a story such as:

- The technology landscape is always evolving and constantly progressing

- As the premier mobile technology company, we should be proud of our achievements, and also push and search relentlessly for better and simpler ways to connect people

This might have focused them on leading the transformation of the world from 2.5 G to 4 G broadband, and connecting every person on the planet instantly by video and internet.

Defining Cause

It is necessary to be really specific about your Cause, which encompasses:

- **Vision:** that which we truly want to achieve, which is inspiring to all stakeholders. It is a future destination, a place to be.

- **Purpose:** what we are fundamentally here to do and what we must do every day to achieve our vision.

- **Mission:** the tools, equipment, skills, financial resources, scale and general wherewithal we need to have or obtain, in order to achieve the vision and deliver on the purpose.

- **Goals/Objectives:** the specific measures that will show that we are on the right track.

Here are some examples of pretty good Cause statements:

> "I believe this nation should commit itself to achieving the goal, before this decade is out, of landing a man on the Moon and returning him safely to Earth."

> John F Kennedy

This is a vision statement, with a clear destination and no components of mission.

> "To create the most compelling car company of the 21st century by driving the world's transition to electric vehicles."

> Tesla Motors

The "most compelling" is more statement than mission, the point appearing to be that they have to be the world's most compelling car company in order to achieve the vision. The world's transition is something you would know you had achieved and works as a destination.

> "SpaceX <u>designs, manufactures and launches advanced rockets and spacecraft.</u> The company was founded in 2002 **to revolutionize space technology**, with the ultimate goal of enabling people to live on other planets."

> Space X

The underlined text is the mission + the bold text is the purpose + the vision is in plain text.

Most organisations will need other detailed sub-goals in pursuit of their ultimate goal.

Our suggestion would be for a wide education in integral leadership to take place as precursor to defining the central messages. Daily business should be maintained whilst foundational work continues, unless there has been some momentous crisis that needs immediate attention. But even then, there is still time to get things right.

Focus first on the language and permissions for leadership, then select appropriate significant symbolic acts that leadership teams can sponsor, alongside the creation of a unifying, powerful Context, Cause and Conditions. The delivery of such is then placed firmly within individual teams as the unit of organisational performance. Each team can then interpret how to deliver against this vision from their individual place within sustained success.

Creating Conditions

We dealt comprehensively with the creation of Conditions in Chapter 6.

The Cause and Conditions you need to create will combine the organisational vision and direction, plus what you need to achieve locally, in order to deliver the change. This means defining the change to a granular level. Best examples seamlessly break a Vision down into manageable actions and activities. Leaders of these tasks must constantly ask if the delivery is in line with achieving the Vision, and great leaders halt activities that do not contribute towards the Cause.

If you are a regional or local leader, some elements of the Cause and Conditions will work directly for your part of the organisation, others will need to be 'subsidised' with local components that remain in service to the organisational Cause and Conditions, and contribute effectively to local culture.

The best use of Cause and Conditions is to inform operational and strategic decision-making, as well as structural and system design. Organisations that follow this through will align all of their HR systems and procedures to support the desired culture, using the Cause and Conditions to guide strategic decisions. Leaders, managers and other contributors will apply it in day-to-day operations. An integrated Cause and Conditions example:

Cause and Conditions Example - Google (global)

Organisational Vision:	To provide access to the world's information in one click
Organisational Purpose:	To organise the world's information...
Organisational Mission:	...and make it universally accessible and useful
Organisational Objectives:	• What we do for you (products) • What we do for business (offerings/services) • What we do for the web (culture & environment)
Our Values:	"Ten things we know to be true"
Our Behaviours:	Google have written deeply about their culture and they do not restrict it to bullet points. Amongst their 'ten things' are: • Focus on the user and all else will follow • It's best to do one thing really, really well • Fast is better than slow • You don't need to be at your desk to need an answer • Great just isn't good enough Google use full sentences and descriptive words to characterise their beliefs about the world and business, including issues such as profit is not evil, the democracy of information, and cross-border collaboration. Their culture is effective and now a destination for employees worldwide.

(Whilst the aim of a corporate culture must be some degree of uniformity and predictability, it must also account for the local cultures and customs where people go to work. So it must be broad enough and specific enough to account for a global context with local nuance.)

A template of this nature enables clear leadership of decision-making and alignment towards organisational direction.

Change Comes Next...
Context, Cause and Conditions are the blueprint for leadership action across the whole organisation. They are also the foundation for agile change. Once these are in place, organisations need to:

1. Disseminate an agile change methodology to drive (not just react to) constant change

2. Upgrade leadership bandwidth across the board

3. Inculcate Authentic leadership principles; Boss and Ruler behaviours need to be identified, minimised or eradicated. Integral and Authentic leadership language and methods need to permeate all change activity to feed back into the desired culture

"Cooperation is the thorough conviction that nobody can get there unless everybody gets there."

Virginia Burden

CHAPTER 13

SKILLS 5: THE TEAM IS THE UNIT OF AGILITY

Granular, daily, sustainable organisational change is not just about setting visions and writing down the organisational purpose. It goes beyond the behaviour of the leadership team, and it takes more than the establishment of new digital processes. All these things are necessary, but they are not enough. True change, i.e. making positive progress on innovation, culture and performance, occurs in the domain of teams and team working.

Once the direction and purpose (Cause) is set, our ways of working (Conditions) are clear, and some key strategies have been put in place, the most valuable three activities any leadership team can do are:

1. Support systematic up-skilling of team leadership and teamworking

2. Delegate appropriate accountability (within a framework) to the right people and teams, then get out of the way

3. Put into place robust, iterative feedback loops on change and progress

Like leadership, there are thousands of ways of looking at teams to understand them and how they work: Google's research into psychological safety (Project Aristotle); Tuckman; Belbin; the Lencioni dysfunctions; profiling methods such as Relationship Awareness Theory, Strengths Deployment Inventory, TMSDI, Firo-B, Performance Climate System; the Gallup Q12; Stephen MR Covey's *The Speed of Trust*; Barry Oshry's power lab and others. Pick and mix from these varied and highly validated team development approaches, as each has something to offer.

All of them also say the same thing at their heart: teams thrive on trust. This makes immediate sense, both rationally and emotionally. We know instinctively that trust is both useful and necessary. And yet, as we have explored above, our many individual ways of viewing the world mean we may all have slightly differing definitions of effective trust. So how do we build such a complex thing between us, given that relationships, autonomy and meaning are so intertwined within it?

Perspectives on Trust

Definitions of trust vary depending on Perspective. Trust is an individual unit of currency, a building block of relationships and working together. Trust is not a contract or a guarantee, but something intangible, an essence, some sort of connection between people or peoples. Yet trust is so valuable that every single major mechanism of our daily lives uses it to help ensure success. Trust underpins most electoral systems, the transfer and use of power, the exchange of money (whether paper or electronic), the relationships between Church and State, marriage and the social contract. We have charters and constitutions and so on, but they are just paper; what really makes such covenants work is trust. It is so intrinsic to our ways of working that when trust is missing or betrayed, our very sense of self can be challenged.

In 2008, the trustworthiness and honour of the global banking system came into question. It emerged that imaginative packaging of housing debt had been sold on so widely that the accumulated debt burden was threatening the very existence of banks. Fractional reserve systems had been shown to be unsustainable when used in ways that were not trustworthy. The banking sector suffered a catastrophic collapse in trust that persists to this day. As an industry, it is now burdened by some of the heaviest regulation ever seen in that system, affecting not just banks but everyone else too. The term 'banker' became an insult, and the breach in trust affected the entire system of money.

In 2018, the President of the United States of America seemed to side with one of America's oldest enemies, Russia, in declaring that he believed the views of the Russian government, rather than the FBI, on the topic of meddling in 2016 US elections. This sent most observers into tail-spin of incredulity and outrage. This was so shocking because it unseated 70 years of Presidential 'top cover' for the US Intelligence Services. This was not a series of bold actions, such as the movement of armies or a collapse in diplomatic relations. Rather it was the accretion over the previous two years of doubt and confusion, followed by several statements during a single Presidential visit to Europe, the UK, and Russia. Spoken words... and a breakdown of trust.

Into the mix of who and how we trust we also have to add two key psychological biases. Confirmation Bias and Fundamental Attribution Error. Confirmation Bias says that most of us will only seek out and see things that confirm our pre-existing beliefs. If we believe someone is clumsy, we will always notice when they trip, and fail to notice when they dance nimbly. Fundamental Attribution Error says that we will tend to interpret our own performance (or that of our in-group) more favourably than that of others (our out-group). And that negative interpretations of others are more likely to be seen as character flaws than behaviours. So, if we see someone trip on a pavement we will interpret that they are clumsy by nature, whereas if we trip ourselves, it was because the pavement was uneven.

Trump detractors cannot believe the frequency and scale of his lying. Trump supporters often trust him as much as their own family members. Both sides seek out and see evidence to confirm their bias. Both sides have a positive interpretation of why their in-group does what it does, and a negative interpretation of their opponents'.

In building trust in and between teams we must consider these two biases very carefully.

Trust is so critical to our way of viewing the world that it is never just a 'nice to have'. Nothing gets done effectively and sustainably without it.

The most basic level of organisational trust is: if I turn up five days a week on time and carry my shift, then I trust that you will remunerate me to our agreed amount every month. An average amount of trust says: if I give more effort than my job description requires, make friends with co-workers, come up with ideas to improve our environment, and deliver results that outperform others, then I trust you will take notice of this and advance me to some more responsible or higher paid role. A high level of trust says: we believe in each other, and both come to work willingly and for the Cause. We will give it our all, technically and emotionally (as much as our limits on life sacrifices can allow), so we can both make money and meaning from what we have done together.

Levels of trust between individual team members and individual leaders define performance. One toxic relationship can poison the performance of a team, a department or even a whole organisation.

What levels of trust are you giving as an individual? What levels of trust are you expecting?

Trust is never contractual. Trust is rarely explicit. Yet trust is always vital. Trust, or lack of it, directly impacts your speed of work, ease of work, fun at work, effort at work, performance at work and results of work.

To an **Integral** Perspective, trust is assumed. You are counted on to bring your whole self to work and to deliver by the standards and disciplines of the Cause. Not to do this would be to exclude yourself from participation.

To an **Interdependent** Perspective, trust is an investment into mutual vulnerability and the quality of the relationship: trusting, open Authentic relationships, are far more durable and reach a better long-term level of performance than relationships based in competition.

To the **Independent** Perspective, trust may be offered as 'currency' to gamble my way into a situation where I can win (with the risk that trust may be lost); or, alternatively, with that Perspective I may not need your trust because I only expect us to be professional colleagues without intimacy or friendship.

To the **Dependent** Perspective, trust is based on our transaction: If I am your enforcer and give you loyalty, then in exchange you promote or prefer me above others. If I give my loyalty and you betray me once too often, then I will turn on you and punish you.

To the **Self** Perspective, trust is a fool's errand because only I can be relied on. What would I need trust for?

Defining Trust

All of this begs the question: *what is trust, precisely?* Stephen MR Covey, in his book *The Speed of Trust*, creates a beautifully simple description of trust that can also be applied in reality: Character + Competence. Think of any quality we may trust in someone, and it can be placed into one of those two columns. We trust some personal characteristic they have, (such as their values, shared beliefs, like-ability, similarity to us, and so on); and/or we trust what they can do, (their knowledge or expertise, ability to deliver, consistent personal standards, their addiction to quality, exactitude, or some talent).

In organisations, we need both Character and Competence for trust to be present. You may like me very much and we may be friends who go on holiday together, but if I do not deliver for you in the workplace, you will only trust me so far. It is the same the other way around; I may be The Terminator in terms of execution and never let you down or see a client go wanting, but if I trample everyone to do it and make enemies as I go, the list of the things you trust me to do is going to be quite short. Thus, self-interest is a determining factor in trust.

The Trust Equation deepens this way of looking at trust:

Trust = Competence + Reliability + Intimacy
Self Orientation

- **Competence** - can this person do what they say they can do?

- **Reliability** - will this person do what they say they will do?

- **Intimacy** - do I know them well enough to judge?

- **Self Orientation** - to what extent is their behaviour self-serving?

The kind of trust we need in high performing teams is going to combine Character and Competence across each member of the team, and knowing each other well enough for it to fully gel. This can take time to forge authentically. If a group of Interdependent Authentics are led by an Independent Boss, trust will be present between team members, but there will be little trust in the Boss or between the Boss and the team.

If a group of go-getting Independents are led by an unskilled, relational Authentic, the Authentic will be attempting to get them to trust in each other's performance, but the team will be stepping on each other to succeed. If the Independent team members are also remunerated or rewarded for individual achievement, Authentic leadership may get nowhere.

Many teams and organisations use a variety of psychometric tools such as MBTI™ or Insights™ to help people get to know themselves and each other. These tools are extremely helpful giving us language and frameworks to discuss character. However in organisations where the culture triggers people to lower levels of Perspective - from Interdependent at home to Independent in the office, for example, the profile is likely to show the authentic character rather than the triggered one and this needs to be taken into account.

The Holos Recipe
Only hire Authentics, only promote Authentics and Visionaries, and only reward team performance. What might happen then...?

Holos recommends building team structures on this basis in order to start a team practice based on trust and psychological safety. In an environment of constant change, lack of a change model or process increases the likelihood of failure to 'high'. Trying to succeed in constant change without trust in the culture increases the likelihood of failure to 'certain'.

Constant change demands that organisational Context, Cause and Conditions sit above team process, and all team activity should be aligned to achieving that. From that we can derive our local priorities or strategies for delivery; each member of a team then takes on functional or role specialisations that define what they must deliver to contribute to that overall vision. These may change often, and we must be prepared for that.

Once we have set our minds to an agile approach, we then need to understand who is in the team with us, and work out a way of delivering all of this together. We often cannot choose who we work with, and there is no template, as Google found out, for selecting individuals in an effective team. What we need to do instead is focus on how we work together *with this group of people.*

Change one thing in a system, and the whole system changes. If one member of our team changes, the whole team changes. Whether working in a long-established team or inaugurating a new team, we are constantly sussing everyone out to see whether or not they are (still) trustworthy. The second thing we do is work out how we can perform, both individually and together.

Goals, Roles, Processes
The leadership of teams is a fundamental skill for those who aspire to make change. It must be studied and improved consciously and daily. As a team leader, our primary responsibility is to see further, and guide better, the decisions we make in pursuit of the Cause. This is the essence of effective performance. So, the fair and efficient running of a team is the basic unit of leadership performance.

Teams look first for clarity. What do we need to achieve overall? What is our team role in that? What is my role in this team? Then, how do we work together, what are our daily rituals and routines? How do we systematise and rely on, within reason, common processes of working that we all understand? How do I get paid? How do I get my expenses paid? How do we communicate with one another?

These critical questions can be segmented into three key components of transactional or functional ways of working: the Goals, Roles and Processes we all understand and must work to.

Goals, Roles, and Processes may already be set out for us to a large extent; in large systems the vision is already set, the main departmental goals defined, the bureaucracy and processes clearly staked out (usually by others and we can have little effect on them). We may not agree with these processes, or would not have designed them that way, but we have to remember that things have usually been set in place over time and sometimes for good reasons. However, large systems tend to stop adapting well when historical accretions of processes lay one on top of another. Such systems can be very hard to break and may be a change frontier of their own. If we are lucky, we can enter a relatively white space and design all of these processes to be modern, relevant, and adaptive.

A constant change environment puts a new lens on the way in which we hold, or trust, team process. In a constant change environment, as we change our operational role or practices towards the new digital environment, for example, it is likely that the pay, appraisal, bonus scheme, pension and investment portfolio of the whole company will also simultaneously need to be under review. In a constant change environment, Goals, Roles and Processes can no longer be relied on to last long term, in the way they have been.

Therefore, leadership needs to be looking further out. To see, anticipate, and include our team colleagues in what may be coming down the line, and to mentally prepare the team for increased ambiguity and uncertainty. It is important this is done in ways that protect morale and resilience. This is why we declare 'culture is the strategy'. If structures change, the only reliable thing we can control in that ambiguity is our culture.

Leaders who lack bandwidth are unable to curate culture, so a key element of effective leadership is the creation and protection of leadership bandwidth. Leaders should not seek to be busy, they should seek to be alert to change and effective with teams.

In 1988, when Mark was in the armed forces, he did a tour of active service in Northern Ireland. The basic activity of team working in the Province was patrolling: sending a number of small sub-units out into the streets or fields for several hours at a time in order to maintain a visible presence. Daily events would impact the patrolling schedule in interdependent ways; an incident in the city would impact what happened in the countryside, would impact what happened in permanent vehicle checkpoints, and so on.

The patrolling schedule published on Day 1 of each week would be extremely unlikely to happen by Day 7. Mark tried many ways to prepare his teams for this ambiguity, including increasing levels of control and direction. This did not get him very far, and he slowly became aware of more and more grumbling - not about the schedule, but about him (which to his mind felt grossly unfair). During an inspection, Mark glimpsed a colleague's patrolling schedule posted in a different Troop's barracks. Written boldly in marker pen on the top page were the words: "*Oh well! How about this?* - a starter for ten!". He had forgotten the primary leadership responsibility of leading for change.

Instantly, Mark learned a very valuable lesson in how to better handle constant change in a team environment: mindset. Humour, a sense that we are all in this change together, and mentally preparing his teams for adapting to coming change had been missed.

Adaptability, Connection, Resilience
We have limited control over the rate of change to do with Goals, Roles and Processes. However, we do have complete autonomy over the ways we work together. These areas are typically called the 'soft' skills. We acknowledge that they are skills, and can be learned, but there is nothing soft about them. Introverts can do them just as well as extroverts, technical novices just as well as masters. And if culture is the main lever for performance this is an important bit of autonomy.

Adaptability is our preparedness for change and our ability to deal with change. Again, this is in the context of constant change: adaptability becomes a benchmark justifying the trust we have in the people around us; flexibility is an essential personal skill for which every company must hire, and as Yuval Noah Harari says, an essential personal skill in the age of Megatrends. Connection is the degree to which we operate together and relate to one another; it fuels pride and identity in our team and teamwork. Resilience is our ability to cope, individually and as a unit, with high levels of stress and adversity, and a measure of how quickly we bounce back in difficult conditions.

Resilience must not be mistaken for hardiness, where we become so used to adversity that it changes us for ever. Highly stressed systems create hardy people, who eventually either burn out or leave, creating more problems overall. In Chapter 5, Mammalian Perspectives, we showed that humans are not built for constant, all-pervasive states of hyper-vigilance; remaining in stress for too long results in masking or inauthentic behaviours that eventually lead to personal burnout. In fact, the practice of resilience and mindfulness has been one of the most potent treatments in the effort to create healthy business systems and authentic cultures.

Leadership to support these states of being is of paramount importance. A team with adaptability, connection and resilience can truly claim to be an effective unit of change, agility and performance. A team with Authentic transformational leadership is forward-facing, adaptable, optimistic, deals with conflict quickly and equitably, openly discusses feedback and dips in performance, and frequently rotates leadership according to specialisms. It uses agile processes to try things out, gain feedback and learning, then improve and iterate again. These teams see themselves in a state of 'permanent beta'; nothing is ever perfect, but everything is always getting better. These teams understand that leadership is one attribute of team performance, not the exclusive preserve or responsibility of one person. There is little judgement, and when one person is failing, the team morphs without rancour or blame to cope with that dip, enabling the individual to recover more easily and come back stronger. The psychologically safe team then recognises that individual failure is not part of a healthy, high performing team and examines its own processes to understand why such a thing happened. The focus is on avoiding exclusion or overload from negatively affecting any one person in the future.

In these teams, the substrate underpinning all of this high performance is trust.

Leadership Skill - Systemic Coaching

How do we create a high performing, adaptable team? If human organisational history has preferred Bosses and control, how do we break the cycle of being in Fix or Reliability and head out into the open waters of trust, interdependence, adaptability and change? How can we all skill ourselves up for that, and not retreat at the first failure or follow our confirmation bias and seek evidence that it will not work?

One of the strongest methods we have discovered is systemic coaching. We have seen executive coaching adopted in many organisations as a beneficial route to personal growth. This, however, is too often offered as a remedial process, or used on those who do not yet quite 'meet the mark'. Yet the essential premise of coaching is that every one of us would benefit from it. Indeed, those at the top in any discipline from tennis to teaching, writing to war-fighting, seldom get there without the help of a coach.

Coaching individuals is not the best route to high team performance. Each person has different limiters and blockers, opportunities and enablers. Each person will, instinctively or unconsciously, have taken up some role in the team beyond their appointed one. There will be the caretaker, the entertainer, the thinker, the drinker and so on. These roles will be linked closely to individual identity.

Team performance is an amalgam of the obvious attributes linked to title, position, given role and deliverables, and the hidden or unspoken attributes linked to the unconscious roles individuals adopt in order to gain self-worth and fit in.

While individual coaching has limited impact in shaping team performance, systemic coaching is a very effective way of surfacing all of these seen and unseen attributes and making them part of the everyday team conversation. It involves assigning an executive coach to every person in a team and coordinating between those coaches, whose shared focus is on assisting each team member to develop their awareness of where they have been holding themselves and the team dynamic back.

We provided coaching to every member of one leadership team over six months; one 90-minute session per person, per month. We discovered at least three huge interpersonal issues that had effectively put a cap on that team's performance. The issues had badly eroded trust in the team.

Working initially with each individual to explore where they were and how they saw their own performance, we then carefully brokered different kinds of courageous conversations between individuals who had not raised such trust-related issues in years. This created a steadily increasing level of trust, then openness, then direct conversation, and the exposure and healing of long-standing relationship sores. This coached 'catharsis' led to new ways of working together that transformed the organisation. The organisation is now moving into profit for the first time in five years and has unleashed an incredible surge of optimism and creativity that is setting a positive and sustainable future.

Coaching that system was not overly long or expensive. It was intense and felt vulnerable, but the success of the systemic coaching was ultimately down to the character, intent, and courage of the individual team members in response to the coaching. They wanted to improve. The team leader, the CEO, had to swallow a couple of big pills: vulnerability and feedback. But with Interdependent humility and the knowledge that everyone was going through the same coaching around their innermost self, business performance was transformed.

Independent of the coaching experience, better conversations emerged, individuals became highly self-aware and their impact on others more deliberate. Self-coaching began to take place, and the quality of Interdependent leadership improved swiftly. The system began to monitor and upgrade itself through the push-pull of everyday conversations and the smallest of individual, personal leadership moments and self-aware decisions. The team and business moved from fragile to anti-fragile.

Systemic coaching is by far the most powerful tool we have found to engender change and increase performance at team level.

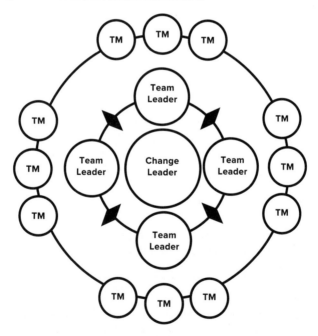

Change Agility focused around ripples, or waves, in creating autonomous team performance. (TM = Team Member)

Sustaining Transformation

- Delivering constant change in the post-conventional context is no longer an activity leaders can deliver from the side of their desks. In constant change, we need tools to help us take strategies off the page and into daily working lives.

- Adaptation requires a wholly informed and engaged system in which as many employees as possible are aware and agile in nature. This creates high degrees of skill and ownership, as well as diversity of thought and an iterative approach based on experimentation.

- To make such change easier, Holos has developed an online digital toolset that combines the development of culture with overall change progress tracking for change leaders.

Adaptive Change Modelling

As with teamwork, there are many change models: theoretical, science-based, experiential, researched and instinctive. The Holos change model is founded in our real-time observation and research into how teams and organisation become adaptive. We acknowledge and accept that many other change models can work, and the best of them all share key elements because the factors in play rarely differ. No one builds anything alone - as practitioners we all stand on the shoulders of those who have gone before.

We would like to thank the tens of thousands of individuals, senior and junior, young and old, from all corners of the globe, all races, creeds and beliefs, whose discussion, objections, reflections, practices, trust, arguments, rejections, challenges, fears, tears, joys and sharing of experience have honed the ideas below. This model is offered in the spirit of making life a tiny bit easier for you. This is not the model but a model for successful, sustainable, constant change.

Change Agility Model (CAM)

The model articulates the stages and phases of change to create Sustained Success. It contains three hierarchies of activity (with specific credit to Simon Sinek's 'Golden Circle'), all designed to help us behave in the right ways to get to the fourth layer: the intended outcomes.

Once the Leadership Team has understood the model and embodied it, it should be disseminated, trained and coached into the business by every leader as the template for every single team to become adaptable. Systemic coaching should be employed to up-skill personal contribution and team performance, alongside an agreed team process that incorporates both transactional and transformational data points.

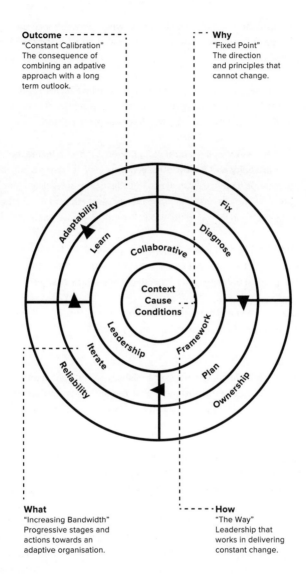

Outcome
"Constant Calibration"
The consequence of
combining an adpative
approach with a long
term outlook.

Why
"Fixed Point"
The direction
and principles that
cannot change.

What
"Increasing Bandwidth"
Progressive stages and
actions towards an
adaptive organisation.

How
"The Way"
Leadership that
works in delivering
constant change.

1. Why is at the core = **A Fixed Point**, i.e. what cannot change during change: the organisational vision for moving forward and the resources to get there.

2. How is the cultural vision = **The Way**, i.e. what we believe and how our leaders collectively need to behave to succeed: the behaviours, standards and disciplines by which we deliver the vision.

3. What moves us up the ladder of Sustained Success = **Increased Accountability and Bandwidth**, i.e. progressive leadership activities and actions, taking us from Fix to Reliability then spreading leadership outwards into the organisation to deliver ownership, and from there to autonomy in following the vision in order to create Adaptability.

4. The outcome = **Constant Calibration**, i.e. a cycle of feedback loops and incremental actions that adapt and improve business states, keeping us competitive or taking in new thinking that enables change leadership.

Allied to this are a series of four helpful stages that all leaders will need to consider and utilise to flesh out the broad process:

1. Diagnose
Prepare the organisation to move from Reliability to constant change, or Adaptability. Understand how the global, regional, local and sector Megatrends are affecting you - create a narrative for this Context and what it means for different divisions and departments.

Agree at a senior level the Cause and Conditions you need to work to, define the story and narrative (the new mythology) that will bring people together in shared habits and behaviours to achieve this, and attract new joiners to the Cause.

Understand in detail your current organisational state and readiness as against this adaptive vision, and in relation to Sustained Success. If your organsiation is in the 'Fix' stage, don't try to change and innovate yet. First, create stability and predictability.

- Calibrate the leadership potential of existing managers and help them realise it

- Calibrate the complexity of the change required, and socialise the depth of the change in advance so leaders can create bandwidth to cope skilfully with the changes ahead

2. Plan

Upgrade behaviours from Management to Leadership. Develop leadership capability and skill, especially around visioning, influencing and change skills.

Celebrate the elements of culture that are working and should be kept. Understand levels of current performance and create a definition of the performance upgrade required.

Select and share a single change model (the Holos model or any other simple model that works for you), to standardise the vocabulary of change and allow cross-calibration on progress. Ensure the change model adopted creates adaptability, rather than a new steady state that will require another expensive change in two or three years.

- Develop the plan in detail: create a change goal that aligns to adaptability, create time horizons and work streams, and share the plan as widely as possible

- Plan a series of significant symbolic acts - 1-3 high profile leadership or tactical actions that signify this change

- Identify how you will utilise teamwork, how empowerment mechanisms will work, and what key characteristics or behaviours will build trust; establish team level frameworks for autonomy and delivering high performance; realign measurement and reward systems to deliver team rewards.

3. Iterate

Employ trial and error tactics; get everyone used to not knowing. Forget the 'grand launch'. Start the change though significant symbolic leadership acts and seek immediate feedback. Focus on opening up leadership culture and practising what you preach.

Execute change actions based on the plan, using 80/20 principles and removing the need to be perfect. Work on leadership and cultural conversations at team levels, and try out new ways. Hold feedback and experimentation sessions to role model the new way; share whatever is learned.

- Iterate and experiment, iterate and experiment, iterate and experiment, both in what you are doing and how you are doing it. Socialise this 'permanent beta' state as your chosen way of working towards sustained success

- As you discover what gets you towards the vision, standardise both behaviour and tasks, and continue to share and socialise these ideas

- Decide where true innovation takes place, and where continuous improvement is sufficient. Segment them. Protect and sustain 'cranking the handle' methods to generate profit and set a portion aside to support innovation

- Be rigorous about habits, behaviour and culture within the leadership team. The leaders must be exemplars who reliably embody the change, before seeking to enrol the next organisational level.

4. Learn

Embody agility, embed best practice. Create a cyclical and local approach to appraising context and realigning action to the vision.

- Constantly calibrate your leadership and the overall culture against the destination

- Use data and feedback to maintain agile process and embed agile ways of working

- Continue to loop through Iterate and Learn while holding true to the Context, Cause and Conditions

- Resist assimilation. Resist assumptions and fixed beliefs. Do not become the supertanker

- At the right point - a point that will only become evident when it arrives - go back to Diagnose to ensure the Context, Cause and Conditions remain true, then go through the whole cycle again. Doing something once is experimenting. Repetition brings learning

Change Agility Toolkits (CAT)

In support of this process, it may be a good idea to have a toolkit that provides common understanding of the language, skills and process of constant change. This enables the whole flotilla to change together and collaboratively - rather than awaiting orders and explanations from the tanker.

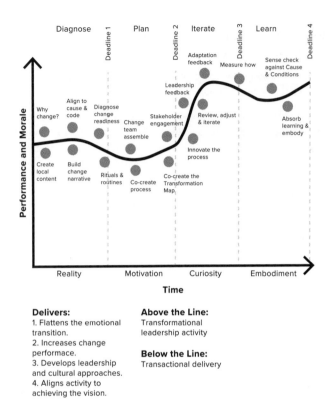

Delivers:
1. Flattens the emotional transition.
2. Increases change performance.
3. Develops leadership and cultural approaches.
4. Aligns activity to achieving the vision.

Above the Line:
Transformational leadership activity

Below the Line:
Transactional delivery

It would be advantageous if the change toolkit were online, and supported by a dashboard so that those running the change could see, at any time, the progress of individual teams or divisions.

Further, the ideal toolkit would contain tools that supported activities around cultural change and more effective leadership, such as creative workshop templates for alignment to Cause and Conditions, behavioural development, transformation mapping tools, leadership feedback snapshots and iterative learning events. Such a global unifying approach to change would address cultural and systemic needs at once.

Holos has developed the Change Agility Toolkit or CAT, to assist leadership of adaptive, iterative change over time (rather than simply management of Fix or Reliability).

www.holoschange.com/CAT

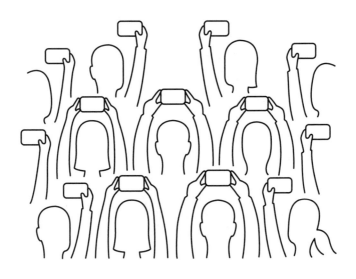

"The most exciting breakthroughs of the 21st Century
will not occur because of technology, but because of an
expanding concept of what it means to be human."

John Naisbitt

CHAPTER 14

MEGATRENDS FURTHER READING

It is critical that leaders pay attention to Context and continuously share it with teams. Leaders must create the bandwidth to do the necessary horizon-scanning and stay up-to-date with anything that might impact the future of their organisation. This is your job as a leader.

In practice, this mostly this means reading articles. There are books and videos that are highly relevant, but inevitably these date quickly, so best practice is to identify appropriate news sources, scan them daily, read interesting stuff and share the most relevant bits around your organisation. Appropriate topics are not just the Megatrends we have highlighted but whatever is relevant for your organisation.

Digitisation is well covered in publications such as *Wired, Fast Company* and *Inc*. For decarbonisation and ageing you have to hunt a little harder, but online news such as Electrek and services like the *CIA World Fact Book* are good sources. The easiest thing to do is to use a personalised newsfeed such as Google News, Apple News, Flipboard, or similar, and set it up to follow the topics relevant to your sector.

Staying up-to-date yourself is not enough. To be truly change agile we also need our people to stay abreast of both the internal and external context. When we all understand the impacts of innovations that are going on in robotics, artificial intelligence and big data, we are already far more amenable to organisational change that responds to those impacts. Just because you have your finger on the pulse, do not imagine that other people do.

For three years, Neil ran a regular session that included Megatrends for high potential middle level leaders in a large multinational. Only about 10% of participants had any meaningful knowledge of the Megatrends discussed, even the ones that were directly relevant to their business.

Typically this percentage rises slightly with seniority in organisations. What is not clear is which comes first: are people who pay attention to context more likely to get promoted, or do people who get promoted pay more attention to context?

> "Have no fear of the future. Let us go forward into its mysteries, tear away the veils which hide it from our eyes, and move onwards with confidence and courage."
>
> Winston Churchill

Neil's Afterword

I hope that you have found some valuable ideas as you have read this book. Our intention in writing these words is to help you our readers to be better leaders and to be more selective about who you follow.

Every time I read the news I grieve at the destruction that is caused and the opportunities that are lost by Boss and Ruler style leaders in business, government and education. It does not have to be this way. All it takes is for us to stop electing, selecting, appointing, promoting and most importantly following Boss and Ruler style leaders. And a parallel stepping into our own authentic leadership potential for those of us who want to. Once we commit to only following and being an authentic leader at work our work changes for the better. Once we commit to only supporting authentic leaders in government our world changes for the better.

#campaignforauthenticleadership is a rallying cry for all of us who have suffered at the hands of bosses or rulers and all all of us who have felt uncomfortable as leaders. It is time to create a society where everyone is supported to be the very best version of themselves and where no one feels that need to be what they think other people expect them to be. It is time to create a society where sustained success is universally pursued and celebrated and stealing from the future is regarded as a crime.

To join the campaign all you need to do is to avoid following boss or ruler style leaders and/or to take your own journey of authentic leadership and share your stories using #campaignforauthenticleadership.

Mark's Afterword

This book has been for the most part an illustration of a rational and reasonable case for authentic leadership, and a handbook for sustained, agile change. Our overwhelming intent has been to create a sense of possibility about tackling these issues.

Although the book has dealt with the emotional transition through everyday change, our narrative has not addressed the vast, subterranean grief and helplessness many feel about the slow build-up of the threats to the world. In 2018, we are in the middle of an extinction event as grave as that which occurred 65 million years ago. This extinction event is unique because it has been brought about by us, and is all the more troubling because governments and blocs are not acting quickly enough to stop the destruction. It is not "just" the environment that is under threat, but our own food chains and hence our very ability to sustain our growing numbers.

Throughout writing, events across the world have moved at a pace we could not keep up with. This evidenced itself both in positive stories to mitigate and ameliorate pressing global challenges, and in retrograde or backward leadership steps. For example, both the election of Trump and the vote for Brexit occurred after we had written early drafts. If the issues were pressing in 2015, how much more urgent are they in 2018, given some of the decisions taken between then and now?

The crisis of leadership we face goes way beyond voting in one set of decision makers over another, and reaches into our own lives and choices with two penetrating questions:

What are you prepared to do?
What are you prepared not to do?

The responsibility for action lies with all of us, and the future is by no means certain. We are on the fulcrum of a see-saw, and we could tip one way or the other.

The crisis is at the heart of our individual connection with the planet and our own sustenance, into our integrity and foresight, and, ultimately, our individual and shared self worth. In some ways our collective awareness needed to have made this journey. For three or four hundred years, as a species we have experimented with the idea that we are supreme. What we have come to know by 2018 is that any illusion of supremacy will be short-lived. We connect and interdepend with every other aspect of this world, from its moving crust to its atmosphere and ability to provide air, to the local climates and geographies that produce shelter, food, and water. The essentials of life are not how large we can make our flatscreen or turbocharge our V12 engine, but whether or not we can breathe, drink, eat, and procreate.

The crisis of leadership has been perpetuating a model that by its own nature takes from our species' future to give ourselves the illusion of plenty now. We have grown so used to this state of affairs that we are prepared to tolerate the intolerable, defend the indefensible, and argue forcefully for the dangerous, just so that we in this generation, and perhaps our children in theirs, can enjoy the standards of living we have grown accustomed to.

Hard choices lie ahead.

Any therapist or psychologist will tell you damaging emotion that remains unresolved profoundly affects our decision making in the present. Healing requires that we face into, understand, move through, and integrate the meaning of the species-level trauma we are experiencing in order for us to be able to surpass it. This will only occur when a conscious enough leadership, that is global in reach and inclusive in nature, is able to both address the trauma in us all, and legislate to enforce a set of social and industrial standards that do not yet exist.

I am grieving. I am angry. Yet I have moved through my depression. Whilst not yet hopeful, I am purposeful.

#campaignforauthenticleadership

GLOSSARY

Adaptability	An organisational state that embodies both high reliability, in which those processes that can be managed are being so, and those activities that require leadership are receiving equal attention. Both management and leadership contribute toward the achievement of the long-term vision and the organisation may be a disruptor in its market. Decision-making and ideas are widely distributed and several business models may exist contemporaneously.
Agape	Agape (Ancient Greek, agapē), a Greco-Christian term referring to love, "the highest form of love, charity". It embraces a universal, unconditional love that transcends and persists regardless of circumstance.
Authentic	Leading from a place of personal authenticity and enabling it in others.
Authenticity	Knowing yourself and being it skilfully in all situations.
Bandwidth	The capacity to devote time, focus and attention.
Boss, Bosses	A leadership style motivated by status, competition and achievement.
Cause	The reasons an organisation exists - includes Vision, Purpose and Mission.
Conditions	The conditions we work within - including principles, behaviours and habits.
Consciousness	A combination of self awareness, other awareness, maturity and global perspective.
Context	The things that are going on in the world and our organisations that must be taken into account in pursuing the Cause and leadership.
Dependent	A perspective that takes decisions by looking to others for validation, direction, or shelter.
Extractive	A mindset that takes value from natural and human resources while offering little or nothing in return.

Fix	An organisational condition in which there is duplication, crisis or panic, and too many tasks. Processes and practices are not fit for purpose and there is no leadership bandwidth for anything except execution.
Independent	A perspective that takes decisions primarily from the primacy of the self, possibly in competition with others, and usually for the short term.
Integral	A perspective that takes decisions by considering all available interdependencies, causes, and effects, to the maximum possible good of all life over the very long term.
Interdependent	A perspective that takes decisions by considering the connections around us and creating mutually beneficial results, usually for the longer term.
Leader	Individual personalities who seek to disrupt and make change.
Leadership	Enrolling and aligning people around disruption and change.
Management	Enrolling and aligning people around steady-state reliability and efficiency.
Median	The point at which there are as many above that number as there are below it.
Mission	The resources required for the pursuit of the purpose and vision.
Motivation	What truly underlies your intentions in wanting to effect a change; usually aligned to either status or purpose.
Ownership	An organisational state in which culture is beginning to become the medium for success. Delegation and empowerment has moved out of decision-making centres and teams are beginning to align towards the achievement of a long-term vision. There is leadership bandwidth to horizon-scan and to pay attention to becoming fully Adaptable.

Perspective	How we take decisions in relationship to our current level of self-awareness and the awareness of our interconnectivity with others and the world.
Psychological Safety	The quality of feeling safe to speak out and act authentically in groups.
Purpose	The reason why we exist as an organisation or team; the thing we are fundamentally here to do.
Reach	One's ability and capacity to affect sizes of systems, for example yourself, a family, a team, an organisation, a region, a country, a bloc, the world - etc.
Reliability	An organisational condition in which internal processes and practices are as reliable as external ones. Goals are being met and promises being kept. Management is the preferred medium for achievement and leadership bandwidth is minimal.
Ruler, Rulers	A leadership style motivated by status, control and the maintenance of power.
Self	A perspective that takes decisions with only self-interest in mind.
Universality	An organisational state that exists beyond Adaptability, in which the general dreams and aspirations of humanity may also be bound up in the organisational purpose and reach, with business activities become relevant and useful to all.
Vision	The destination, insuring to all stakeholders, we may seek to reach through the pursuit of our purpose.
Visionary, Visionaries	A leadership style motivated by purpose, creating new power-bases, and the pursuit of an audacious vision.